TABLE OF CONTENTS

INTRODUCTION   ix

Part I • Because We Are Loved

Chapter 1
HOPE FOR THE MAINLINE CHURCH   1

Acknowledging the Bad News • Power At Work In the Mainline Church: A Mindset For Mission • Identifying the Maintenance Mindset • The Age-old Oscillation: Between Mission and Maintenance • The Power Of God • A Passion For Excellence: Ten Marks Of Growing Churches • How to Assess Your Growth Potential

Chapter 2
KINDLED BY FIRE AND BLAZING WITH HOPE: THE POWER
OF A PERSPECTIVE   17

The Gospel Loving, Mission-Minded Perspective • The Maintenance Mind-set • Hope On the Horizon • Old Christ Church: Historic and Mostly Traditional • St. Peter's in the Woods: Brand New and Growing • St. Thomas: Deep America Rural • Clergy Leadership Makes All the Difference • Checklist: Taking Action To Diagnose Your Church

Part II • Telling The Old, Old Story

Chapter 3
ALWAYS SURROUNDED BY THE LOVE OF GOD   35

Preparing For Evangelism: Church Programs That Don't Help • Identifying Divine Interventions • Mission-minded Christianity: More Than Fellowship • Evangelism: Introducing God To God's World • What Evangelism Is Not • Introductions In A "Chance" Encounter • Evangelism From the Perspective of Jesus' Life and Ministry • Nicodemus: Touched By Love and Changed • To Speak Of God: Learning To Use A Language Of Faith

Chapter 4
STORIES OF LOVE TO TELL...TODAY   51

Preparing To Exercise The Ministry of Introductions • God's Love Right Before Our Eyes: A Wedding • Hearts Set On Fire • A Dad Dies: And God Makes Things Right

Chapter 5
SUSAN, I'D LIKE TO INTRODUCE YOU TO A FRIEND OF
MINE   61

Evangelism From Scratch • Good Fortune or God's Providence? • Introducing Love Right Before Our Eyes • Looking For Turning Points • Always With Us: Immanuel • God Keeps Company With Us: The Companion • The Friendship of God: Ruth • God Supplies Our Needs: Providence • God's Favor Invites Our Attention: Grace • God Walks With Us and Talks With us: Conversation • The Wind of God Rustles Our Lives • Networking Relationships: God's Spirit Acts • Taking Action: Celebrating Evangelism With A Study Group

Chapter 6
WHY DO BAD THINGS HAPPEN IN GOD'S WORLD?   77

Answering A Question That Burns • Renewing Our Images of God • Freedom in the Universe • Sin: Not Able to Listen to God • Sin is "Original Equipment" • God's Love and God's Powerlessness • The Adversary of Scripture • Evil and the God Of Love: A Cosmic Drama • The Solace Of Prayer • Taking Action To Learn the Ministry Of Introductions

Chapter 7
DEVELOPING YOUR STYLE OF PERSONAL EVANGELISM   93

Story Telling Or Story Listening? • Determining Your Style Of Personal Evangelism • Checklist: Developing Your Style of Evangelism

Part III • Leadership At Work: Building Up the Church

Chapter 8
WORSHIP: O GOD OUR HEARTS ARE READY   103

Maintenance-Minded Worship: A Short Take • Mission-Minded Worship: A Short Take • Preaching the Power Of God • Always Pushing For Better Worship • For God's Sake Do Things Well • Educate, Educate, Educate • Taking Action To Make Plans

Chapter 9
MISSION-MINDED CLERGY LEADERSHIP: ENTHUSIASTIC
AND INTENTIONAL   121

Maintenance-Minded Clergy: A Short Take • A Joyful Celebrant • A Skillful Liturgist • A Visionary Steward • An Able Educator • An Enthusiastic Administrator •

Maintenance-Minded Clergy Burnout • Educating Clergy for Ministry • Revisioning Theological Education • Calling A Mission-Minded Pastor For Parish Leadership • Evaluating Clergy Prospects: Help For the Calling Committee

Chapter 10
HELPING NEWCOMERS FIND A HOME: THE MINISTRY OF HOSPITALITY   143

What Brings Us To Church? • Responding To Visitors: Nothing Is Left To Chance • Step One: Valuing God's Ministry To the First Time Visitor • Step Two: Talking To Newcomers • Step Three: Return the Visit While Interest Burns Hot • Step Four: Orienting Newcomers — The Newcomer's Class • Step Five: Tracking and Sponsoring Newcomers • Step Six: Still Later — Membership Classes • AggressIvely Seeking Out New Members: A Community Canvass Works! • Initiate A New Baby/New Mother/New Father Ministry • Confident and Growing: Putting It All Together • Welcoming Visitors: A Program to Prepare Your Congregation

Chapter 11
REACHING FOR THE DROP-OUT, THE DISAPPOINTED AND THE BROKEN-HEARTED   165

Why Do People Drop Out Of Church? • Molly Leaves: A Result Of Current Hurt • The Healing Conversation • Bitterness Beyond Redemption • Stress and the Dropout • Taking Action: Ministry in Response

Chapter 12
THE CHURCH IN THE WORLD: EVERY DAY WHAT WE DO MATTERS TO GOD   175

Helping God Take Care Of God's World • Why Don't I Get What I Want? • Valuing God's Action In Our Lives: Look For Turning Points • Taking Action: Determining God's Hand At Work In Your Life • Education For Children and Teens: Looking Toward Their Future

Part IV • Education In the Mission-Minded Church: Equipping the Saints For Ministry

Chapter 13
ORGANIZING A PARISH FOR CHRISTIAN EDUCATION   189

Escaping Failure • Prayer Book Perspectives On Christian Education • One Of Many Success Stories • Using Store-Bought Curricula Materials: Recognizing the Dangers • Wedding Worship and Sunday Morning Christian Education

Chapter 14
SKILL BUILDING FOR EVANGELISM'S MINISTRY OF IN-
TRODUCTIONS: WITH ADULTS AND TEENS   199
  Why Do Episcopalians Fear Evangelism? • Three Kinds Of Evangelism • Episcopal
  Church Evangelism: What It Looks Like • Organizing an Evangelism Study Group:
  For Adults and Teens • Always Use Stories • Taking Action: What Next For Episco-
  palians?

Chapter 15
MAKING BELIEVERS OF CHRISTIANS: NEWCOMER AND
MEMBERSHIP CLASSES   211
  Classes To Welcome Newcomers • Classes To Make Members of Newcomers • The
  Portrait Of A Mature Christian • Constructing A Membership Class: Working
  Toward Maturation • Believer's Confirmation • "Kiddie" Confirmation: Robbing
  the Church Of Strength

Part V • Making Plans for the Future

Chapter 16
FROM MAINTENANCE TO MISSION: MAKING LOCAL
PLANS   227
  Generating A Mission-Minded Parish Conversation • Learning From The Trends In
  Your Congregation's History • Becoming Intentional: Celebrating Your Patterns Of
  Ministry • Announcing the Kingdom of God: The Ministry of Publicity • A
  Clergy/Parish Annual Evaluation • Creating A Program Calendar • Worksheets

INDEX   243

INTRODUCTION

If you hunger to know more about God and the difference that God makes in your daily life...

If you want to feel more confident and comfortable with the ministry of evangelism...

If you are a pastor who wants more for your congregation than their limited vision of fixing the roof, repairing the plumbing and filling the holes in the parking lot...

If you are presently thinking about calling a pastor to leadership in your parish...

If you want to pay careful attention to issues like church growth and the quality of your congregation's life...

You will find help in this book.

Every year I travel in the mainline church. And I listen to what is happening.

For the most part my travels are occasioned by church retreats and the leadership of conferences in the fields of Christian education, evangelism and church growth. I don't sit in the wood-paneled offices of denominational officers discussing things like ecclesiastical politics or general church programming. I visit in the local parish, and I work with folks like you.

I've heard you speak with longing hearts about what you hope will happen in your church, and I've heard anger about what is not happening. I've also heard some good news about things that work, and I ask "how come" and "why" questions. And you tell me.

Regardless of demographics and the local economic climate (and sometimes in spite of both), in the midst of declining numbers a number of mainline Protestant congregations in America are dramatically expanding while others mark time or decline. Why is this so?

I've discovered that what I call a "mission perspective" marks growing churches. This designation distinguishes their common life from congregations marked by what I call a "maintenance mindset." *Church Growth and the Power of Evangelism* explores these two perspectives and shows them at work.

The mission mindset is not what is commonly understood by the word mission, that is, the "work" of carrying the gospel into foreign places, or the "work" of formulating and implementing mission programs. Rather, a mission mindset values God's here-and-now presence and ministry in the church and world today. God is close and mission-minded congregations know it. They also love to talk about it, and their ability to speak of God generates all kinds of interest in newcomers and visitors.

Christian congregations always begin with a commitment to mission. In their lives God has done a marvelously new thing; they have been touched by grace, they know it, and they love to talk about it. But as soon as any new congregation convenes, a concern for maintenance arises. This is as natural as night following the day. In large measure this concern is stirred by the chatter of anxious hearts, wondering, "Who will look after us?" But maintenance is not mission.

A maintenance mind-set is a necessary component in parish ministry. But even the slightest interest in maintenance tends to subvert a commitment to mission, and it has done so in every age since the first century. Hence, mission-minded congregations make every effort to keep the maintenance mindset in its place. And it is always a second place.

A mission mind-set shows itself most readily in a congregation's ability to speak of God's presence and ministry in the here and now of everyday life, not in highly intellectualized and abstract language, but in terms easily understood in the marketplace of life. This is, of course, the ministry of the church commonly called evangelism. The following chapters discuss this ministry afresh.

"The big failing in churches is that they haven't helped people with their own spirituality, their own life with God." So says Wayne Schwab, Evangelism Ministries Officer of the Episcopal Church. Yet at the same press conference Schwab noted that there is evident in almost every part of the church a request for spiritual help and guidance.[1] Part II in this book is devoted to helping both individuals and congregations *make plans* to discern and celebrate God's every-day ministry among us. Spirituality like this is a striking mark of every mission-minded congregation.

You will also be introduced to the concepts of *preevangelism, primary* and *secondary* evangelism. Each one helps us value the rich opportunities we are given to reach out to one another and to God's world, and each one is different. Few of us might be skilled or much interested in all three: But for the sake of the world and God, mission-minded congregations value all three as parts of a whole.

Church Growth and the Power of Evangelism is also written with other practicalities in mind. You will find specific suggestions about helping any parish welcome and incorporate newcomers, and special instructions about reincorporating those who have slipped from active membership. One chapter is also devoted to a discussion of the ministry of the laity that mission-minded congregations value, and recommendations are made to help you involve your parish in this important deliberation.

In still other chapters you will find a discussion of the quality of worship and clergy leadership found in mission-minded congregations. As a result, you will be able to evaluate more accurately your congregation's pattern of worship, and clergy will find suggestions and perspectives to help them assess their ministry and take better care of themselves.

In every chapter of *Church Growth and the Power of Evangelism* you will find encouragement to reexamine the shape of the ministry of your congregation, and specific suggestions about how to proceed.

If, by the time you have finished reading this book, you find that you're interested in helping your congregation catch a new vision of mission and its ministry, or if you simply want to help your people become more precise with the vision they already have, put a copy of this book into the hands of every member of your parish. Chapter 16 helps you plan this educational ministry. And if you are interested in exploring further some of the ideas about Sunday morning Christian education in mission-minded congregations, my book *Christian*

Education Made Easy is a description of what I have found in such congregations.

Every church is at a different place in its life, with different needs and opportunities. But by presenting a full range of the perspectives and possibilities that mark growing churches across the land, I hope that your imagination will be teased about opportunities before you which you never before thought.

The following pages don't agonize or say "ain't it awful" (even if it sometimes is) about the decline experienced by mainline Protestant churches in the last twenty years. Rather, *Church Growth and the Power of Evangelism* shows why the decline has taken place, poses some fresh ways to assert God's presence, and helps interested churches make plans to put into practice the discoveries made by growing congregations.

1. "Good News in Gallup" in *Episcopal Life* (April 1990): 5.

PART I

Because We
Are Loved

Hope for the Mainline Church

Acknowledging the Bad News • Power At Work in the Mainline Church: A Mindset For Mission • Identifying the Maintenance Mindset • The Age-old Oscillation: Between Mission and Maintenance • The Power Of God • A Passion For Excellence: Ten Marks Of Growing Churches • How to Assess Your Growth Potential

hat marks the difference between those mainline churches doing well and those just limping along? Are some congregations merely blessed with good luck and good fortune, or is there something more at work in their common life? In fact, declining numbers mark many mainline Protestant churches in America.

But in more than a few places the tide is turning. Although generally unnoted in the midst of bad news, growing mainline congregations are beginning to show themselves: their budgets are increasing, often their numbers are growing, and they are making a significant impact in their local community. And even if they are not growing in numbers or in budget, they are blessed with a spirit of joyful expectation. Their Sunday schools work well and parishioners look forward to going to church.

The following chapters detail the power into which a growing number of mainline congregations are tapping, the power of God to make things new, using tools as old as the early church.

In the following chapters you'll find a wealth of ideas to help you

• develop your capacity to identify and celebrate God's everyday ministry in the world (commonly called the ministry of evangelism),

• evaluate your congregation's welcome of newcomers and help them become active members,

• construct an exciting and satisfying educational program for adults and children, one that centers its attention on celebrating God at work in the world.

If you've ever thought that things could be better in your congregation, and if you've had trouble putting your finger on what might be wrong and what might be right, this book will offer you all kinds of practical insights gathered from congregations "in the know."

Acknowledging the Bad News

According to the 1989 *Yearbook of American and Canadian Churches* the Roman Catholic Church and a number of conservative churches continued to grow in 1987 (the latest figures available), while many "mainline" Protestant denominations experienced another year of membership losses.[1]

This same article in *The Living Church* notes that in 1987 the Episcopal Church shrank by 1.69%, losing 42,000 members, while declines also marked the United Methodist Church (0.74%), the Presbyterian Church (USA) (1.3%), the United Church of Christ (0.81%), and the Disciples of Christ (1.81%). And in December, 1989, *The Anglican Digest* noted that the Episcopal Church is no longer listed as one of the ten largest church bodies in the United States.[2]

More, lay members in the Episcopal Church might be surprised to learn that the reasons for the decline of the Episcopal Church are for the most part unattended by either theological education (where women and men are prepared for leadership in the church), or by their diocesan leadership—except for some hand-wringing. Yet seminaries, of all the resources in the church, ought to be focused on what modern day business calls research and development.

Pollsters like George Gallup suggest that the declining membership of mainline congregations is rooted in a return of their parishioners to fundamentalist denominations.

In the last two decades many middle-class Americans have left mainline churches, with their emphasis on social programs, and joined the evangelical movement, attracted by a more inward-looking faith and clearer, stricter instruction in moral values.[3]

During the period 1965 to 1985, the Assemblies of God (formerly the church of Jimmy Swaggart and Jim and Tammy Bakker) grew from 500,000 to a few more than 2,000,000, while the Southern

Baptist Convention expanded from slightly less than 11,000,000 to 14,500,000.

In this same interval:

• the United Methodist Church lost 2,000,000 members, declining from about 11,000,000;

• the Presbyterian Church (USA) lost 25% of its membership, down to 3,000,000 from a high in 1965 of 4,000,000 members; and

• the Episcopal Church declined from about 3,400,000 to 2,900,000 communicants (losing an additional 400,000 members in 1986). In fact, the Anglican Digest notes that since 1968 there has been a decline of 33% in Episcopal Church numbers.[4]

Two million members, one million members, and a loss of one third of its membership. From the looks of these statistics it seems like pollsters like George Gallup might be right.

Mainline church leaders are concerned. A group of wardens and treasurers in the Episcopal diocese of Colorado, for example, meeting with their bishops, listed as a first priority the ministry "Evangelism and Incorporation" as the item with which they needed the most assistance.

> These leaders went on to say that they wanted help "retaining existing members, integrating and retaining new members, [and] motivating 'Sunday-only' people to deeper, more active commitment." The concerns of these local church officials are also the front-burner interests of leaders in other mainline American denominations.[5]

But happily, more than a few mainline congregations are *not* shrinking. Indeed, some show growth in numbers and commitment *even* in economically stagnant areas, places where population increases don't naturally drive up Sunday morning attendance. Though my research has generally centered on Episcopal churches, the following pages describe some of the common denominators that I've found marking growing churches in what we call the mainline denominations. And fundamentally what I have discovered is this:

"Where there is no vision the people perish" (Prov. 29:18 KJV)

Power At Work In the Mainline Church: A Mindset For Mission

Every year I travel in the mainline church, and while I journey mostly in Episcopal circles, I also visit with other denominations. And no matter where I go, I don't much sit in the offices of denominational executives discussing strategies or programs. I'm present in congregations a lot like yours, and as a result I see a number of congregations "doing things right."[6]

And this is what I've discovered. Growing, enthusiastic-about-ministry congregations are marked *mostly* by what I have learned to identify as a *mission mindset* of hope. Declining congregations are marked *mostly* by a maintenance mindset; they are more concerned with repairs and programs than celebrating God's everyday presence and ministry, and they are mostly concerned with what they "ought" to do.

Mission-minded congregations:

• celebrate God's presence and ministry in the here and now of everyday life,

• celebrate the presence of newcomers in their midst as gifts of God,

• celebrate with worship that sets hearts on fire, and

• celebrate what goes on in the Sunday school classrooms of their children. In maintenance-minded congregations, Sunday school is generally a necessary obligation, and those few good-hearted folks who give their lives to this effort often burn out. And then they drop out.

Even if these enthusiastic-about-ministry congregations aren't blessed with expanding numbers, they are celebrants because each one is marked to some degree by a "mission-mindset" of hope: God is close, these congregations know it, they enjoy talking about it, and this knowledge fuels their common life with enthusiasm and old-fashioned commitment.

Six years ago, when St. Thomas' Episcopal Church (Dubois, Wyoming) gathered for worship at 10:00 AM, about twenty-five people opened their prayer books and hymnals. Then they called a mission-minded priest to serve them as rector. And they began to talk about God.

Now instead of one worship service on Sunday morning, they have two. About twenty persons gather for an 8:00 AM eucharist, later at 10:00 AM the small church building bulges with about seventy (more or less), and at 9:00 AM about thirteen or so gather for an adult Bible class. And at the 1989 Sunday School Christmas festival, the church was jam-packed with one hundred and thirty seven children and adults. And before you jump to the conclusion that Dubois is exploding, let me note that this wild-west town's population is expanding at about the rate of a dead-slow trickle.

One reason that congregations like St. Thomas' are growing is this: they make every effort to identify, welcome and incorporate Sunday morning visitors (both children and adults), no matter how few come during the year. They do this not only as an act of human generosity, which it is, but because they know that God has a hand in bringing all visitors to church. It is God who accompanies these newcomers through the front door of the church on Sunday morning and, in response, the welcome these mission-minded Christians offer is a faithful act of worship directed to the Sovereign God of the universes.

Nor do these congregations simply offer a good-hearted general welcome. It is more than a "take it or leave it" approach. Indeed, mission-minded congregations make all kinds of careful plans to incorporate these newcomers into parish life. Recent studies show the wisdom of their method.

> Interviewing 50 active members and 50 persons who had left the church, one study discovered that the number of friendships developed in the first six months is critical in maintaining and strengthening a relationship between the visitor and their new congregation.
>
> Of the active members surveyed, all could name three or more friends made during the first six months. Thirteen new members could identify seven or more friends, and twelve could identify nine or more friends.
>
> But of the 50 persons who had left the church, eight had established no such relationships, fourteen could name only one friend, and eight could name three friends. Only one drop-out could name six friends.[7]

Still more investigation corroborates this finding. Church growth leaders note that:

• Newcomers are looking for circles of intimacy. If the ways and means to connect with the life of the parish are not readily available and identifiable, these visitors will not likely return. These folks want to participate not only in the on-going life of the congregation; they want to make friends.

• Searching families are likely to turn away from a church that is so crowded (80% of capacity) that they can't conveniently sit together, a church that doesn't have a bright and inviting nursery, and a church that doesn't have a parking space they can find on the first try.

• Newcomers also look for strong preaching. They want to know more about God in the here and now of their life, and they want preachers to enjoy using the Bible. They want sermons relevant to their everyday life situation, sermons that ask, "Who is God and what difference does a knowledge of God make in my everyday life?"

• Newcomers want worship that welcomes. They find a predominantly pre-1940s diet of church music hard to take. But they don't want guitars either. They do like the use of instruments and the piano, and synthesizers are finding an increasing use around the church, both large and small, and particularly in small congregations that couldn't normally afford more than a tinny-sounding electric organ.

Identifying the Maintenance Mindset

On the other hand, declining mainline congregations are often marked by an overly conscientious concern for maintenance, whether buildings or program. Over the course of years these congregations have become more interested in themselves than interested in God. I've come to call this ailment a "maintenance mindset," and it stands in sharp contrast to its opposite. So, you ask, "What are some of the marks of this mindset?"

In the extreme, maintenance-minded clergy tend to be strong on telling their congregations what to do and what not to do. "I don't want flowers on the altar;" meaning there will be no more flowers on the altar. "We must develop a soup kitchen," they might say, and

"Our committee meetings are running too long"—or not long enough. "This year we will have an Easter Vigil," or "Next year I want brass on Easter Sunday morning," they say with brass.

These members of clergy have opinions about a lot of things. But their opinions are most often centered on what they want done, which becomes what "ought" to be done. Such clergy are fundamentally self-centered. They don't much care about the hopes and desires of their congregation, and they have little knowledge of what it means to pray together *with* their people to discern the hopes of God's holy spirit. In their heart of hearts they know that given such prayerful conditions, God's holy spirit will likely generate a variety of expressions, a sum too rich for them to handle. They fear a loss of control.

With this kind of leadership, maintenance-minded congregations *learn* to worry about things that "ought" to be done. "The parish hall needs a new roof," says the buildings and grounds committee, "The Sunday school needs a new curriculum to work well," another says, or "We have got to have a more successful stewardship drive this year," says still another. You will not hear in these congregations much talk about God, but a lot about what the church "ought" to be doing.

POINT. Congregations marked by enthusiasm for ministry first of all set their sights on God's ministry in their midst. They know how to identify it and they love to talk about it. And only then do they pay attention to things like repairing the roof and providing new curriculum materials. These congregations know that both mission and maintenance perspectives always mark their common life, but they can tell the difference of one from the other, and they know that a mission perspective always walks first in the kingdom of God.

Every chapter in this book is devoted to a discussion of these two perspectives, and shows why a mission-minded attitude makes all the difference. Vision is at issue here.

The Age-old Oscillation: Between Mission and Maintenance
From its first-century beginnings, the Christian church has oscillated between the perspectives of mission and maintenance. This is a

given: After any group of people gathers for any reason, in short order they become concerned about taking care of themselves. However, the more Christian churches concern themselves with self-preservation, the less likely they will value the identification and celebration of God's ministry.

If Christian congregations generate because of a joy for mission, once buildings are constructed a concern for space takes over, or more space, for the roof, for the plumbing, for new members to help us "grow" even more, and the list goes on and on.

For example, the Church of the Heavenly Rest (Episcopal) began thirty years ago as a mission. Since their founding they have had two presiding priests, and their current minister has been there twenty-six years. In their earlier days they were surrounded by the angels. Every Sunday brought new people and new opportunities. God was close and they knew it.

But as the suburbs expanded and as city life encroached on the once-quiet neighborhoods surrounding this church, members (many of them founding members) moved away to more distant suburbs. The number of those returning shrinks a bit with each passing year. Their priest has also grown older. He's no longer as aggressive in his ministry as he once was. Nor is the congregation. They are happy with their friendships. But one founding member recently noted that when their minister retires, she and her husband will no longer pass the many Episcopal churches between their new home and Heavenly Rest. "We will probably transfer," she says, "but not until our minister retires."

Recently a newcomer visited the Church of the Heavenly Rest. But she left after the early service not quite feeling the fulfillment for which she hoped, so she attended a neighboring Methodist church. And there she found the welcome for which she had been looking. "The people at Heavenly Rest were cordial enough, but the people at the Methodist church were truly friendly. They were glad to see me, and I had never even been there before."

At Heavenly Rest, mission has given way to maintenance. And when their present minister leaves they will probably lose many of their current members. There will be a period of remorse, regret and

soul searching, particularly as they find their common life impoverished by a flight of members and the loss of their "spark." God
is of course still bringing newcomers and visitors to Heavenly Rest.
But they are no longer welcomed as they once were. The fire of mission is gone.

POINT. If a new church begins because of the power of a mission
perspective, it often declines the more a maintenance perspective
asserts itself.

The following pages show why a mission perspective makes the
difference between excellence in ministry, and ministry that just
limps along. Often I treat the maintenance mindset as a foil, marking
it as "bad." I exaggerate for effect. But don't forget the truth of the
matter: maintenance and mission mindsets mark every congregation's life, but to the extent that maintenance rules, congregational
life suffers.

The Power Of God

Underlying the vitality of mission-minded congregations lies the
power of God. Now I don't mean even remotely to suggest that the
loving power of God is not present in the most intractable maintenance-minded congregation. But what mission-minded congregations have learned is this: That it is a celebration of the power of
God that generates joy in their common life, not the necessity of
fixing the roof. Strong-willed maintenance-minded congregations
have lost this vision.

Hans Küng describes the presence of God's renewing spirit this
way, and teases the imagination about the way in which God is
working to form congregations marked with a mindset for mission.

> Perceptible and yet not perceptible, invisible and yet powerful, real like the
> energy-charged air, the wind, the storm, as important for life as the air we
> breathe: this is how people in ancient times frequently imagined the
> "Spirit" and God's invisible working.
>
> According to the beginning of the creation account, "spirit" is the "roar-
> ing," the "tempest" of God over the waters....
>
> "Spirit" as understood in the Bible means the force or power proceeding
> from God, which is opposed to "flesh," to created, perishable reality: that
> invisible force of God and power of God which is effective creatively or

destructively, for life or judgment in creation and in history, in Israel and in the Church.[8]

God is keenly interested in our lives. Mission-minded Christians know this, and mission-minded mainline congregations are being blessed because they preach this message above all others.

A Passion For Excellence: Ten Marks Of Growing Churches

What factors make for hope and fervor in mission-minded congregations?

1. Mission-minded congregations are marked by a passion for excellence. But these congregations don't simply say to themselves, "We must be excellent." Excellence is a by-product of their close walk with God. And because they know God is near, nothing is left to chance. In large measure these congregations take their marching orders from a comment made by Jesus: "You, therefore, must be perfect, as your heavenly Father is perfect." (Mt 5:48)

But mission-minded congregations are not deceived into thinking that Jesus is asking the church to be flawless. They know that Jesus asks only that we be whole, or complete, even fully grown up, a better translation of the Greek text than the word "perfect."

2. Adult parishioners in mission-minded congregations are learning to enjoy identifying and celebrating God's everyday presence and ministry. More, they are being equipped for this ministry by clergy preaching and teaching. These Christians know that God is not an object or an idea to be debated. Rather, God is known as a Subject who engages the world in the here and now of life today. Mission-minded Christians have been touched by God's love and it has made a difference in their lives. They know that God's kingdom is at hand; they have been taught to recognize it and they can comfortably talk about it.

3. Because these mission-minded Christians know that God is always with us, they value evangelism as a ministry of introductions. Evangelism is not, for them, a high pressure sales pitch. This kind of evangelism sounds more like the angels announcing the birth of Jesus than it sounds like the fervent, closing argument in a court case that many Christians have come to fear.

4. A mission-minded congregation's ability to speak of God marks their life with celebration. They like nothing better than to thank God for one thing or another, and as a result they begin to thank one another for everything. The altar guild is praised for its work, and the work of the Sunday school is regularly celebrated by the parish at large (it is never hidden away in a back-hall classroom). Indeed, parishioners learn to give thanks and offer praise to one another because they see it modeled by clergy leadership.

5. Newcomers to Sunday morning worship are immediately identified, welcomed and incorporated into the life of the congregation. Mission-minded congregations know that every newcomer is accompanied to Sunday morning worship by God keenly interested in us.

Nor does extending the glad hand of welcome cease with this initial welcome. Newcomers classes are designed to continue the process of inclusion, and these newcomers aren't simply asked to "call the church office to let us know if you'll be present." They are personally invited, and in many cases accompanied by a parish sponsor.

Lapsed members, when they are identified, also receive attentive response in mission-minded congregations. In fact, I find that mission-minded Christians tend to reach out more quickly, for the sake of love, to both newcomers and the lapsed.[9]

6. The generosity of the celebration makes education a joy in mission-minded congregations. And education is shaped three ways.

• Whether a mission-minded congregation is large or small, Sunday school is highly valued and it is well done. Visiting parents are generally "sold" on a new ongregation because of the commitment expressed toward Christian education, and because the plans they use work.

• The adult capacity to speak of God with clarity and in easy, spontaneous ways is enabled by classroom education, Bible study and prayer groups.

• These mission-minded Christians have also been taught to understand that in their daily occupations they help God take care of the world, their neighborhood and their community. They have learned that the ministry of the laity is more than just a synonym for serving on the altar guild or the vestry.

7. Pastoral care is an important priority, but in growing congregations it ranges more widely than simply responding to the sick and those who are hurt, as important as these ministries are. Much of parish pastoral care in mission-minded congregations takes shape in small group settings.

Large congregations who don't honor this need tend to shrink. For example, five years ago the United Methodist Church of Whitefish Bay, Wisconsin, found that it had experienced a 45% membership decline from a peak of 2000 in 1976. Seeking help, they turned to Church Growth Inc., of Monrovia, California. Today, in an area where population has continued to decline, membership has settled at about 1400. Sunday school attendance has jumped from 300 to 700 and average worship attendance from 400 to 560.

What made the difference? Pastor Richard Jones considers the ninety *small groups* formed by church members as one key to growth. There are traditional *Bible study* groups as well as those offering things like *aerobics* for women. Church dinners are held at least weekly, with *Wednesday night meals* usually attracting between 150 and 200 people. These include families who stay on for choir practice or other activities.[10]

8. Outreach is an essential ministry. Growing churches count it a joy to offer assistance and care to the surrounding community. Church facilities are regularly used by garden clubs, Alcoholics Anonymous, Al-Anon, Mothers Against Drunk Driving, and Sons Against Drunk Driving. There may be a day care program for working parents, or a kindergarten or school, and those not able to put bread on their table may be fed at a soup kitchen.

9. Sunday worship celebrates God's love in song, prayer, preaching and praise, whether in formal or informal settings. Members look forward to "going to church," and every effort is made to make worship familiar and comfortable for the newcomer.

The following does not happen in mission-minded congregations:

> One parishioner noted that his rector conducts church worship "by the book." She never announces page numbers, and there is very little wel-

come, either at the beginning of worship or at the time of the announcements. She doesn't want to disturb the 'purity' of the liturgy."

"And," he continues, "we don't attract or keep many newcomers."

10. Clergy are enthusiastic, articulate leaders with whom people
can identify. Underline the word *leadership*. It seems to be *the* significant ingredient that enables the development of a mission mindset. These women and men know who they are and Whose they are.

Each of these ten points is discussed in the following chapters.
And in those chapters you will also find suggestions to compare and
contrast your own attitudes and procedures to those found in mission-minded congregations.

How to Assess Your Growth Potential

We do a grave disservice to ourselves by thinking that church
growth will only take place when we bring a friend to church on
Sunday morning, a notion that has done more to disable the ministry
of evangelism than any other.

Here's what is wrong with the idea of basing church expansion on
the primacy of our invitation to others: measuring church growth on
the basis of our invitation simply values "our" ministry (which we
are wont to do, are we not?), as opposed to the ministry of a loving
God always inviting visitors to grace our doors. Mission-minded
congregations, on the other hand, have discovered an age-old truth;
when they welcome those newcomers God is always stirring to look
us over on Sunday morning, the church of God is quite likely to expand at a pace that keeps us busy.

In fact God is always gracing our doors with new people looking
for a home, and by now you may want to test how well your congregation is responding—or not. To test the effectiveness of your
stewardship, simply take the number of newcomers who graced your
doors during the last twelve months (I hope you know how many),
subtract from them the number who joined with your fellowship, and
divide that number by the total number who visited. And don't count
visitors from out of town, or family visitors on holiday outings. Use
your common sense.

For example, St. Martin's, a small church in the suburbs, counted 17 visiting units (families, couples and singles) in the previous year. These folks were new to the neighborhood and out "shopping" for a church. 5 are now active. By dividing 17 into 5, the actual growth of St. Martin's is 29%, while the growth potential of St. Martin's (dividing 17 into 12) is 71%. How would you evaluate the job they did?

Unfortunately, thinking about church growth may trouble some congregations who don't deserve to be worried. St. John's, for example, was last year visited by only two new units, a family with two small children and one single adult. And both stayed to become members. The *actual* and the *potential* growth of St. John's are both 100%. St. John's is located in a rural area on the edge of suburbia, and except for visitors from out of town, only occasionally do newcomers attend.

The plain fact is this: God is always about the business of bringing folks to church on Sunday morning, a point made over and over again in the following chapters. We are at our best when we honor this Godly ministry, and mission-minded congregations make every effort to do so.

End Notes

1. *The Living Church* (September 10, 1989): 10.

2. *The Anglican Digest* (Advent-Epiphany 1989): 49.

3. Laura Sessions Stepp, "The Evangelical Challenge: Many Americans Leave Mainline Churches" in *Washington Post* (17 August 1987): 1.

4. *The Anglican Digest* (Lent 1989): 2. Similar figures were supplied by the Commission on Evangelism and Renewal, and reported to the 1988 General Convention of the Episcopal Church.

5. *The Colorado Episcopalian* May/June 1988.

6. I often travel to diverse places in the American church, mainly conducting and participating in Christian education workshops. To name a few, I have visited both large and small congregations in such places as McAllen and San Antonio, Texas; Honolulu, Hawaii; Breckenridge, Colorado; Baton Rouge, Louisiana; Dubois, Wyoming; Montclair, New Jersey; Logan, Utah; Topeka, Kansas; Shawnee, Oklahoma, Meridian, Mississippi, Wilmington and Chapel Hill, North Carolina; Sewanee, Tennessee; Blacksburg, Va., and near my home in the Washington, DC suburbs of northern Virginia.

Most times I travel to these places because I am invited, but more and more I invite myself. My teaching leadership in a seminary of the church demands that I remain current with contemporary pastoral ministry in the local church, no matter what shape it takes, and the only way to do this is by direct observation. I cannot teach what I do not know.

7. Win Arn and Charles W. Arn, "How to Uses Ratios to Effect Church Growth" in *Church Growth: The State of the Art*, C. Peter Wagner, ed. (Wheaton, IL: Tyndale House, 1986), pp. 97-98.

8. Hans Kung, *On Being A Christian* (Garden City, NY: Doubleday, 1976), pp. 178-9.

9. A. Wayne Schwab. "The Decade of Evangelism," 11/4/88.

10. *The Washington Post* (21 October 1989): 6.

Similar material is noted in The Anglican Digest, Late-Pentecost A.D. 1988, page 28-29, *Worshipers Back for More*, Dr. Erwin J. Kolb. Kolb calls the immediacy of response the "36-hour principle." When lay persons visit the homes of first-time visitors within 36 hours, 85% will return to worship the next Sunday. When the visit is delayed for 72 hours, only 60% return, and when delayed 5 to 7 days, only 15% return.

CHAPTER 2

Kindled By Fire and Blazing with Hope: The Power of a Perspective

The Gospel Loving, Mission-Minded Perspective • The Maintenance Mind-set • Hope On the Horizon • Old Christ Church: Historic and Traditional • St. Peter's in the Woods: Brand New and Growing • St. Thomas: Deep America Rural • Clergy Leadership Makes All the Difference • Checklist: Taking Action To Diagnose Your Church

Contemporary growing congregations are tapping into ancient, God-with-us themes powering the church for 2000 years. I've learned to identify the capacity to celebrate God's presence and ministry as a "mission mind-set," a perspective sharply distinguished from its opposite, a "maintenance-minded" ministry. This chapter shows maintenance and mission mindsets at work in the life of the church, and what happens to the spirit of a congregation when either one or both is exercised.

As noted in the last chapter, on more than a few occasions in this book I treat the maintenance mindset as a foil, a straw man, and mark it as "inferior." I do this for effect. But don't forget the truth of the matter: maintenance and mission mindsets mark every congregation's life, but to the extent that maintenance rules, congregational life suffers. Every church will have some of each attitude, but the mission mind-set is the edge that makes the difference in all growing congregations.

The Gospel Loving, Mission-Minded Perspective

The notion of a mission mind-set does not mean what is commonly understood as mission: sending missionaries into the world, developing programs in the world, or otherwise giving away time, talent, and money to the world. These tasks will naturally follow the development of a mission mind-set, but they do not precede it.

Mission-minded Christians first of all value their relationship with God, and they enjoy their capacity to speak of God in plain, market-place language. They know who God is, they have come to expect God to be present in the midst of life, and they know that worship takes place every time they say "thank you" for a happy coincidence, or for the advent of good fortune. Mission-minded Christians know that God is doing infinitely more in our midst than we can ask for or imagine (Eph.3:20). They enjoy centering their attention on God's everyday action in the world, and, as the Westminster Catechism states, they know that the chief aim of the church is to love God and enjoy God forever.

When knowledge of God's presence and ministry is valued as most important in the local congregation, and when the first order of business is that of seeking *to celebrate* God's presence and ministry in the world, all else falls into place. Furthermore, a church learns to be mission-minded because ordained clergy provide mission-minded leadership. Make no mistake, the clergy model is all-important. Now this is not a pitch for a clergy-centered ministry. But across the church I have found that when the clergy model is missing, the likelihood of a mission mind-set developing in any parish is small. Furthermore, a parish commitment to mission is easily destroyed with the advent of maintenance-minded clergy.

A potentially divisive issue provides the illustration of a mission-minded rector at work with her congregation's executive committee. Here we find ourselves at a meeting of the church executive committee. The agenda item is a presentation of the architect's plan for a new sanctuary, and the committee's response is generally favorable. Discussion is drawing to a close, but as it does one member of the board announces, "I just can't go along with all this. I haven't said much to this point, but I just can't remain silent any longer." He is strongly set in his views.

Without a second thought, the pastor immediately says, "Let's listen to [and she names him], because God may be speaking to us here. Please tell us what you're thinking, and maybe we can also help you put things into words."

She soon discovers what has upset this hesitant member of the committee: The architect's drawings show a building substantially larger than the present one, and older members are fearful they will lose some of the informality that they have learned to love on Sunday morning.

With no fear on her part about a contrary opinion or the failure of a growing consensus, this pastor carefully explains to the board that here is an opportunity to think even more deeply about God's invitation to consider the construction of a new building. As a result of the ensuing discussion, the vestry directed the architect to return with plans that made better provision for informal conversation and fellowship in the new building.

Mission-minded clergy and the congregations committed to their care know four important things:

• the world belongs to God;

• God is present in the world and God is always stirring us to new visions of opportunity;

• signs of God's ministry abound in the here and now of everyday life—to eyes that can see;

• their capacity to speak about God's ministry without embarrassment, and in ways that generate the interest of others fuels their mission thrust.

The Maintenance Mind-set

As necessary as the mission perspective is, a maintenance mind-set is generally more evident in most mainline Protestant congregations. As you might expect, these are task-centered churches. Leadership spends much of its time worrying about conservation. Members often complain about being tired of requests for more money, noting that repairs never end. They also report that they like the way things are, and wonder why others aren't so interested in joining their common life.

The Episcopal Church is a mainline denomination whose common life illustrates a maintenance mind-set at work and shows how it develops. From 1850 to 1900, the Episcopal Church grew at a pace three times faster than the general population in the United States. In those decades worship and preaching were valued and done well, Sunday morning "church" was a special event, and Christian education, particularly for children, grew to be an important ministry. Social action was also much a part of this denomination's life.

St. Andrew's Episcopal Church in Meriden, Connecticut epitomizes what took place in those decades. To house its growing Sunday school, in 1888 St. Andrew's constructed the first parish hall in the Episcopal Diocese of Connecticut. This congregation also sponsored a widely acclaimed boys' choir, planned and provided worship that brought in more and more members, and built both an orphanage for children and a home and infirmary for the widows of factory workers. Every one of these ministries were developed with funds generated by grateful church members.

The story of St. Andrew's was repeated with variations across the country in the years before the turn of the century by congregations in all mainline denominations. Hospitals were built, Sunday schools begun, and some of the most majestic church buildings in America were erected as an expression of thanksgiving to Almighty God.[1]

Every congregation begins this way, with a mission mindset firmly in place. God is close and they know it. But the longer any congregation exists, the more likely it will engage a maintenance mindset, and run the risk of being consumed by it. The natural progression from mission to maintenance shows itself in two ways: a legitimate concern with expanding maintenance needs, such as repairing the roof or fixing the plumbing, and a healthy common life that turns into an unhealthy "static triumphalism."[2]

Static triumphalism believes that the way things are is the way things ought to be. The more this mind-set takes shape, the more church maintenance becomes the order of the day. It is rooted in what we Christians call sin, our need to cling to "what is" for the sake of safety in the future. Unfortunately, the more we obsessively cling to what we like now, the less able we are to respond to the many opportunities God is placing before us today.

The following statistics paint a grim picture of static triumphalism in the Episcopal Church. After a time of great expansion in the nineteenth century, from 1900 to 1980 (even thought the American population was expanding) Episcopal Church growth merely kept pace. In the last twenty years membership in this denomination has declined by 33%.[3]

Year	US Population	Baptized Members
1860	31,433,000	146,500
1870	38,558,000	220,000
1880	50,152,000	338,000
1890	62,481,000	509,000
1900	76,295,000	715,000
1910	92,284,000	928,000
1920	105,710,000	1,074,000
1930	122,775,000	1,261,000
1940	132,164,000	1,449,000
1950	151,326,000	1,657,000
1960	179,323,000	2,028,000
1970	203,302,000	2,239,000
1980	226,547,000	3,020,920
1981		3,014,982
1982		3,015,000
1983		3,024,105
1984		3,002,416
1985		2,972,607
1986		2,504,507

The declining figures are countered by recent numbers showing that although total membership is down, attendance at Sunday worship is up, and so is the amount of pledged income. Some say that these new numbers show a greater commitment to the gospel and the church's ministry, and well they might. But when the increases of growing congregations were removed from these totals, the statistics present an even bleaker picture.

Static triumphalism tends to win out in older denominations. But why does God let such things happen?

To apply a farming image used by Jesus in the gospels: The more we fill our personal barns—no matter what those barns may be and what they may contain—with the good things that matter to us, the more that self-absorption will characterize our common life. Jesus puts it this way:

> There was a rich man whose land yielded heavy crops. He debated with himself: "What am I to do? I have not the space to store my produce. This is what I will do," said he: "I will pull down my storehouses and build them bigger. I will collect in them all my corn and other goods, and then say to myself, 'Man, you have plenty of good things laid by, enough for many years: take life easy, drink, and enjoy yourself.'" But God said to him, "You fool, this very night you must surrender your life; you have made your money—who will get it now?" (NEB. Luke 12:16-21).

Like many other mainline congregations, the Episcopal Church shows triumphalism and a maintenance perspective in such things as:

• An inability to identify and celebrate God's here-and-now ministry in the world. Many sermons in the Episcopal Church focus on who we are and the complexities of everyday life. Keen psychological insights are offered and social responsibilities outlined, but conspicuously missing is any identification and celebration of God at work in the world. Episcopal preachers aren't often able to offer this perspective, not because they don't want to do so, but because they were never taught how. For the most part Episcopal clergy grew to maturation in maintenance-minded congregations and were not equipped for a mission-minded ministry by their seminary education. In short, they give to others what they got.

• Placing less and less emphasis on welcoming newcomers at Sunday worship, or making Prayer Book worship itself more hospitable. We print an order of worship in the Sunday bulletin, but expecting newcomers and visitors to balance several books, follow a tightly constructed bulletin and do both while an unfamiliar liturgy marches on is not only naive, but unfair.

• Interest in new members merely as a way of filling out the list of pledging units. "We *need* new members," these congregations say, and listening more closely, it quickly becomes clear that new members will simply ensure that the congregation will not shrink to nothing, or that the parish budget will be guaranteed. Maintenance-minded congregations tend to treat visitors and newcomers as objects.

• Coffee hours which, if they are held at all, are focused not on the people God is bringing to church for a first time visit, but as opportunities for old friends to greet and exchange the gossip that helps all community life continue. This latter maintenance task is important, but coffee hours are better valued as an expression of both mission and maintenance.

Hope On the Horizon

Fortunately, hope is showing again in some mainline American congregations. One report describes it this way:

> A few months ago I met a young couple at a conference who excitedly told me and anyone who would listen about their parish. They praised its spirituality, the Bible studies, the innovative programs linking personal piety with social action, and the opportunity for and expectation that every parishioner would discern and use his or her spiritual gifts.
>
> I asked where this wonderful parish was and discovered the couple drove forty miles, crossing parish, diocesan, and even provincial lines, to attend their church.
>
> Since then I have heard variations of this story frequently enough to know that the artificial political boundaries of the Episcopal Church no longer hold. People no longer attend the neighborhood parish out of obligation or the Episcopal Church because their parents did. People attend church because they are hungry and are looking for parishes to feed them, not denominations to be identified with.
>
> The plain and simple truth is people are searching for answers to the tough questions of living in today's world, answers that are not found on TV on Sunday mornings or in sermons summarizing the latest book read by the rector. People are asking to be fed and discipled, not managed and entertained.[4]

Both mission and maintenance perspectives are important. What we "should" and what we "ought" to do are to be valued. But so is the ministry of simply identifying and celebrating signs of God at work in the world. In fact, to the extent that this ministry does not walk first in our midst, to that degree the church is impoverished and in need of renewal.

Craig Dykstra writes as follows about this newly kindled movement:

> If a fresh awakening is taking place and if I am right about its character, pastors and theologians need to be prepared. Many of those who are

searching may be coming in our direction. They may turn to us for help, wanting to see if there is any food left in the cupboards of religious institutions they long ago may have left. They may even come with a sense of hope and anticipation. But they will be testing us to see if we know what the idols are—including religious ones—and to see if we are willing to call them by their names. If they sense we do not and will not, they will go away again, perhaps more cynical than before. If they sense we do and will, they may become interested.

But even this is not enough, for they are asking for something more. The deepest question they are asking—and may not yet dare to ask out loud— is this: Do you know God? If they sense we do not, again they will go away—perhaps this time more sadly than cynically. And if they sense we do, it will not be because we *say* we do. It will be because they see it in the way we live, in the manner of our speaking, and in our willingness to listen and to search. They will see it in the freedom this knowledge provides and in what this knowledge commits us to.

All this is true not only of the "thirtysomething" crowd who may have been reading the paper and buying bagels on Sunday mornings instead of going to church. It is true as well of people of all ages who populate the pews from week to week or spend their money on religious books and magazines. They want to know theological things. They want to know God.[5]

The world is hungry to hear about God in our midst. And when a word about God in our midst is offered, faithful response will increasingly take the shape of action, whether in the church or in the world. But inevitably, the social action of the church will shoulder aside mission until God acts afresh in our behalf.

Old Christ Church: Historic and Traditional

Traditional congregations across the land are among the churches that are growing. Christ Episcopal Church, Alexandria, Virginia, is one such example. Although George Washington worshipped within its walls, Christ Church is now marked more by current enthusiasm for ministry than by a remembrance of the past, though memory does run deep and traditions are much valued. In the last ten years its membership has almost doubled, and while a decade ago there were less than 100 children in the Sunday School, there are now more than 300 present on Sunday morning. On festival occasions Sunday worship is generally a standing-room-only affair. Christ Church is also located in an already jam-packed city where it is impossible for the population to expand at anywhere near the same rate as nearby Fairfax County.

Neither the people nor the clergy at Christ Church would likely identify their common life as an expression of "renewal." But in fact a spirit of infectious enthusiasm pervades their worship on Sunday morning. Bible preaching characterizes the sermons, and prayer is much a part of the way these folks live. God is near and they know it. More, a majority of parishioners eagerly participate in congregational activities, another mark of a mission-minded congregation. In fact, the church itself is like a second home for many.

St. Peter's in the Woods: Brand New and Growing

St. Peter's in the Woods is a brand new Episcopal church located in densely populated western Fairfax County, Virginia. From the beginning I was privileged to be part of their journey, remaining for a year until they called a permanent vicar. The church began as mission for the Church of the Good Shepherd in Burke, Virginia, a neighboring community. At the urgings of the rector of Good Shepherd, and as a result of prayer and meditation (including a retreat for those who were thinking with him about establishing a mission congregation), about thirty members chartered the church.

Meeting at the Bonnie Brae elementary school, one year later St. Peter's numbered about one hundred people for Sunday worship. Where their Sunday school at first numbered less that ten children, in a year it numbered near thirty, and more than fifteen teenagers regularly gathered for youth group meetings. How did this happen?

In part they have grown because their community is expanding. But there is more.

Worship is an event to which the members of St. Peter's look forward. They know that in church on Sunday morning they will hear about God, and find there the encouragement to come afresh to the throne of grace always hidden just behind the shadows. Make no mistake; there have been occasional problems. Yet the problems themselves point toward the way in which mission-minded congregations characteristically turn problems into opportunities. For example, at the end of their first summer a member of the vestry expressed concern that young families were not identifying with the parish. They came once and did not generally come again. Why? The answer was easy to discern.

Greeters at the door of St. Peter's identify newcomers, and then these visitors are introduced to others who still later sit nearby during worship. Next, a follow-up telephone call is made within two days to express joy at their first time visit, and to find out:

• How did things go on Sunday morning?
• Did you find a welcome?
• Did we leave anything undone that should have been done?
• Do you have any questions that I can answer now?
• Will you worship with us again?

Follow-up telephone conversations revealed that parents with children were concerned with our fledgling Sunday school. They wanted something more secure for their children.

We at St. Peter's knew we were doing good work with just a few children, but unless we were able to communicate that to visiting parents, we were going to continue to lose them. So we put on our thinking caps. Because our children enjoyed Sunday school during the Liturgy of the Word, giving parents an unhurried time to worship and enjoy the sermon, our few children had been quietly entering worship at the time of the Peace to join their parents for communion. To give a better witness to our Sunday school program, we instituted a student entrance processional with hymnody at the time of the Peace, and, when children brought to church some of the produce of their classroom (a banner made, a picture drawn, a question answered), we played a bit of show-and-tell with their classroom crafts at the time of the Peace. From then on visiting parents began to stay.

POINT. When Sunday school is valued, visiting parents stay for more. And the value of a Sunday school will show best when it is acknowledged with regularity.

St. Peter's also makes a parish commitment to wearing nametags—even for layreaders and clergy. For they know this: the more intentional any church about community building, the more likely community will form.

This congregation hosts a coffee hour in the entrance hall right next to the school cafeteria in which they worship. When people leave church, to get to the outside door they must first pass near the welcome provided by a bright presentation of cookies and cakes. The coffee hour is truly a time of celebration, and it becomes the clincher for people thinking about coming again. When and if you rethink your coffee hour ministry, or if you are planning on building a new church or parish/social hall, make sure that the place of coffee hour and fellowship is right next to the place of worship. You will not be disappointed by what results.

St. Thomas: Deep America Rural

Church growth and the celebration of a mission mindset are not limited to cities and suburbs. The town of Dubois, Wyoming, is located in the upper reaches of the Wind River Valley. It has not seen a population increase in recent memory. "We're about the size we've always been," inhabitants say, and the 1980 United States census put this town's population at about one thousand people. If you want to see what rural America is like, take a look at places like the Wind River Valley of Wyoming.

But in recent years something else has happened in Dubois. Six years ago when the folks at Dubois' St. Thomas Church gathered for Sunday morning worship twenty-five people opened their prayer books and hymnals. Then they called a mission-minded minister to serve them as priest. Sunday morning worship became a priority, the celebration of God's everyday presence and ministry took an articulate shape, and a commitment to community life grew. A small dayschool and nursery was begun, in itself an excellent tool to create an interface with the surrounding community.

Now instead of one worship service on Sunday morning, St. Thomas has two. The Sunday school which once numbered seven children now counts more than twenty on a typical morning, and adult Bible study is also popular. St. Thomas' Church is a small congregation, but it is burning with hope and enthusiasm, and across the country small congregations play out similar stories. The plain fact is this: the majority of mainline Protestant congregations are small churches of under 150 people, and they do not get a lot of attention. Yet small church mission-minded congregations know their ministry of presence in their community is an important-to-God expression of God's care. By their buildings and numbers (as small as they may be), these Christians know that they are everyday reminders of God at work in the world.

Also, because their open door policy is known to the community, each of these small congregations tends to attract community newcomers. They have learned that even in "no-growth" areas, people tend to come to places where they hear the welcome mat is out.

THE BOTTOM LINE. Mainline church leaders now recognize that the majority of their congregations count less than 250 members. Issues of church growth and "success," whatever success might be, are often troublesome to small congregations. "Big is better," our culture believes, and "small is failure." But this is the plain truth: there are a whole bunch of small congregations in America full of spirit and enthusiasm. They are not static and they are not going to vanish.

Clergy Leadership Makes All the Difference

Whether congregations are large or small, clergy leadership makes the most important difference in why some churches are spirited while others are not. Now again I say, this is not a pitch for a clergy-centered ministry. And I'm not suggesting that all lethargic congregations find their rest in clergy leadership. But my emphasis on the importance of clergy leadership does acknowledge what I see more and more around the church.

For example, St. John's Episcopal Church in McAllen, Texas, is a church bulging at the seams with children and adults in their Sunday school. They have a program that works because their clergy have given it all kinds of support. And new parents are quick to join this congregation on the basis on their children's welcome. Worship on Sunday morning is also packed, because these expectant Christians have learned that their clergy are enthusiastic about feeding them with the bread that lives. And when they gather to party at occasional church supper groups, the camaraderie simply reflects what transpires on Sunday morning. Clergy leadership makes the difference.

Or listen to this. The former rector of St. Michael and St. George in St. Louis, Missouri recently described the life of the parish he served and the ministry he encouraged: "I never go after people to come to this church. If we are doing what we ought, the people will hear of it and come on their own."[6] In large measure growth has occurred because the rector advised his parish to take itself $600,000 into debt to hire more staff. $600,000 into debt to hire more staff to support the life of congregation committed to his charge! You won't find maintenance-minded fellowships operating in this fashion.[7]

But the fact remains that among clergy who grew up in traditional churches more concerned with maintenance than mission, the chances are good that they will exercise a maintenance style of leadership in their adult years. In fact, these clergy are likely to mistake caretaking for leadership.

POINT. Maintenance-minded congregations long for a caretaker, and they are more than happy when a caretaking ministry takes shape. If:

• Sunday morning Christian education was not important in their formative years, it is not likely to be so now.

• preaching was not much valued as a ministry by the clergy with whom they grew up, it is not likely to be so now.

• leadership meant telling people what to do, they are likely to be autocratic now.

• there was no parish focus on a welcoming ministry, they are likely to perpetuate this model in their present congregation.

In many ways we members of clergy are reflections of our past. And if we do not learn about our past and critically assess it, we are doomed to repeat it.

Checklist: Taking Action To Diagnose Your Church

To make the points discussed in these first two chapters more immediately helpful to you and your church, use the following guides.

These questions are designed to help your discussion develop; they are not intended to provide specific plans.

1. Briefly discuss the marks of mission-minded congregations that show in your common life. Write them on newsprint.

2. Next, what words describe your congregation's attention to maintenance? Examine and discuss them.

3. Always remember that every church contains some of both perspectives.

4. With this discussion in mind, and considering the spirit of your congregation, where would you place your congregation's ministry on a scale between maintenance and mission?

Mission 1 _____ 10 Maintenance

2   3   4   5   6   7   8   9

5. Now the more important question: Where would you like your congregation to be?

6. What changes might be in order?

7. What will help you get to that place?

POINT. Growing churches also are concerned with maintenance and conservation, but it is a priority that falls behind their interest in the ministry of enjoying and bearing witness to signs of God's presence and ministry in the world.

End Notes

1. Cultural anthropologists also tell us that at least some of St. Andrew's nineteenth-century growth was fueled by the influx of non-English speaking immigrants. English speaking communities, fearful of losing their identity as an "English people," met their needs for community and identity by joining the Episcopal church. It represented things English.

2. I'm indebted to Martin Bell, author of *The Way Of The Wolf*, *The Return of the Wolf*, and the recently released *Wolf* for the concept of static triumphalism.

3. Statistics are compiled from figures published in the Episcopal Church Annual for the years under examination.

4. David L. James, "Hunger spurs search for renewed parishes," in *The Episcopalian/Professional Pages* (November 1989): A.

5. Craig Dykstra, "A Fresh Awakening?" in *Theology Today* (July 1989): 127-128.

Dykstra thinks that a third spiritual awakening is perhaps beginning in America. The first Great Awakening took shape in the seventeenth century. Among others, Jonathan Edwards gave expression to an American hunger for God, and in one of the greatest spiritual feasts in this nation's history, people found God and churches were built. What followed this rise of joy was a renewed commitment by the people of God to their everyday social responsibilities. But mission gave way to maintenance, and the fire was lost. This same pattern of mission giving way to maintenance in the churches occurred after the Civil War. It may now be that the American church stands at the front end of a third awakening. Certainly the excesses of some of the TV evangelists give expression to the excesses that often characterize the beginnings of all renewal.

6. "Evangelism Now!" in *The Anglican Digest* (Early Pentecost A.D. 1989): 5.
7. "Large Parishes" in *The Living Church* (May 21, 1989): 6.

PART II

Telling the Old, Old Story

CHAPTER 3

Always Surrounded by the Love of God

Preparing For Evangelism: Church Programs that Don't Help • Identifying Divine Interventions • Mission-Minded Christianity: More Than Fellowship • Evangelism: Introducing God to God's World • What Evangelism Is Not • Introductions in a "Chance" Encounter • Evangelism From the Perspective of Jesus' Life and Ministry • Nicodemus: Touched By Love and Changed • To Speak of God: Learning to Use a Language of Faith

Many mainline congregations are shrinking because they have lost their capacity to speak of godly things. Instead, now they are more concerned with ministry items like feeding the poor or setting the captives free. Now don't get me wrong and make no mistake: these are important works for Christians. And so is fixing the leak in the church roof.

But the good works of the church are not the fundamental work of the church. Fundamental is the task of identifying and celebrating signs of God's presence and active ministry in the world, so that the world might see, and seeing, believe.

In Part II you will read about the ways and means to identify God at work in the world, and you will be encouraged to conceive evangelism as a ministry of introducing God to God's world. This chapter will present an important New Testament understanding of evangelism often used in mission-minded congregations. I call it the ministry of introductions, and it is simply the ministry of introducing God to God's world, using signs of God's presence and ministry in the world as a springboard for witness. This ministry is widely practiced in mission-minded congregations (though not necessarily by the name I give it), and it is based on the work of Jesus, St. Paul and St. Philip.

I am much attracted to this way of thinking, and my appreciative bias shows.

Preparing For Evangelism: Church Programs that Don't Help

Many mainline, modern day Christians have lost the capacity to speak personally about God. Denominational leaders are concerned, but often what poses as denominational help offers little preparation. One Christian makes just this point.

> I recently attended an Evangelism Conference. We had great speakers, we sang a lot, and there was fellowship all around. As a result I'm convinced about the importance of evangelism. But I still don't know how to do it.
>
> What we did at that conference happens on Sunday in my church. We sing, we pray, we hear about God and we learn about God, so I can relate what I learned to Sunday worship, and I also see how we can improve some of the things we do. But I went to this conference hoping to learn more about the practice of personal evangelism. I'm an electrician by trade, and I was looking for something that would help me talk about God with other people. I didn't get any of that.

The confidence that skill-building generates is what Christians long for when thinking about evangelism, but skill-building is what they seldom get. What they do get are evangelism workshops offering more hype and hoopla than substance. Participants sing gospel songs, they share together in small groups, they begin to tell their stories about God's action in their lives, they eat together, worship together, and they end up with all kinds of good feelings about themselves and God. But good feelings don't get us very far when there's work to be done. The story of much hype and little substance is repeated elsewhere. For example, recently I was contacted by a person who had been asked by her denomination's leadership to be a workshop leader at an all-day evangelism conference. When she rejoined that she didn't know what to say about evangelism, she was told, "Just help the discussion." Immediately she telephoned me. She had recently seen an article in which I had discussed evangelism, and if possible she wanted at least a little bit of preparation.

"Can you help me with just a basic definition? I hate to ask you for your time." Because I was busy when she telephoned, I couldn't respond with the kind of explanation she deserved. So I asked her to call me early the next morning.

The next morning arrived, but she did not call. The time period we set passed, and I prepared to leave home to run some other errands. "But," I thought, "maybe she will still telephone." So I proceeded to answer some correspondence, a task I usually put off until the evening hours. A short while later the telephone rang.

"A friend of mine died last night, and I've been running behind all morning long. I'm sorry to be so late." After we talked briefly about the loss and her grief, at her request I proceeded to develop a fifteen minute short course in the ministry of evangelism, its definition, and the work of the ministry of introductions.

Finally, to show the ministry of introductions at work in the here and now of her life, I inquired about how she heard about my work, and why she thought about calling me. She told me the story of reading the article, filing it in her memory, not remotely aware that she would ever need to make use of it. But God might have known.

Then I told her about my being ready to leave the house for my other office, and my decision to remain at home instead. Now, you be the judge. Is this a story of God's love in action, or not?

This chapter is written to show why I think the preceding story records the shape of God's ministry, and to introduce to you evangelism's ministry of introductions.

Identifying Divine Interventions

God is a living presence in the here and now of everyday life, a point made on every page of the Bible. And what the Bible pictures about God "then" is a description of the way in which God acts in our world today. Mission-minded Christians, therefore, know they are never alone in the world, even if they sometimes feel that way.

For example, many of us are struck by odd, even fortunate coincidences. At still other times we benefit from blessings that don't seem to be deserved and haven't been anticipated. And as a result of these occurrences, many of us end up wondering "Why?" At precisely these points mission-minded Christians are offered an opportunity to speak of God, as the following two stories illustrate.

In 1969 Sue Scott woke up suddenly in the dead of a December night. She had just dreamed that her brother, an Air Force navigator named Doug Ferguson, had been involved in a car accident somewhere in the United States, that he was in serious trouble.

"I told myself," she recalls, "that it was all right. Doug was not in the United States, he was somewhere in Southeast Asia."

That afternoon her family received a message from the Air Force: the plane to which Doug Ferguson was assigned, an F4, had been shot down over the Laotian jungle while flying at only 500 feet. The crew was missing.

"I figured out the time difference," Sue says, "and I had the dream about the time the plane went down.[1]

At a recent church conference, Connie, a woman in her late thirties, recounted a similar episode. Traveling home with her husband late one rainy night, suddenly Connie was clutched by a cold fear that something terrible had happened to her mother. Next, she stunned her husband (and herself) by bursting into tears. As soon as they reached their home Connie telephoned her parents. Neighbors reported that her mother had just been involved in a bad accident, and that both her parents were now on their way to the hospital.

"Later," she said, "I figured her accident was exactly the same time as my premonition."

"But," you say, "I've heard about things like this before. It's no more than what some folks call mental telepathy." In fact we've all heard of things like these. But because of what the Bible and the church have to say about God's interest in our lives, you won't ever find me trying to discount these kinds of episodes.

POINT. God meets us where we are just as we are. And for just the briefest of moments these two women's heart were stirred about a painful reality about which neither had a reason to know. No one but God does things like these.

The holy communion that the church celebrates on Sunday morning is far more than the sharing of food, for what happens in communion simply signs the shape of God's ministry in the universe. We are already seated, everyone of us, at a banquet table far richer than we yet know, and at this banquet we are joined with the mind of

God. Though I don't pretend to know how such things as these happen, they do happen, and they are not divided from God's providence.

Evangelism's ministry of introductions likes nothing better than an opportunity to engage stories like these.

Mission-Minded Christianity: More Than Fellowship

Now to return briefly to Connie's story. I kept informal contact with Connie throughout this conference, and still later she and I spoke about the way in which mission-minded congregations like to converse about God.

> Well, I've never had the courage to tell the story I told you to my parish. They might laugh me right out the door. Now don't get me wrong, I love my church and we are a real family. But we just don't seem to be encouraged to think much about God.

Connie is a life-long Episcopalian, a Sunday school teacher, a former Sunday school superintendent and former member of the vestry of her church. Now she is the president of her church's Association of Women. "I've just never been taught," she said, "or even encouraged to think about how God might be present in my everyday life, but I know God is. And I knew that night that God was present."

Connie is a member of what I have come to call a fellowshipping church. Though its common life looks like joy-filled mission, in fact it is a maintenance-minded congregation. Every year this parish schedules a ton of activities. There is communion everywhere you look. Supper groups are well attended, there is joy galore, and on the surface everything looks hunky-dory. But this beauty is only skin deep.

Press a little and you hear that children don't like Sunday school much, while church leadership always seems to be asking for more money. As for worship on Sunday morning, many of these good-hearted folk come to church to chat with one another. And they may not much like "new things" or "the new liturgy."

Social life falls short of the goal for mission-minded congregations. They too like good times, but they also know that living bread tastes far better. Connie's congregation would be an even brighter light in God's church if its life had a more explicit spiritual dimension, and the capacity to identify and celebrate God's everyday presence and ministry would be just that step.

Evangelism: Introducing God To God's World

Mission-minded congregations invest much of their interest and energy in learning to speak conversationally about God. But speaking of God conversationally is not like speaking of God from the pulpit, and that's where attempts at evangelism often go wrong. Because most of us hear about God through the church's preaching ministry, often when we think of evangelism the image of a preacher jumps immediately to mind. But not many like to be preached at when conversation is what they hope for.

POINT. Better than a pulpit model or a "sales pitch," the words "conversation," "introduction," and "interpretation" best describe the ways and means of marketplace evangelism today.

For example, the New Testament word "evangel" is derived from the Greek *euangelion*, which simply means "good news" or "gospel." More, the Greek word *angelein* is the root of the word "angel." Above all else an angel is a messenger. So is every evangelist, and the song they sing sounds a lot more like angels sweetly singing to the shepherds (Luke 2:8f) than it sounds like a hard sell of the Christian gospel.

"But if an evangelist is a messenger," you say, "then what is the message we proclaim?" Simply put the message is this: God is with us, God acts in our behalf, there is never a time when we are alone, and in the flesh Jesus shows us the shape of God's everyday presence and ministry. This basic vision empowers mission-minded congregations. Evangelism is simply the ministry of introducing God-in-the-world to God's world, and it rejoices in using everyday stories and events. If this method was good enough for the angels, it is good enough for the church today.

Hence, mission-minded Christians first of all cultivate their capacity to speak of God in plain, everyday language, knowing that signs of God's presence and ministry are richly present in the world.

St. Paul knew this well. In fact, there is no better New Testament illustration of evangelism at work than Luke's record of Paul's visit to Athens. And although we have only one account of Paul working this way, there's every reason to believe that what he did at Athens probably characterized his general approach to evangelism.

Here's what he did. Paul was new in Athens, and the town may have been strange to him. But the more he looked around the more he found himself provoked that no one knew the God of Abraham and Sarah, the same God and Father of the Lord Jesus Christ. Scholarly Athenians had a reputation for being current with every new idea, yet twenty or so years after the resurrection they had not heard of it. As a result, Paul saw *need* and *opportunity* come together, a sensitivity that marks evangelism to this day.

"But how can I make an introduction?" Paul likely wondered.

Now he could have gotten the attention of these scholars by condemning their ignorance, or he could have told them what they "ought" to believe, two approaches that all too often characterize what passes for modern-day evangelism. But if Paul had responded in either of these ways, quite likely he would have been run out of town, or at the least he might have been written off.

POINT. Evangelism values folks as they are where they are, just as God does.

So what Paul did was this: he listened, he found an object around which a conversation could be built, in this case the Athenian's "Altar To An Unknown God." Next Paul offered evangelism's ministry of introductions by introducing them to the God he loved and knew. It worked, and as a result several Athenians stayed to hear more, folks by the name of "Dionysius the Areopagite and a woman named Damaris and others with them" (Acts 17:34). A small church was born.[2]

Some scholars don't attach a great deal of importance to what Paul did at Athens even though it was important to Luke, because Paul didn't begin a "name church" there, like the church at Corinth or Ephesus. But what these scholars miss is the way in which a new and tiny church did in fact begin. Christian congregations always begin this way: the gospel is spoken, it is heard by a few, and a community begins to gather. Cathedrals don't come until later, and until we get rid of the notion that "big is better" we will never be satisfied to begin with small.

Modern-day evangelists do well to follow Paul's lead. We must be content with beginning where people are—knowing that signs of God's presence and ministry are already here, and we must be satisfied with beginning in small ways. And finally, there is no place in the ministry of evangelism for abusive or pushy behavior.

Paul himself makes this same point, and shows the breadth of his respect for others in his letter to the Christians at Corinth:

> I am a free man and own no master; but I have made myself every man's servant, to win over as many as possible.
>
> To Jews I became like a Jew, to win Jews; as they are subject to the Law of Moses, I put myself under that law to win them, although I an mot myself subject to it.
>
> To win Gentiles, who are outside the Law, I made myself like one of them, although I am not in truth outside God's law, being under the law of Christ.
>
> To the weak I became weak. Indeed, I have become everything in turn to me of every sort, so that in one way or another I may save some.
>
> All this I do for the sake of the Gospel, to bear my part in proclaiming it (1 Cor. 9: 19-22).

Paul shows the church four important marks that make up effective evangelism:

1. He was patient. If he had not been, Paul might have rushed headlong into a confrontation—which too many evangelists too often do.

2. He knew he could expect to see signs of God's presence and ministry all around the world. The world belongs to God, and we all belong to God whether we know it or not. The evangelist never walks into a place where God is not present; there is always an opportunity to bear witness.

3. He knew that it is important to listen to those we seek to serve. Evangelists value people just as they are where they are, not where they "ought to be."

4. He saw that around the world there are already billions of altars to an unknown God, waiting to be used. Just like the other writers in the Bible, Paul had mastered the art of taking life events and seeing in them signs of God's action. We don't know the questions he asked at places like Athens, but I bet they sounded something like:

• What signs can I see of God's ministry in the here-and-now of this present experience?

• How can I describe it?

POINT. Evangelism's ministry of introductions works best when it does not focus on ideas or debate, but on an event from real life interpreted from the perspective of the Bible through eyes of faith.

What Evangelism Is Not

Now compare Paul's approach with that of a young Christian more excited by *her* own conversion than by the ministry of evangelism.

"I challenge people to accept Christ as their savior, and I am willing to argue to make sure that they do. I have always worked this way and I always will." She calls this pressure-packed ministry "evangelism."

She is wrong. What this twenty-four-year-old new-born, fervent Christian is describing is not evangelism, but an exercise of argument and power (perhaps appropriate and even expected in the adolescence of faith). But as a result of folks like her, many fear that evangelism means that they will be "put on the spot" and pushed around. Arguments tend to generate an adversarial relationship; one person will be the winner and one the loser.

Argument and evangelism won't mix. Instead of God being glorified in the here and now of everyday life, the focus is on right belief or the affirmation of creedal formulae. Now Christians may argue with one another about creedal statements like "Do you accept the Lord Jesus Christ..." and Christians may argue with non-Christians about the same thing, but this is not evangelism's good news about God at work in the world.

The angels announcing Jesus' birth did not argue with the shepherds. Instead they announced their message about what had already taken place, sang a song of invitation and left the shepherds free to respond or not. That was good evangelism. And it still is.

Introductions in a "Chance" Encounter

Paul is not the only New Testament person who practiced a ministry of introductions. Luke also includes in Acts the story about Philip meeting an Ethopian businessman (Acts 8:26-39). Here's the story, and while you read it, look for turning points. To eyes of faith expecting to see signs of God's presence and ministry in the world, turning points can identify God's action.

Philip was traveling the Gaza road on a trip from Jerusalem. Soon he came upon a wealthy traveler pulled over to the side of the road reading from a book. Philip had no idea what he was reading nor who he was, but he was moved to stop and ask.

Immediately the evangelist wonders "What's going on here?" Do we have here simply good luck, or is Philip's pause simply an expression of

> give an infinite number monkeys an infinite number of typewriters and one of them will, theoretically, come up with the itinerary for a trip from Jerusalem to Gaza,or a trip involving a meeting between one person who needed help with another who could give it, and the list can go on and on. The plain fact is this: random chance offers an infinitely random number of possibilities.

"But," thinks the evangelist, "perhaps Philip paused because he was stirred by God's holy spirit."

These are the facts we have: Philip was on the road and he stopped to make inquiry, only to learn that this Ethopian national:

• had just come from Jerusalem,
• had been to the temple,
• was interested in the Hebrew Bible,
• was reading Isaiah,
• did not understand it,
• wanted to understand it, and
• needed help.

After inquiring about whether an explanation would be helpful, Philip explained what Isaiah meant, the Ethopian believed him, and next he asked to be baptized.

Evangelism's ministry of introductions always looks for turning points in any story from life. For turning points offer opportunities for imagination to paint bright pictures of God's love and care in ways that are both factual and easy to understand.

Now you tell me, is this story simply a tale of good fortune or good luck, or in this story are there signs of God's presence and ministry?

Like Paul, Philip also teaches us to pay close attention to life. But for Philip, evangelism plainly takes the shape of a patient conversation. The word "conversation" itself is rooted in the Latin *con* and *versari*, and it means "to travel with." A conversation is more than a simple exchange of words, it is a thoughtful and sensitive walk with another person. The task of evangelism requires a careful listening to the life of the other person, and it always tailors its response to what is needed.

POINT. Pure and simple, a patient, interpretative conversation that takes life events seriously becomes an experience in which God acts to form belief. It happened for the Ethiopian, it happened for several listeners at Athens, and it has happened for folks like you and me.

Evangelism From The Perspective Of Jesus' Life and Ministry

Jesus himself describes God's care this way. Because it was customary for young men to read in the synagogue from Scripture's witness, on a return trip home and at worship one day, Jesus stood, took the Torah, and read:

> "The Spirit of the Lord is upon me, because he has anointed me to preach good news to the poor. He has sent me to proclaim release to the captives and recovering of sight to the blind, to set at liberty those who are oppressed, to proclaim the acceptable year of the Lord."

> And he closed the book, and gave it back to the attendant, and sat down; and the eyes of all in the synagogue were fixed on him. And he began to say to them, "Today this scripture has been fulfilled in your hearing" (Luke 4:18-21).

What Jesus read was a description of God's everyday ministry in the world, and for the rest of his earthly life he traveled the Judean countryside offering sight to the blind, freedom to the crippled, careful, active concern to those who were oppressed, in which they could begin to begin to hope, giving over to him their despair and hopelessness.

What Jesus did God still does. And because of Jesus' life and ministry, once and for all the shape of God's ministry in our midst is clear, and our natural, blind ignorance is washed clean by the bright light of his presence among us. Whenever the evangelist sees

- vision where there was formerly none, an
- idea where there was once a question,
- movement where there was once stagnation, and
- concern where there is hurt,

evangelism recognizes a sovereign God's ministry in the here and now of everyday life. God is an invisible presence in life, and though signs of God's care are all around us, we'd have no reason to identify it or expect it unless God first revealed its shape. Christians believe that Jesus is God's best revelation, because Jesus is Immanuel, God with us.[3]

The servant ministry of God's Christ always points beyond itself to the One he came to make known. Paul makes just this point in Philippians 2: 9-11:

> Therefore God raised him to the heights and bestowed on him the name above all names, that at the name of Jesus every knee should bow—in heaven, on earth, and in the depths—and every tongue confess, "Jesus Christ is Lord," to the glory of God the Father.

It is always God to whom Jesus points us, and so it is with modern-day evangelism.

POINT. I have never healed a palsied limb and I have never opened the eyes of the physically blind. I have never made a deaf person hear and I expect I never will. But I have seen the deaf hear, I have watched the blind receive their sight and I have seen the lame walk. And I know the author. This is the message that evangelism's ministry of introductions offers to God's world.

Nicodemus: Touched By Love and Changed

Patience must always mark evangelism's ministry of introductions. The story of Jesus and Nicodemus is a beautiful expression of God's work in the world, and the way in which, over a long period of time, those of us who are spiritually blind, like Nicodemus, begin to see the things of God.

Still, some evangelists (like the fervent, new-born Christian a few pages back) still push for immediate conversion. But the story of Jesus and Nicodemus makes a mighty case for patience in this ministry, and nods clearly toward the task of trusting in God to do the inner work of conversion. God acts and lives are changed, and for many the change is a long time coming. But God didn't make the world in one day, either.

Nicodemus ("Conqueror of the People") was a Pharisee, and just as his name suggests, he probably had every reason to feel secure and comfortable, on top of the world. He was a teacher, and his stature demanded community respect.

Nicodemus first appears in the Bible when he visits Jesus under the cover of night. Tradition has it that Nicodemus was embarrassed, maybe because Jesus was not recognized by other Jewish teachers as one with legitimate teaching authority. As best we can surmise, Nicodemus had been watching Jesus quite closely from a distance. He is clearly interested in what Jesus was teaching, and in some important way it had struck a chord in his own life. Christian faith often begins this way.

But on this night Jesus confounds Nicodemus with talk about a second birth and God's spirit blowing where it will. Perhaps because the hour is late, or maybe because *he can't quite catch the meaning*, Nicodemus leaves. He may have even been a bit disappointed (John 3: 1-20).

We hear no more from Nicodemus for a number of months. Maybe even a year passes.

Then Nicodemus shows up again. Jesus is being harrassed by the Pharisees, and Nicodemus is among them. But even though he still suffers from some of the fear expressed in his earlier visit to Jesus, courage and love also show. For when his peers push too far, Nicodemus confronts them: "Doesn't the law demand that we give the other person a fair hearing?" Now we find Nicodemus defending Jesus, and in doing so he is rejected by his peers (John 7:45-52).

A "conqueror of the people" is being conquered by love.

Nicodemus did not turn away from Jesus between his first visit and this event in chapter seven. In fact his questions continued. Yet some were evidently answered, because by the time of his second visit he is clearly more supportive; he is even beginning to love. Nicodemus is being transformed, and it occurs slowly over a lengthy period of time. Moreover, Jesus seems content to let this happen. Nicodemus was being touched, and we can plainly see signs of his growth in both knowledge and love.

Nicodemus appears only once more, after Jesus' death. Along with Joseph of Arimathea Nicodemus takes Jesus' body for burial. Joseph provides the tomb, and Nicodemus provides the myrrh and aloes used in wrapping the body for burial. Though still named "conqueror of the people," Nicodemus has by this time been conquered by love.

What Nicodemus could not comprehend when we met him in the gospel's third chapter, he began to understand because love grew. God was moving in his life. Over the course of John's gospel Nicodemus becomes a new creation; he is born again. And we are teased to imagine God's holy spirit blowing through his life, answering in love the questions Nicodemus first brought to Jesus. Tradition has it that Nicodemus and Joseph are the two disciples that the early church called "secret."

Evangelism can't force love, as if love can ever be forced. Nor can evangelism force belief, because forced belief is called brainwashing. But when evangelism is treated as a celebration, and when signs of God' presence and ministry are offered, there is a good possibility that the world will also be conquered by love today. Nicodemus would know this better than most.

To Speak of God: Learning To Use A Language Of Faith

In order to speak of God we must have a language to do so. And because God is an invisible presence, one whose identity is known only to eyes of Christian faith, mission-minded congregations also know that the capacity to speak of God takes work. Nor does it develop overnight. A simple-to-use language of faith must be employed.

When we go to buy a new car, we use the language of the automobile industry to determine which vehicle is best for us, and which model best honors our pocketbook. So too when we visit a medical physician: we don't use the language of sunset and roses to describe the sharp pain in our tummy. Similarly, all through this book picturesque, traditional and easy-to-use images and metaphors are employed to describe God's ministry among us. Mission-minded congregations value these perspectives, although some images may be used more in one congregation than another.

Nor will you hear these Christians use multi-syllable words when an everyday expression makes more sense. Rather, you'll hear them use stories to speak of God in life today, stories like those spread on every page of the Bible, and their current interpretation of God's action will not be any different than the interpretation that Scripture makes.

The capacity to speak of godly things in a way that welcomes dialogue is as old as the Christian church. Paul puts it this way: "If I don't know the meaning of the language, I shall be a foreigner to the speaker and the speaker a foreigner to me" (1 Cor. 14:11). Mission-minded Christians enjoy using language that supports easy discourse about God, and when they gather, speaking of God becomes affectionately commonplace.

The remaining chapters in Part II of *Church Growth* are devoted to helping you become more proficient in your capacity to identify and celebrate God's presence and ministry in the here and now of everyday life. The ministry of one-on-one evangelism is discussed and illustrated. Still later in Part II you will find help with the task of defining your personal style of evangelism, as well as support with the task of learning to identify God's action in everyday life.

End Notes

1. James Conway, *The Washington Post* (July 23, 1984): C1.

2. Paul's careful approach in presenting the Christian good news also shows in his presentation to King Agrippa (Acts 25:13-26:32). Paul wanted to go to Rome, figuring that a hearing before Caesar would get the Christian gospel all kinds of good press. Under arrest and on his way to that great city, Paul met with King Agrippa and his wife Bernice, and at that audience Paul said, "I consider myself for-

tunate, King Agrippa, that it is before you that I am to make my defense today upon all the charges brought against me by the Jews, particularly as you are expert in all Jewish matters, both our customs and our disputes."

Notice the way Paul cultivates Agrippa's attention. Then, having gained Agrippa's favor, Paul next presents his life story from childhood to the present, including his conversion and subsequent work on behalf of Christ. He uses his story as a window into God's action in his life, yet only after he has gotten the interest of the king. But while he was speaking thus, Festus, Paul's adversary, speaks up: "Paul, you are raving; too much study is driving you mad."

"I am not mad, Your Excellency," said Paul; "what I am saying is sober truth. The king is well versed in these matters, and to him I can speak freely. I do not believe that he can be unaware of any of these facts, for this has been no hole-and-corner business. King Agrippa, do you believe the prophets? I know you do."

Agrippa said to Paul, "You think it will not take much to win me over and make a Christian of me?"

"Much or little," said Paul, "I wish to God that not only you, but all those also who are listening to me today, might become what I am, apart from these chains."

With that the king arose and said to Festus, "This fellow could have been discharged if he had not appealed to the Emperor."

Paul had made his point, and his respectful approach to Agrippa is the same method he employed in his response to the people of Athens.

3. The Book Of Common Prayer, p. 849, On God the Son.

CHAPTER 4

Stories of Love to Tell...Today

Preparing To Exercise The Ministry of Introductions • God's Love Right Before Our Eyes: A Wedding • A Dad Dies: And God Makes Things Right

T he Christian church has a story of love to tell. Many people in the world are anxious to hear about godly things, they want to know who God is and how God acts, and they want practical insights into the difference that God makes in their lives. Evangelism's ministry of introductions is a response exactly right for the times. It has always been so.

There is no better way to tell the story of God's love than by looking for signs of God's action in the world about us. This chapter, along with chapters 5 and 6, shows what mission-minded Christians already know; once signs of God's action are identified, the ministry of evangelism takes an easy shape.

But make no mistake. Not every member of every mission-minded congregation is as proficient with evangelism's ministry of introductions as everyone else. Yet taken as a whole, these congregations admire the capacity to speak of God, they have been taught to do so by clergy example, and they know it is Christian worship at its best.

Preparing To Exercise the Ministry of Introductions

Just as running a successful business means being familiar with certain rules and regulations, faithfulness to the ministry of introductions means knowing how to exercise it. A businessman offers this perspective.

"I travel a lot in my daily work," he writes, "so I put a lot of miles on my car. I am also a Christian, and I see some similarities between good sales and effective evangelism.

"Up until recently I drove an old economy car with no air conditioning. That can be deadly in Houston, Texas. After finding myself broken down on the side of the road for the third time in three weeks, my mechanic and I both agreed that I needed better transportation.

"If you've been car shopping lately, then you know there are lots of makes to choose from. I could have chosen a Chrysler, Ford, GM, Toyota, Datsun, or Subaru, but I chose the model I'm now driving for three reasons:

1. The seller knew the car and knew it well. Questions were answered that I did not think to ask, and I'm fairly knowledgeable about autos.

2. He drove the same model himself. He could have chosen other demos, but he liked this particular model. And he was able to tell me about his experiences, good and bad.

3. I drove the car to try it out, and what I experienced matched up with what I had been lead to believe.

"Now I didn't meet an exceptional salesperson. What he did was practice what folks successful in sales have practiced for years. He:

• knew his product,
• used his product, and
• believed in his product.

"It's more than a little difficult to present a product you don't understand. And it's even more difficult if you wouldn't use it yourself. And although more than a few salespersons operate this way, according to my friend their return business is near zero.

"Now the Christian gospel is not a product, and Christian faith is not something to be conveyed by a sales pitch. But sales principles do illuminate an important perspective when we consider the task of bearing witness to God's presence and ministry in the world. We must know the shape of God's work in the world (and the Bible is like a big picture book of it), and we must be comfortable talking about it."[1]

So what do we learn from this businessman's commentary? Just this: an effective use of evangelism's ministry of introductions means that Christians must

1. *know* the shape of God's presence and ministry in the Bible and the here and now of everyday life,

2. *identify* in the experience of others the shape of God's presence and ministry, and

3. *answer* questions people pose, so that others might see, and seeing, perhaps believe.

As a good presentation takes hard work and careful preparation, as good doctoring means careful preparation and hard work for the medical physician, and as being a good parent entails hard work for parents who care, so careful preparations are necessary for the ministry of introductions.

THE BOTTOM LINE. When clergy leadership takes seriously the identification and celebration of God's presence and ministry, mission-minded congregations are born and grow.

God's Love Right Before Our Eyes: A Wedding

Every year a large number of couples thinking about marriage "shop" for a church to provide a setting for their wedding. And every time they do, they show God at work in the world. Now, couples shopping for a place to celebrate their marriage may think that their search is simply an expression of their wanting the best for themselves, or it may be a family tradition, or it may be because it just seems to be the right thing to do. Any one of these reasons (and more) may be operative.

But it is also true that no matter what the reasons *seem* to be, God is also an active participant in their decision to reach out to church. They may not know this, but we do. And for evangelism our knowledge makes all the difference.

Fred and Helen are one such couple. "Very utilitarian reasons brought us to church," said Fred. "We needed a place to be married, and neither one of us was interested in a Justice of the Peace. I'm a builder, so when we went shopping for a church, I found myself paying particular attention to workmanship and architecture. And we didn't want anything modern."

"We could have gone to any denomination," said Helen, "but I figured that since I was an Episcopalian, we could start there. So we went shopping on Sunday morning. We'd go to one church one week, and another church the next week. And we kept looking for one that we liked, and a minister who seemed friendly."

"And finally we found just the one we were looking for. Helen liked the minister. It was also a Gothic stone church and, to be frank, I was impressed with the woodwork and the stained glass windows. I wanted the very best for us. And this church seemed to exactly fit what we were looking for."

Fred and Helen were both upwardly mobile people. They were "making it" in the world, and they didn't want anything second best. They got what they were looking for, too, and as Helen comments, "a whole lot more."

Fred is now a priest in the church of God.

More than a few clergy would have turned away shoppers like Fred and Helen. Some do so because they don't want the church to be "used": "We are not up for rent." Here sounds a note of generous protection for integrity of the church. But to the extent that this concern is not modified by a generous appreciation for God's hard work in behalf of shopping young couples, to that degree this clergy concern is mostly an expression of a self-serving, maintenance mindset.

POINT. I have found that clergy who *simply* turn away shoppers like Fred and Helen without much of a second thought aren't able to value God's here-and-now action in the world. I don't know what was in the mind of this priest of the church, but what he did was right and faithful. And if he were a mission-minded minister, he probably also offered a ministry of introductions shortly after sitting down with this couple. To do so he would have looked for turning points, new ideas and thoughts, fresh perspectives and hope, and at those points he would have wondered with them about love right before their eyes. Altars to God (unknown to many) abound in God's world, and mission-minded Christians enjoy identifying them.

I also suspect that at least part of the reason Fred and Helen were searching for a church was because of this word from God: "You are good folks and I love you. Come on home, it's a good place for your wedding. You'll like it."

"But," you say, "are you suggesting that God actually speaks to us, people like you and me?" I am indeed. But I am not going to suggest that this is an accurate verbatim of the godly conversation. Still, even if the words are not accurate, I'll bet that they are an accurate summary of God's conversational interest in the lives of these two children God chooses to call God's own.

Now this is not to say that once God presents an opportunity to any of us, we are obliged to say "yes." For example, God did not *make* Helen and Fred come to church. Force is not of God. The plain fact is, we are free to listen to God's invitation or not, or listening, respond positively or not. Our motives for seeking help are never pure. They are always a mixture of a lot of hopes and fears.

POINT. At deeply unconscious levels God touches us just as we are where we are. The ministry of introductions always looks for signs of these encounters resulting in new ideas and perspectives.

Now some Christians shy away from making these kinds of biblical declarations. It makes God "too active," they say, or they add, "God has better things to do than be interested in my life." But these folks miss an important point: Jesus didn't seem to have any question about a sovereign God's close interest in our lives, for if he did he would never have said anything about sparrows that fall from the sky or the number of hairs on our head (Matt. 10:29-31), or the sheep that got lost (Matt. 18:12), and the list goes on and on.

If God were not interested in the life of the universe, neither present in our lives nor touching us at all points with God's presence and interested conversation, the Christian church would have nothing to proclaim. But because God does love the world, and because signs of God's presence and ministry are richly present, concrete signs powered by faith show that we are never alone.

THE BOTTOM LINE. God *is* interested in us, and the Bible shows this on every one of its pages. The world is waiting to hear perspectives like these, and mission-minded congregations are growing as a result.

A Dad Dies: And God Makes Things Right

Alone now, Bette stood by the bed of her dad. She had just come straight to the hospital from a long day at the office, and her day wasn't made any better by the prognosis she'd been just given.

"Perhaps," said her physician friend, "your dad has one or two more days."

Her father's simple cold had quickly become pneumonia, and though the drugs had worked wonders, compared to just two weeks ago he was now a shell of the man she had grown to love.

Eighty-four, she thought, is a more than adequate span of years. Her father was prepared to die, but still... Bette was not ready to let him go.

He roused himself a moment, still lucid, but not as aware as he'd been the day before. Their eyes met. He was glad to see her and it showed.

"My tiny little girl," he said. The words lanced clear through to her heart. She was not so tiny, but now he was, lying there a bit like a child, though still her dad. For fifty-nine years she'd known his love, felt its comfort and security. Bette tried to remember when she'd first heard the words, "my tiny little girl." Maybe when he first held her after birth. Or maybe in a later year at five o'clock in the afternoon, gathering her in his arms after a day's work at the shop. Maybe this was the time they were first heard. Who can tell?

And Bette remembered more. She remembered the hugs in adolescence. More than once he'd said, "Even if you're eight feet tall, you'll always be my tiny little girl."

His words made her a little mad at the time—it was tough to want to grow up so badly, but she loved him all the more because of it. And now it had come to this.

She bent down to kiss his cheek. And she lingered there, for just a moment. His hand touched her head and held her close. "My tiny little girl," he said. The voice was thin, but the resonance was as strong as ever.

She shifted her weight a bit to sit on the edge of the bed, just what the nurse said never to do. And then she nestled closer to his side. Her shoes dropped to the floor, first one and then the other, and her legs curled next to the edge.

"I hope no one sees," she thought, "but just for a moment. Oh God, only for a moment." Once more she told him how much she loved him. And she was again his tiny little girl.

Memories of the past flooded in. Mom was dead. So was her brother. And she was next to last, soon to be the last. All things considered their lives had been good. Not perfect, but "really good," she thought.

He stroked her hair once more. And though her eyes could not see it, she knew that he was smiling. And she knew what he was thinking.

Bette cried later, telling me about it. "It was the most special moment. I was embarrassed, afraid someone would come in, but I wanted so much to feel his arms again and have him hold me. It made everything all right.

"He died a day later, just like the doctor said, but it was OK. It hurt, I don't mean to say it didn't. It hurt like hell, but it was OK, too.

"I didn't realize what had happened between my dad and me until later. We said goodbye, though we never used the words. He knew it, I'm sure he did. And in that moment I knew that everything was going to be all right. Even though he was going to die."

God is, of course, powerless to stop the onslaught of death, and powerless as well to stop Bette from feeling the loss of her dad. But God was close, and at least part of God's care took this shape.

Though Bette was tired and near a time of day when it would have been far easier to go home first, on this day she chose to visit her dad late in the afternoon. And there, she was in place to hear a word of caution from a physician friend who happened to be finishing up his late afternoon rounds. And then, in the right place at the right time, in the fullness of time, Bette and her dad said goodbye. No one but God does things like this.

Suppose Bette had come later, maybe after a warm bath and dinner, and after the rounds of her friend were complete. And what if she had not heard her friend's word of caution? Why do we take one path and not another? Is it simply good luck or good fortune, or is there more to be said of God's action?

Maybe this is how it happened. Bette was tired by the time she got to the hospital. The day had been long, and it left her ill prepared to hear the doctor's prognosis. His opinion humbled all her hopes. No one saw the tears that filled her eyes. So what of God's ministry to her dad when Bette appeared at the door to his hospital room? Perhaps this word of comfort to him...

"There's your tiny little girl. Isn't she great?"

God didn't force this thought on her dad, but simply offered it to a heart pinched by the loneliness of death's approach. And so her dad spoke...and Bette heard. A host of memories flooded her thoughts, while next God may have said something like,

"He loves you. And hasn't it been good? Why not give him a hug?"

In the twinkling of an eye God offered Bette and her dad an opportunity to give up the painful loneliness they felt about a loss soon to come, and exchange it for a moment of communion and tender love. God didn't force Bette's action, because force is not God's way. But God did offer her an idea that generated a new vision. And because of God's initiative and Bette's accepting response, their loss was, in that moment, forever shaped in her memory by a moment of communion.

Above all else, evangelism's ministry of introductions celebrates God's love at work in the world, knowing that by pointing out signs of God's action in the lives of others, what was formerly unrecognized in their lives is known, and once known, given an opportunity to be loved.

If by now you are interested in helping others identify and celebrate God's presence and ministry in the world, remember that you must:

1. *know* the shape of God's presence and ministry in the Bible and the here and now of everyday life,

2. *identify* in the experience of others (or our own experience) the shape of God's presence and ministry, and

3. *answer* questions people pose to us, so that others might see, and seeing, perhaps believe.

More complete suggestions to assist with the development of this ministry are given in the next four chapters. Using the story of a young woman arrested for drunk driving, moreover, the next two chapters illustrate the ministry of introductions at work in a one-on-one setting.

To speak of God takes work. But it is some of the most joyous work there is.

End Notes

1. From an unpublished paper contributed by the Rev'd Dale Hirst, a mission-minded Episcopal priest residing in Virginia Beach, Virginia.

CHAPTER 5

Susan, I'd Like to Introduce You to a Friend of Mine

Evangelism From Scratch • Good Fortune or God's Providence? • Always With Us: Immanuel • God Keeps Company With Us: The Companion • The Friendship of God: Ruth • God Supplies Our Needs: Providence • God's Favor Invites Our Attention: Grace • God Walks With Us and Talks With Us: Conversation • The Wind of God Rustles Our Lives • God's Spirit Acts: Networking Relationships • Celebrating Evangelism With A Study Group

O pportunities to speak of God are always present for mission-minded Christians. Along with the next chapter, this hands-on chapter is written to help you strengthen your capacity to speak of God. Both chapters discuss a young woman named Susan's arrest and conviction for driving while drunk, and both show God at work in the world. Together, they also provide the evangelist with a treasure chest of perspectives to introduce to the world God's love right before out eyes. By including this chapter's discussion in *Church Growth*, I hope you will be more confident with undertaking evangelism's ministry of introductions.

"But," asks one person, "why do we need to evangelize?" The answer is simple: We have a story of God's presence and ministry to tell. God's love calls life into being and God's love makes life good. As a result, Christians know that:

• because God keeps company with all five billion of us in the world, and

• because satisfying signs of God's presence and ministry are all about us, and

• because people the world over are curious about the deeper meanings of life, and

61

• because the church see a connection between what is going on in the world and who God is,

evangelism can't help but take place.

In much the same way that it's impossible to see the sun peak over the horizon in the morning and not say, "There it is," mission-minded Christians find it natural to speak when they see signs of God's everyday presence and ministry.

Evangelism From Scratch

The Sunday morning pulpit often (though unintentionally) weakens confidence in evangelism. Here's why. Preachers are expected to preach about God and godly things. But as a result, many of us tend to think that evangelism means "preaching" to others. Yet when evangelism is treated as sermonizing, people turn away. On a one-to-one basis, evangelism ought never take the shape of a sermon.

Instead, think of evangelism as a conversation marked by five qualities. All five show up in this chapter's discussion.

1. The ministry of introductions is a *listening ministry*. Evangelists may have a personal story to tell, but for the most part they set their story aside and *listen* to the stories of others.

2. Evangelism's ministry of introductions pays close attention to life events and *turning points*.

3. Evangelism does not impose belief—that is commonly called brain-washing—and it is never coercive.

4. Personal evangelism requires a basic attitude of *patience*. The ministry of introductions is not accomplished according to a fixed schedule; it meets folks where they are just as they are.

5. Evangelism offers the ministry of introductions as an act of *worship*. At its heart evangelism is the activity of praise. It is adoration and thanksgiving all rolled into one, and it takes the shape of a song celebrating God's presence and ministry in the world.

Each of these five notes is sounded in the following discussion. I hope you'll be alert to them. And don't think that the following story is simply an illustration of a pastoral counselor at work with a young woman in trouble. First, it is a story that illustrates God in action in the world today, working in behalf of a young woman and her family in ways that are incredible to behold. And second, it is a story showing how the splendid images and metaphors of the Jewish/Christian tradition can be used to paint bright pictures of God's action, just as they are meant to do, and just as I hope you will learn to use them.

Good Fortune or God's Providence?

Susan was introduced to me by Bruce, her father. He himself telephoned me one evening from a thousand miles away, and even though he knew little about me, he asked if I'd see his daughter. He was worried about her welfare.

Susan had been recently arrested and charged with drunk driving. She is a young professional woman in her early thirties, single and new in a town a long way from her mid-western family of origin. Stress was an unhappy part of her life, and several months ago she found that a drink with friends at the end of the day was a happy way to cope.

The next evening Susan called me. We made an appointment and began to meet on a regular basis. Our conversation had the effect of ameliorating some of her sharp feelings of loneliness, for both the friendship and the insights that accrue in a counseling relationship make life more tolerable.

At the beginning of our eighth session, however, while I made a place for her to sit in my cluttered office, Susan asked about what I taught. I named off a few of the courses, and she inquired about what I covered in evangelism. I briefly described the ministry of identifying signs of God's presence and ministry in the world, to which Susan remarked, "I could never believe that."

"Well," I said, "if I knew something more about how your dad happened to find my name, I might be able to introduce you to someone I know who loves you a whole lot."

I prepared to listen to Susan's story. And I knew full well I'd be looking for turning points. Susan laughed, and said she had learned a bit more about what had happened to her dad just this week. A wonderful coincidence I thought, how things come together.

What follows is my summary of Susan's story.

Bruce didn't know where to turn or what to do. On a lunch break one day, wandering "aimlessly" (his word as he later described it to Susan), he happened to come upon a church. The building invited entrance, "though I must have passed it a thousand times in the past and never gave it a second thought."

The church itself was a handsome, late nineteenth-century Gothic structure, and the stonework made it look permanent and solid. Maybe, one imagines, the architecture struck a note of security. Said Susan, "His visit was a lucky break for me." Thought I, "More than that."

Bruce stepped inside, not quite knowing why. Perhaps it was a stir of hope from someplace way down deep. And then he heard a voice say, "Can I help you?" An elderly priest was a bit late leaving for lunch.

Neither Susan nor her parents are church people, and although he had no idea what to expect, Bruce soon found himself spilling his fears to this unnamed member of clergy. By now lunchtime had run its course, and to offer one last bit of help, this priest looked through some references and found my name as a pastoral counselor in Alexandria. He gave it to Bruce along with my telephone number, and later that evening Bruce called.

Not for one moment do I believe that it was simply luck and good fortune operating in Bruce's life that day. I believe it was providence. There is more to life than chance and good fortune. God keeps company with all of us, and although events are randomly generated at a dizzying pace in our lives, no random event ever takes shape apart from God's interest and conversational presence. Here is a statement of faith, but all of Scripture supports it. So in our conversation that night I interpreted Susan's narrative from the perspective of God's providence, God's conversational presence among us, and our freedom to deny his care-filled interest and help.

I began to point out the turning points I saw. We wondered together about why this unknown priest was late for his lunch hour that day, and why he had been in just the right place to be seen by her dad. Was it simply good luck and good fortune, or had grace quickened an idea that took the shape of a delay?

Of course we'll never know the actual answers to these questions, but I found myself smiling as I said to her, "More was present that lunchtime hour than your dad and a priest. I also think you know it's true."

Conversation lends itself to this kind of discussion and affirmation, and when important matters are on the table, God's holy spirit stirs human spirit to the truth of things as surely as the sun rises every morning.

Susan was not quick to bite off as true all that I said, as she pointed out to me: "So what about the evil of the world? Why do some folks get screwed for no reason at all?"

I heard this question asked from the perspective of her own painful experiences. But instead of developing that set of feelings, I decided to meet her puzzlement and try to think things through. On a personal level, I said, human freedom means that we have the capacity to destroy ourselves and one another. Then I mentioned William Golding's book, *Lord of the Flies*, which Susan had also read. In that book British school children are shipwrecked on a deserted island, and the reader is encouraged to believe that since they grew up in the British elementary school system, a small replica of the British empire would eventually be established. Quite the opposite occurs however, for in a quest for personal power the boys begin to destroy one another. Order quickly gives way to chaos.

So it is in God's world. We are built to survive, and free to survive even at the expense of one another. Given these fundamentals, it is God's conversational presence that makes the world more symphonic than cacophonic. Because of grace we are encouraged to choose life and mutual fellowship as opposed to death and destruction.

I noted that Susan was free to drink, and even to drink ot excess. "Now I'm not against the consumption of alcohol," I said, "but it is easily abused," and I added a little later, "God wants better for you than drunkenness, or your risking the welfare of others while driving drunk, even while God knows full well that the alcohol deadens the pain in your life."

We talked a while longer about this, and then moved on to some of the more pressing issues in her life. Still later Susan asked me to recommend an Episcopal church to her, and she began to attend. But when that didn't work out to her satisfaction she found a Unitarian church that better fit her needs, and to this day she is there most every Sunday.

Now our conversations are more infrequent, but when we meet Susan still mentions God's presence in her life, almost always plugging it with something like, "I don't feel so lonely anymore." An important and deeply satisfying conversation is still taking place in Susan's life. God's deep is speaking to her deep, and though we are not privy to an accurate account of it, in its essence the dialogue probably sounds something like what Jesus said to Thomas:

> Put your finger here and see my hands; and put out your hand and place it
> in my side; and do not be faithless, but believing (John 20:27).

In its entirety Susan's story is an altar to God, and because evangelism is a ministry that values identifying signs of God's presence and ministry in the world, this ministry listens to stories. It does not argue, and it does not hassle those whom it seeks to serve.

More, the marks of effective evangelism, listed at the beginning of this chapter, were all met in this engagement with Susan.

1. The conversation with Susan centered itself on *listening* to her story.

2. *Turning points* were approached from the perspective of God's action on her behalf. Turning points spark the interest of every evangelist. A turning point is a place in any story when a *decision* is made that makes a difference in the outcome.

• Why did Bruce "see" this particular church for the first time? Was it simply because the granite walls offered solace or security, and is this all there was?

• Why was one member of clergy late for his lunch on that day of all days?

• Why did Susan ask a question that led to the ministry of introductions?

3. Evangelism did not *impose* belief nor did it argue with Susan. It valued God's action, next it sought *to bear witness* when a time presented itself, and finally it trusted in God's action to bring about the birth of belief.

4. Evangelism in this story expressed a basic attitude of *patience*. The evangelist silently noted turning points as they appeared, and when a time presented itself responded to Susan's question.

5. Evangelism offered its ministry of introductions as an act of *worship*. An attitude of praise and wonder took shape as Susan was engaged by God. Subsequently this encounter made more and more of a difference in her life.

The remaining pages in this chapter detail a few of the images and metaphors that help mission-minded Christians speak of God. Most of them were employed in the conversation with Susan.

Always With Us: Immanuel

On the day she was arrested, Susan was in trouble with more than a traffic cop. Her whole life was in disarray and she needed care. Many of us, also and often, find ourselves in similar predicaments.

The word "care" itself is rooted in the Latin *garrier*, meaning "to chatter," and the old Irish *gair*, meaning "a cry." Susan was making all sorts of cries for help, and her life was a'chatter with chaos. But being new in a city far from home made help scarce.

Still, even though Susan didn't know it and couldn't feel it, she also was surrounded by love. The Bible puts it this way:

> God found her in a desert land, and in the howling waste of the wilderness God encircled her, God cared for her, and God kept her as the apple of his eye. Like an eagle that stirs up its nest, that flutters over its young, spreading out its wings, catching them, bearing them on its pinions...(Deut. 32:10-12a).

The breadth of God's love is spread on every page of the Bible. For instance, Immanuel is a name for God first used by Isaiah, and it describes the immediacy of God's care-filled presence in the midst of Susan's life. Neither Bruce nor Susan were unaccompanied on the day of her arrest, and although they were physically separated, they were supported by God's everlasting arms. A collect from the Prayer Book describes it this way:

> O Heavenly Father, in whom we live and move and have our being: We humbly pray you to guide and govern us by your Holy Spirit, that in all the cares and occupations of our life we may not forget you, but may remember that we are ever walking in your sight....(p. 87)

"But," you say, following Susan's lead, "if God is so close, then why do we get pushed around and abused?" Human freedom supplies much of the answer to this question, and to that we'll turn later. But for now keep looking with me for signs of God's immediate care for Susan.

God Keeps Company With Us: The Companion

The more lonely we become, the more our hearts quiver with fear. We are made for relationship, and although it is both good and necessary to draw apart for occasional quiet times of solace and reflection, there is a mighty big difference between being alone and feeling lonely.

Susan felt lonely. And I also know she was beginning to feel a little bit scared. "I look forward to a drink at the end of the day," she said, "and a lot of times I get angry when I forget to put a six pack in the refrigerator. But I can't seem to break this habit, and that's what's really scary."

I suspect Susan's plight was just as frightful to God, for better than anyone God knows the way we happily give ourselves to addictive substances.

The word companion combines the Latin *panis*, meaning "bread," with the prefix *com*, meaning "with." A companion is a friend who breaks bread with us, one who joins us at mealtime. The Book of Revelation describes the shape of God's companionship this way: "Behold, I stand at the door and knock; if anyone hears my voice and opens the door, I will come into him and eat with him, and he with me" (Rev. 3:20).

We are not alone in the world, and we are never far from God's keen and watchful sight. There is not a doubt in my mind that God was working in a variety of ways to help Susan out of her loneliness.

At least a part of God's work might have been that of helping convene a support group that met after work, and certainly that group had several of the signs that mark communion.

But God was also worried about Susan's growing dependence on alcohol. "God was worried?" you say. "Isn't that a bit too much to say about God?" You're free to draw your own conclusions, and as well you can call it good luck to explain Susan's reaching out for help. But I believe her reaching out was a direct result of God's companionable, concerned—even worried—care for her. I also believe Jesus would have worried about Susan's welfare if this story had appeared in the gospels, and if Jesus worries, it is a clear indication, to Christians, of the shape of God's concern.

The Friendship of God: Ruth

Life also seemed friendless to Susan. But there is more to life and what we or she could, or can see. God's everyday presence also takes the shape of a friendship for us, an idea plainly present in the Old Testament Book of Ruth.

God has cast his lot with us, and the Book of Ruth simply illustrates this truth with a song of love. Now because Ruth, Naomi and Boaz are distant forebears of David and Jesus, one might think this is the only reason for its inclusion in the Bible. But there is also more. Like all the Bible's books, the Book of Ruth is fundamentally a story about God's love for us.

We first find Naomi in the land of Moab, where she had moved because of a bad and lengthy famine in Bethlehem. She went there with her husband and two sons. Her sons soon married two Moabite women, Orpah and Ruth, but not long after they began to build homes in this strange land, Naomi's husband and her two sons died.

Now Naomi is left with only her two daughters-in-law. A bit later, however, she hears that times are finally better at Bethlehem, and so she decides to return. But not wanting her daughters-in-law to feel the same kind of pain she once so keenly felt, Naomi asked them to remain in the land they loved. Orpah decided to honor Naomi's offer, but Ruth did not. And the words of Ruth still ring through the ages.

Entreat me not to leave you or to return from following you; for where you go I will go, and where you lodge I will lodge; your people shall be my people, and your God my God; where you die I will die, and there will I be buried. May the Lord do so to me and more also if even death parts me from you (RSV. Ruth 1:16-17).

In Hebrew the word Ruth means *friend*, and the word Naomi means *my joy*. So from this perspective here is what we have: *friend* offered to stay with *my joy* when she considered returning home to Bethlehem. *My joy* would never be alone. In other words, God is *friend* to us who are to God, *my joy*. And although voiced centuries before Jesus walked the roads of Galilee, the thoughts of Ruth echo Jesus' words of love on the cross.

God is a friend to folks like Susan, folks like all of us, and just as a friend is never abusive nor ruthless, neither is God. Over and over, signs of God's friendship are clearly present in Susan's story.

God Supplies Our Needs: Providence

Both Susan and Bruce needed help, and they were unable to provide it for themselves. Susan was trapped in a vortex that was destroying her life, and Bruce could only feel helpless a thousand miles away. Caught in a similar set of circumstances, another person might put it this way: "It's just me and life, and the name of the game is dog-eat-dog. I'm scared."

Providence is a description of God's ministry that has been valued by the church for centuries. Even though the word is used only once in all of Scripture (Acts 24:2), the idea is biblical. Here's why.

The word itself combines the Latin *pro*, meaning "for" or "before" with the Latin *video*, meaning "see," and it suggests:

• God's capacity to see ahead of wherever we are, and

• God's benevolent provision for our welfare long before we have need, or even know we might have need.

The pillars and fire and cloud in the Hebrew exodus from Egypt are visual expressions of God's providence (Exodus 13:21), and physical expressions take the shape of manna and the spring of water from a rock (Exodus 16:13-16, 17:3-7). Now of course we don't see a pillar of fire in Bruce's life that day at noon, but because a godly interest began to brightly burn, his heart turned toward a place where he had little reason to expect help.

So then this question: When Bruce noticed the church and turned in, was it simply random good fortune or was it providence? Or was it some of both? The Bible suggests that God's providence played a strong part. I hope you're beginning to see how easy it is to celebrate God's presence and ministry in the world.

God's Favor Invites Our Attention: Grace

Bruce was in a quandary. He didn't know what to do. The morning had been a busy one, and because busy times demand almost all our attention, he had been mostly free from concern for Susan. But at lunchtime all the cares stored in the back of his mind crashed into consciousness. Maybe because he had no stomach for food he took a walk, and maybe that's the reason he "really saw" a church which he had passed a thousand times before.

But Christians call what happened on this lunch time break an act of grace. The word grace itself describes God's bottom-line, affectionately positive attitude toward us. Just as every loving parent is for their children and wants the very best for them, God loves and cares for us.

Grace is not passive either. God did not look toward Bruce and simply think, "He's in trouble." Grace is an active and aggressive attitude of respect and friendship, and what happens is this: because God prizes us so much, in each one of us—more often than not—our hearts are stirred to creative action, and our minds enlightened to healthy possibilities. So because of what we have learned to call God's grace, Bruce heard a voice without words. And because of God's affectionate and aggressive concern, he did not turn away.

Like Susan, all of us walk a line between order and chaos in the world, and if we tend to lean toward disorder (because everyone of us wants to order things our way), God is always about the task of inviting us toward a more life-respecting order.

God Walks With Us and Talks With Us: Conversation

Of all the pictures of God painted in this book, the word conversation best of all describes God's relationship with us.

The ministry of introductions also knows this: Every turning point in every story lends itself to speculation about the "word of God" in the moments just preceding it. A grand old hymn puts it this way: "He walks with me and he talks with me..."

The Bible reads like a litany of God's conversational presence in the universe:

• Creation begins because of God's word "Let there be...,"
• Israel is formed because of God's call,
• the exodus from Egypt is by decree,
• God kept conversational company with young Samuel, and
• God spoke to Elijah in a still small voice.[1]

In order to take a look at what God might be saying in any situation, get into the shoes of Jesus as the gospels present him and take a prayerful look at how Jesus might respond to the same event. Then you'll have a pretty good idea about what God thinks and feels.

Although God's conversation is never explicit in Susan's story, to the eyes of faith a godly discourse provides the steady driving engine that powers her and her father's every positive action. This is the way I see it.

Bruce was worried, and although he had passed near the solid Gothic walls of that downtown church many times before, this time he turned in. The Christian community had never meant much to Bruce or his family, and though he had been to church once or twice in his lifetime, it had proved to be a waste of time. He had little reason to expect any help this day. But there was another present in his life, a conversationalist and companion who cared.

"Let's go in," God might have said. "We can find help on the inside.

"Now I know you haven't found much help in places like this before, but I think we can work something out now.

"Come on, let's go in."

Bruce had a number of things on his mind, but there was nothing more important than his love for Susan. So God's wind troubled the waters of a father's love, and later the same wind stirred the waters of Susan's life enough that she made a telephone call to a place where she least expected to find assistance.

The Wind of God Rustles Our Lives

The words "wind" and "spirit" are the Bible's inspired way of picturing God's creative participation in life, and the way God works hard to make every opportunity for us.

But if God is so close to us, why don't we sense God's care any more than we do? Here's one reason why. Human consciousness can be pictured as an iceberg. We see only *simple consciousness*, what we know and what we're consciously aware of. Just under the surface there is *semi-consciousness*, or what we suspect and sense, and deeper still there resides our *sub-conscious mind*, what we don't consciously know, but of which we are deeply aware, nevertheless. Of course these distinctions are artificial, but they serve to describe the complexity of our mental processes and the deeply pervasive way God is with us.

Consciousness has to do with what we know: what we see, hear, taste, feel and understand. Bruce was consciously fearful that Susan might be in deep trouble. But something more hopeful than fear was introduced at a point late in the morning. For even though he should have been hungry for lunch, Bruce decided to take a walk that eventually carried him right by a church. Why?

Still later Bruce met another person who could give him the help he so desperately needed. Now the plot thickens. At *sub-conscious* levels God was stirring Bruce to action. Maybe God's word was something like, "Here's a place you can get some help, and if you'll turn in right now we'll find someone to talk to. Come quickly."

At deep human levels there is a lot more communion between God and us than most Christian theology imagines. Bruce's decision to turn in to a church is an expression of this fact.

POINT. Evangelism's ministry of introductions is often built on speculations about the dialogue between human spirit and God's Spirit at the levels of the deep sub-conscious. But given our openness to the Spirit's presence, we consciously know God's touch only now and then, while at deeper levels we sense it all the more.

God's Spirit Acts: Networking Relationships

Question: How could Bruce reach clear back to Washington, DC, and offer the arm of his love to a daughter who was badly hurt? There are more resources for help in the world than we can imagine, but how to get help together with need is always an issue.

Here we have the scene. Bruce is standing before the church, and we know there is also a priest just inside, one a little late for his own noon-time lunch. He lingers (for reasons we do not know but wonder about!) to finish a chore he usually completes after lunch, and Bruce stands outside on the curb wondering what to do with a "ridiculous" idea.

Networking relationships describes the way in which God creates the music of symphony in the midst of worldly noise, and forms the harmony of fellowship between five billion people, each one of us free to write our own music.

God is with us, and God's presence is personal and interested. It stirs us to new possibilities even in the midst of the old always passing away. It rustles our consciousness and sparks shivers of life. We can depend on God, we can prepare for God, we can rejoice in God, but God comes, if ever faithfully, nevertheless unexpectedly.

It was more than a fortuitous idea that crossed Bruce's mind that day. God's Spirit stirred Bruce's interest, just as God's Spirit invited another to linger in order to tidy the pews after mid-morning worship instead of waiting until after lunch.

POINT. As a forest sways as the wind blows through, the evangelist identifies signs of an inspired coherence in the seemingly random and spontaneous events of life. Personal affection and interest always count, and they do in this story, but so does the ministry of God's Spirit to human spirit.

Celebrating Evangelism With A Study Group

Developing the capacity to speak of God takes work, but it is work much loved by mission-minded Christians. To strengthen your ability, discuss in a small group of fellow travelers the images, metaphors and stories used in this chapter and the previous two.

Then with this *brief* discussion completed, pick one story, review it, look for turning points, and then speculate about God's presence and ministry. When thinking of God's ministry, consider the perspectives suggested by the images and ideas of:

• *Immanuel,*
• God's *companionship,*
• Ruth and the *friendship* of God,
• *providence,*
• *grace,*
• God's *conversation,* and
• the *wind of God.*

Once you're comfortable with evangelism's ministry of introductions, and the more you are able to conceive all of life as an altar bearing witness to God's power and love, with your group of fellow travelers pick a story or two from your lives, and look there for turning points and speculate about God's action. Still later, choose to discuss stories from the daily press and weekly news magazines. As a result, you'll be much more confident and comfortable speaking of God, when you see God at work in the lives of others.

End Notes

1. Walter Brueggemann, "Covenanting As Human Vocation" in *Interpretation* (April 1979): 118.

CHAPTER 6

Why Do Bad Things Happen in God's World?

Answering A Question That Burns • Renewing Our Images of God •
Freedom in the Universe • Sin: Not Able to Listen to God • Sin is "Original Equipment" • God's Love and God's Powerlessness • The Adversary
of Scripture • Evil and the God of Love: A Cosmic Drama • The Solace
of Prayer • Taking Action to Learn the Ministry of Introductions

ometimes life is harsh. And because many of us
have not had much explicit preparation in speaking
of God even when things go well, all the more do we
shy away from this task when life is tough. Or if we
do speak, we are apt to say something like, "It must
be God's will."

Mission-minded Christians function differently. They know that
good news is not merely good news "because it happened once upon
a time in a certain place to some people, but because it happens all
the time in all sorts of places to all sorts and conditions of men and
women everywhere."[1]

Given a few traditional tools, the harsh questions that life raises
are not difficult to approach. Many Christians, however, don't know
what to say because they've never had anyone explain it. Using
Susan's story for the last time, the following pages summarize some
of the images that are useful when looking for turning points and at
times when God seems to be absent.

Answering A Question That Burns

When I speak about the positive aspects of God's ministry in the
workshops and conferences I lead, after only a few minutes participants want to know, "If God is so good and so powerful, why do bad
things happen in God's world?"

A recent newspaper article quoted the wife of a man killed in an industrial accident as saying, "It must have been God's will." This is nonsense. Now I know this loving wife was trying to make sense out of a terribly painful personal tragedy, and I wasn't there to witness what happened. But this much I do know; her husband's death was an expression of our freedom in the universe to make decisions, no matter how ill-informed these decisions might be. His death is not an expression of God's love. In fact, I suspect God made every effort to stir this man's senses to the impending doom.

Too often Christians are quick to ascribe an intent to God when in fact we ought to be talking about freedom in the universe, or even what we Christians call sin. Some of our inaccurate opinions are also caused by news reports calling catastrophic events "acts of God." But in fact it is not God who visits tragedy on us. Rather, harsh events may be an expression of natural law (what goes up will come down—so don't jump off of a building without a parachute or a safety net), or they are the result of the abuse we human beings are wont to visit on one another or ourselves. For example, the world's forests are dying because of environmental abuse, and drunk drivers kill because they choose to drink a substance that temporarily impaires their functioning—a natural law. We need to be clear about this.

When mission-minded Christians hear about tragedy, they don't try to explain it away by saying things like "God had a reason for this." They know that God does not function like an abusive parent. Rather, mission-minded Christians affirm God's deep respect for freedom in the universe, and they know well God's commitment to tolerate (in the near term) the destructive results of sin.

The ministry of introductions, when confronted by harsh events, makes every effort to listen to the whole story—the pain, the ambiguity, the questions, the fears and, if it is appropriate, to supply perspectives designed to furnish light to a dark place. So instead of offering platitudes like "This is part of God's plan" to explain something like Susan's loneliness, pain, budding alcoholism and her arrest for drunken driving, evangelism's ministry of introductions looks for signs of freedom in the universe. Out of respect for human freedom, God has placed limitations on divine power.

The plain fact is this: tragedy in the human community is a sign of freedom and a function of sin, not a sign of God's lack of care. Our God-given freedom to create brings with it the freedom to destroy. Before we blame God for it, we do far better to look closely at our own responsibility, or lack of it.

Renewing Our Images Of God

I've found that many adults dropping out of church do so because their knowledge of God doesn't keep pace with the reality of their adult lives. For example: it is often difficult for adult or teenage friends of a person killed by a drunk driver to keep faith if their knowledge of God is no deeper than a first-grade Sunday school image of God as a heavenly, generous parent. No matter how legitimate this image is, it is not an adequate picture of the God who has chosen to love a self-serving, sinful people, a God who respects our freedom even when we choose to destroy one another.

Part of the work of Christian maturation is setting ourselves to the task of broadening our childhood and adolescent understandings of God. In and of themselves there's nothing wrong with our early ideas, but adulthood demands a far richer belief in God than our early years provide. St. Paul puts it this way:

> When I was a child, I spoke like a child, I reasoned like a child, I thought like a child: and when I grew up I gave up childish ways. For now we see in a mirror dimly…(1 Cor. 13:11-12a).

So what can we say about the ways in which our ideas about God change over the course of a lifetime?

Children grow up with ideas about God gleaned from news magazines and papers, parents, and Sunday school teachers. We tend to learn in these settings that God is like an all-powerful parent. Reflecting back on childhood perspectives, adults often remember believing that God had a rule ready to apply to every human situation. God was like a parent who always knew better, one who took control of our lives, bailed us out when things looked bleak, and generally stood between us and adversity. God was also:

• a grandfatherly Santa Claus who brought us gifts if we were good,

• taller than Dad, with a halo and out-stretched hands and arms, bathed in light, wearing flowing robes,

• a genie in an Aladdin's lamp, able to do anything, but comforting and protective and, like our parents, always ready to listen.[2]

These early childhood images of God reflect parental influence, they are informed by cultural perspectives, and they are larger than life.

Now in our early years these images are a blessing and a comfort. But if they are not expanded by the time of our adult years, they can become a curse. Mission-minded congregations pay all sorts of attention to this task: prayer groups, Bible study groups and preaching lead the way.

Our childhood thinking is also encouraged by simplistic use of some very important traditional images of God. For example, we learned in church, or picked it up by hearing others talk, that, like our parents, God was:

• omnipotent (all powerful),
• omniscient (all knowing),
• omnipresent (everywhere), and
• infinite (always and forever).

These descriptions do point toward the truth of who God is. But when they are simply applied to God without other considerations, they better describe the fantasy of a sheriff of the Old West stalking thieves, bank-robbers and rustlers. In fact, these four theological marks of God are simply not adequate to describe the range of God's commitment to us. What these notions don't consider is the tender mercy of God that allows freedom in the universe and tolerates sin.

Our childhood perspectives begin to shift by the time we move into our teenage years, and although these early visions carry forward, naturally added are concerns about power, stability and condemnation. God is:

• a judge and rule-giver,
• a healer and friend,
• always everywhere (like Mom and Dad—there's never enough

privacy),
* fair-minded and forgiving,
* a distant but loving parent,
* stability in the midst of instability,
* one who expects us to be responsible,
* big as the sky, and just about as impersonal.

Issues of personal and community identity are on the front burner for teenagers. For all of us these years are often characterized by a reaction against adult authority and parental norms. Some call it a rebellious time, but in fact this process of negative identification is quite normal, for through it we become more secure in who we are by determining who and what we are not. Our ideas about God during these years often reflect these themes.

By our adult years God is:
* a companion who feels our pain and who needs us to help care for the world,
* more personal than ever, and with a sense of humor,
* a parent who is also a friend.

Adult thinking about God increasingly values God's companionable friendship, and the unmerited grace that often shows to eyes of faith.

Now here is the problem with which most of us struggle. Because our childhood and adolescent pictures of God as a super-parent are too seldom evaluated from the biblical perspectives of freedom, sin and powerlessness, many of us simply continue to assume that because mom and dad were more powerful than we were, knew everything (or thought they did!), seemed to be always around—had always been and would always be—God would be the same way forever. When times are tough and these images don't hold up, many adults are likely to drop out of church.

Freedom in the Universe

Susan's story offers us every good opportunity to consider the range of God's ministry when times are tough. Right from the beginning it must be said that Susan was free to drink, and her freedom played a large part in the mess she created for herself. This biblical concept helps explain a lot of things, and is a useful tool for the evangelist.

We are made in the image of God, and just as God is free to create and destroy, so are we. This fact is as old as the story of Adam and Eve in the garden of Eden, and the Outline of Faith in the Book of Common Prayer makes exactly this point:

> Question. What does it mean to be created in the image of God?
> Answer. It means that we are free to make choices: to love, to create, to reason, to live in harmony with creation and with God.
>
> Question. Why then do we live apart from God and out of harmony with creation?
> Answer. From the beginning, human beings have misused their freedom and made wrong choices.
>
> Question. Why do we not use our freedom as we should?
> Answer. Because we rebel against God (and God's conversation with us—parenthesis mine), and we put ourselves in the place of God.[3]

But the fact that we are free does not mean that God is not interested in what we do, and most of all it does not mean God is silent. It *does* mean, however, that God for the sake of our freedom to create, sets us free to destroy as God never does (and wishes we didn't).

It is a paradox, but freedom shackles human beings. Because of freedom we are free to listen—not to God, but first of all to ourselves and what we want to hear. Our appetites fuel our desire to have things our way. Yet even though we are free, and even though we use our freedom to make decisions that harm us and others, God never deserts us.

Look back at the story of Susan and Bruce. Bruce was free to listen to God or not. In that lunch time hour he could have given himself over to his rapidly rising anxiety. In fact, this may have happened as he decided to walk the city streets. But where Bruce turned and the church he passed made all the difference. As a result, Susan's life was preserved.

Now you tell me: Is this the random chance of good fortune, or is this a sign of a care-filled Voice as broad as the universe?

Susan was free to accommodate a thought about consuming still more alcohol. And too often she did so, until it was almost too late. But even though Susan walked close to the edge of a personal precipice, eventually she *chose* another way to life. And her choice made all the difference.

POINT. We are free. But no matter how much we listen to ourselves, and even though God values our freedom to listen to whoever and whatever, God's interest in us never quits. God never gives up on us. Far more than we do ourselves, God takes us seriously. And because God takes us seriously, we are given every opportunity to become more serious about ourselves.

Sin: Not Able to Listen to God

Just as we do, Susan also struggled with sin. At fundamental levels it was sin that got in the way of her listening to God's care-filled voice.

I hope you'll think about sin as *more* than an action. Sin might be drinking to some, a cuss word for others, or treating God's children, our sisters and brothers, in a shabby fashion. But these actions are better seen as the products of sin.

Sin is fundamentally a human attitude which sets our capacity to choose "our way" over the mutual conversation to which God is always inviting us. The Outline of faith also makes this point.

Question. What is sin?
Answer.   Sin is the seeking of our own will instead of the will of God, thus distorting our relationship with God, with other people, and with all creation.

Question. How does sin have power over us?
Answer.   Sin has power over us because we lose our liberty when our relationship with God is distorted.

Question. What is redemption?
Answer.   Redemption is the act of God which sets us free from the power of evil, sin, and death.[4]

At sub-conscious levels God and Bruce were in deep conversation with one another. How do I know? God is always in conversation with us, and there is no better illustration than the way Jesus used conversation when he worked in the first-century world, just the point made when Jesus joined two disappointed disciples as they trudged toward Emmaus after the crucifixion (Luke 24:13). When we want to know who God is, Christians first look at who Jesus is, knowing full well that Jesus shows us the nature of God.

Even thought God's ministry was unknown to Susan and her dad, God was working to network help to them both. And because connections needed to be made, God was not about to be satisfied with the random possibility that Bruce *might* turn into the church. So God spoke to Bruce, and an idea stirred in his consciousness.

Still, freedom allowed Bruce to struggle on the curbside with several conflicting thoughts. On the one hand, his previous experience with church was not good. The thought of seeking help there seemed crazy. "Surely," he thought, "if I just keep on walking I'll get clear about what I should do. Maybe I'm just too panicky right now."

But this new thought was insistent. "What else can I do?" became his question. Should he march on, or should he listen to "intuition"? He had no knowledge of what was best and what was worst.

POINT. Here is the fundamental shape of sin in life. It is not an action, but our inability to see ahead about what's best for us (and to which God is always inviting us), or even to listen with clarity to the conversation of another who always has our best interests at heart.

Mission-minded Christians know that things go wrong in the world not because God does not care, but because we tend to listen first of all to ourselves, and because the breach between God and us (what Christian theology calls sin) is so wide we cannot plainly hear the conversation that God is always shaping in our lives. We don't hear much about sin in many mainline congregations anymore, mainly because many preachers have lost the vision of God's everyday ministry working in our behalf. But mission-minded congregations know that sin explains a great many things about who God is and who we are, and why harsh, destructive things often happen in God's world.

Sin Is "Original Equipment"

The concept of original sin is simply another way of saying that the human tendency to value ourselves at the expense of God's conversation with us is larger and more pervasive than any one individual life. Just like all the accessories you order on a new auto-mobile are considered to be "original equipment," so sin is a part of our original equipment. It has been a part of human life since the beginning.

The author of Genesis describes the original generation of sin this way, with a story.

> The Lord God took Adam and put him in the garden of Eden to till and keep it. And the Lord God commanded Adam, saying, "You may eat of every tree in the garden; but of the tree of the knowledge of good and evil you shall not eat, for on the day that you eat of it you shall die (Gen. 2:15-17).

And still later:

> But the serpent said to the woman, "You will not die. For God knows that when you eat of it your eyes will be opened, and you will be like God, knowing good and evil." So when the woman saw that the tree was good for food, and that the tree was to be desired to make one wise, she took of its fruit and ate; and she also gave some to her husband, and he ate (Gen. 3:4-6).

From the very beginning God told both Eve and Adam to ignore the fruit of one tree, but now another who seemed to have their best in-terests at heart was saying "It's really OK." Whom was Eve to believe?

You would be wrong to think that God was either silent or passive while this transaction took place. Even though the author of this sec-tion of Genesis does not include God's conversation, we know God cares, and we can be sure that his word was straightforward about the covenant these two had with him.

So now these questions:

• What was Bruce to believe as he walked past the open door to a church?

• What would you believe if you were in his shoes, with his past experience of the church?

• And what was Susan to believe as her dad asked her to call a stranger (and a priest!) in a town far from home?

The plain fact is this: because of our "original equipment" sin it is hard for us to know to whom we're listening—to God, to ourselves, or to others. And so we often "act on faith," or "hope," or simply "trust" our intuition, seldom knowing for certain. Our tendency to not listen to God is a function of our freedom. If we were not free we would not sin. But if we were not free we would not be human, nor would we be made in the image of God.

God's Love and God's Powerlessness

"If God is so good, why do bad things happen?" Questions like this inevitably confront the evangelist. Often they arise at times of crisis, and in part they seem to be rooted in highly idealized pictures of an all-powerful God, not unlike the early childhood pictures of all-powerful and all caring parents.

But no matter what their roots, these questions deserve an explanation. The concept of the "powerlessness of God" can offer a temporary answer. Now I don't mean to suggest that at a time of crisis good pastoral care simply applies explanations about what God may or may not be doing. Good pastoral care first of all listens to pain and seeks in every way to give anguish expression. But often there comes a time, later, when thoughtful questions are asked. For the evangelist and the ministry of introductions, the idea of God's powerlessness provides a helpful, snap-shot picture of the relationship of sin, freedom, and God's love for us.[5]

God is not ultimately powerless, of course, a point made on every page of the Bible. But because of God's respect for human freedom, and because of what we Christians call sin—our freedom to listen to God's conversation or not—the notion of the powerlessness of God catches a bit of the breadth of God's love in a way that talk of God's power does not.

This idea first shows in the dialogue between Adam, Eve and the serpent in the third chapter of Genesis. Eve and Adam were free to listen to God or not. But they chose to listen to another, and in the moment of their decision God was powerless. Jesus himself offers a view of the powerlessness of God when, shortly before his crucifixion, he weeps over the destiny of Jerusalem (Matt. 23:37; Luke 13:34).

So what has the powerlessness of God to do with the suffering of Susan? Given Susan's trauma this seems to be the way God chose to work with it. Though "powerless" to offer effective guidance to her on the day she drank and drove, and though powerless to make Bruce turn into a church building on a lunch hour walk, God did speak to Bruce with all compassionate power, and Bruce did listen. And later so did Susan. And we are left to give thanks for a miracle.

POINT. Christians and non-Christians alike raise questions about why bad things happen in God's world. The notion of God's power-lessness provides a brief snap-shot of theology that satisfies the immediate question. I find it an extremely helpful concept when working with these "Why?" questions, mainly because it also hooks onto the possibility of a later discussion. And when we are introducing God to God's world, what we want are opportunities to engage a conversation. The notion of God's powerlessness offers practical help when the time is right.

The Adversary of Scripture

If God is always seeking to care for us, and if we are free to listen or not, the Bible says that the picture is still more complicated. Evil forces in the world are at issue here. But if you think this section will simply suggest that you say, "The devil makes us do it," you are wrong. We are responsible for our actions, a point the Bible makes clear through and through.

We could also ignore the topic of evil, but that would not be fair to the Christian tradition. We could simply acknowledge evil as the natural human tendency to look out first for ourselves, and, when we think thoughts like "Go for it" or "Me first" or "I deserve the best and to hell with the rest," could see these thoughts as simple signs of our serving our own best interests. There is a streak of meanness in just about every one of us. But is that all there is? The Bible says no.

Jesus himself engaged a demonic spirit, and stories of a demon are spread all through the pages of Scripture. Even the Book of Common Prayer notes "the works of the devil," and it warns about "forces of evil" in the baptismal office.

Question: Do you renounce Satan and all the spiritual forces of wickedness that rebel against God?
Answer: I renounce them.

Question: Do you renounce the evil powers of this world which corrupt and destroy the creatures of God?
Answer: I renounce them.

Question: Do you renounce all the sinful desires that draw you from the love of God?
Answer: I renounce them.[6]

Personifying evil makes it easier to talk about. And more, personifying evil helps us deepen our perspectives on God's love. I prefer to use the scriptural term "Adversary" when speaking about "Satan" or "the devil," mainly because I don't want to confuse the Bible's perspective with modern-day cults and their weird practices.

In the same way that a loving God stands at the door of our lives and knocks, according to the Bible, so does another. But while God offers us bread to eat, the Adversary eats us up (1 Pet. 5:8). Whatever you think of the issue of evil, this fact remains; the church of God through the centuries has been concerned about a force for evil that destroys human life and community.

So what might have been the shape of the Adversary's ministry to Bruce that afternoon? He might have spoken this way: "Turning into church is a crazy idea. You're simply too concerned right now for Susan's good. Take a deep breath and let's walk a little further together. Clear your thinking a bit, you'll be much more effective after a short walk." One can also imagine the Adversary's word to Susan during the long afternoons at a job she was not yet enjoying, "We'll be out before long, hang in and wait for the happy hour."

Putting words in the Adversary's mouth may be a troublesome endeavor to some. Maybe you say, "It's just a myth undeserving of our attention." But the reality of evil deserves all the attention we pay to it.

There is a crazy chaos just below the surface of everyday life. Folks who lived in Hitler's Germany in the decade before World War II describe a presence of evil best called demonic. Many of us also experienced this same evil presence in America in the hostile crowds that gathered during the intense days of the 1960s, when civil rights were at issue and the war in Vietnam conflicted our common life.

Evil and the God Of Love: A Cosmic Drama

Mission-minded Christians know there is more to life than what we can see with our eyes or hear with our ears. To some degree or another, every event gives expression to a cosmic drama, a drama never acknowledged in the daily newspaper, but nevertheless described on every page of the Bible. This drama includes a companionable God, an Adversary, people like you and me, freedom and sin.

In the drama taking shape as Bruce walked near the church, God did not for one minute like the possibility that he might consider not responding to an opportunity right before his eyes. And so I suspect there was a clear note of urgent judgment in God's word of address. It might have been on the order of: "Don't pass by this church. For the sake of Susan's life, turn in and let me take care of you."

But at the same time the Adversary of Scripture might have rejoined, "The idea of going inside really is preposterous. You need to take a break, my friend. Let's walk a little further. What help can you find on the inside of that empty building? There's nobody there. You're wasting your time and you know it."

Although Bruce did not want anything but the best for Susan, like the rest of us he naturally tends to listen to God in terms of what makes best sense for him.

Still, this truth remains: At a very important level Bruce was in communion with God, and when we are in communion with God, if it is at all possible, things tend to work better. St. Paul puts it this way: "In everything God works for good with those who are in communion with him" (Rom. 8:28). As a result of this communion Bruce put aside what seemed like a rational argument based on his past experience with the church, only to find out later that his best interests were those he served best of all.

The Solace Of Prayer

Prayer sums up all that we have been discussing in this chapter. When we pray, in an important and powerful way we are given every opportunity to become accessible to God. More often than not, however, Christians tend to confuse the action of prayer with talking; we have something to say and we hope God is listening and will act in response. But far more than talking to God, prayer is listening to God, as the following story illustrates.

> One evening when I was complaining about a particularly tough problem in my trucking business, my sister asked, "Have you prayed about it, Bill?"
>
> "Sure," I quickly replied. "Whenever I can."
>
> "You mean 'catch as catch can,' don't you?" she said, knowing I was constantly on the run between work and home and any number of other things.
>
> "The Lord can hear me just as well when I'm running," I answered.
>
> "Yes," she said, "but can you hear Him?"[7]

Harried lives breed anxiety, and more than anything else anxiety gets in the way of a listening prayer. We kick and flail away, and the more we work at prayer the less satisfied we become.

Still, Jesus assures us that "the kingdom of heaven is at hand," and to take advantage of it, simply "come to me, all you who labor and are heavy laden, and I will give you rest" (Matt. 11:28). Prayer means surrender, a surrender of our interests and a focus on listening to God—not only to what God wants from us and for us, but what God is already doing in our behalf to bring those things about.

Maybe on occasion you've found yourself so confused that you simply did not know what to do. At times of stress we're overwhelmed by an overabundance of input, much like the trucking executive in the story above. But Jesus offers a model for prayer at times like these; he drew apart for quiet and reflective meditation, to take advantage of listening to One who knew far better than he the ways and means of dealing with whatever current trauma engaged his heart.

Susan and her dad would not have called themselves praying people. But out of the depths and with broken hearts, both of these children cried to a God in whom they did not believe, and whether they knew it or not, God was closely listening to them, and already laboring to make things right. All of life is wrapped-up in a cosmic drama, and we are not alone in it. A mission perspective acknowledges and happily celebrates this drama, and enjoys nothing better than an opportunity to bear witness when ears are ready to hear and eyes to see.

Taking Action To Learn the Ministry Of Introductions

Developing the capacity to speak of God takes work. But it is a work much loved by mission-minded Christians. This chapter has discussed a few of the ways I've learned that mission-minded congregations speak of God when things are tough. My affection for these tools shows, because they are concrete and they generate all kinds of discussion and perspective.

To strengthen *your* ability, discuss in a small group the images, metaphors and stories used in this chapter and the previous three. But pay particular attention to:

• the way in which we are made in the *image of God*,

• *human freedom*, and the notions of

• *God's love* and *God's powerlessness*. Look closely at the way in which

• *sin* disables us, and consider afresh

• the *Adversary of Scripture*, along with the idea of a

• *cosmic drama* in which all of us are involved. And finally, consider

• *prayer* as the wonderful solace it is.

After your brief discussion, just to reach some point of common agreement, pick a story from your own life, and share it with your small group. Share your speculations with one another, and still later choose to discuss stories from the daily press and weekly news magazines. As a result, you'll be much more confident, and comfortable, speaking of God when you see God at work in the lives of others.

End Notes

1. Bishop Michael Marshall, *The Anglican Digest* (Late Pentecost A.D. 1989): 2.

2. These descriptions of childhood, adolescent and adult descriptions of God are drawn from Howard Hanchey, *Christian Education Made Easy* (Wilton, CT: Morehouse-Barlow, 1989).

3. The Book of Common Prayer, p. 845.

4. *Ibid.*, p. 848.

5. Thomas C. Oden, *Pastoral Theology, Essentials in Ministry* (San Francisco: Harper and Row, 1983), pp. 223-48. A brief and thoughtful discussion of the relationship between God's power, God's powerlessness—or self-limitation—and human freedom, written from the perspectives of pastoral care.

See also Dietrich Bonhoeffer, *Letters and Papers from Prison*, ed. Eberhard Bethge (London: SCM, 1967), p. 196.

6. The Book of Common Prayer, p. 302. See also Proper 27, p. 184.

7. Bill Watkins, "Coming To A Halt" in *Guideposts* (August 1988): 13.

CHAPTER 7

Developing Your Style of Personal Evangelism

Story Telling or Story Listening? • Determining Your Style of Personal Evangelism • Checklist: Developing Your Style of Evangelism

ou may have chosen to skim the preceding two chapters, figuring they were not quite as "practical" as you think you need. But in fact, the first six chapters in *Church Growth* provide the background to help you develop confidence with evangelism's ministry of introductions.

POINT. We can't identify the many signs of God's presence and ministry in the here and now of everyday life unless we know what we're looking for. And we can't begin to speak of God until we have a language adequate to the task. Mission-minded Christians know this well.

This is also a "how to" chapter. It is written to help you formulate a personal understanding of the ministry of evangelism, and begin to develop your skill with it. Increased confidence should result.

Story Telling or Story Listening?

Many of us grew up with the notion that evangelism means telling our story, and getting others to believe what we believe. I hope that by now you are beginning to see some alternatives to this way of thinking. Telling our story can be an important part of evangelism, but the ministry of introductions is better served by story-listening than story-telling.[1] Here's why.

Telling our story has two limitations hard to overcome. First, it does not directly value the experience of the other person. It values our experience more. Second, the more we tell our stories, the more people are likely to avoid us as we avoid those who always want to show us their old movies and slides of family life. Determining when to share our story is at issue here.

One evangelist writes the following. As you read her description of an encounter, keep in mind the distinction between story-telling and story-listening, and consider which best serves the ministry of evangelism.

> Once I took a taxi in New York City, and when I told the driver that my destination was the Church of the Resurrection, he commented, "It would be nice to believe that, wouldn't it?"
>
> Sliding right into the opportunity, I said, "Well, I do believe it because it happened to me—not a physical resurrection, but a resurrection in my life."
>
> Then I went on to tell him how Christ had completely changed my life when I totally surrendered it to Him several years before. I never knew if the seed I planted contributed to a spiritual harvest later, but that is God's business, not mine.[2]

We do not know the outcome of this witness, but we do know that the evangelist made a decision in that moment to tell the news about what God in Christ had done in her life.

But for most of us most of the time, story-listening is the ministry of choice. Indeed, story-listening shows more explicitly the care for the other person that we are likely to feel. This same taxi cab opportunity also could have been approached from a story-listening perspective, making use of turning points and offering a ministry of introductions. Here's how this event could be recast into a story-listening incident. The evangelist could have:

• chosen to marvel at the connection taking shape between the taxi driver and herself,

• paid a more explicit interest in the story behind what the taxi driver said, and

• identified the new life that showed itself in the very question the driver used when the conversation began, and the way in which God had worked to bring them together.

Such a listening conversation might have also taken this hypothetical shape:

Taxi: Where to, lady?

Rider: Can you take me to the Church of the Resurrection on Sixtieth Street?

Taxi: Church of the Resurrection. OK. (There was silence as he pulled into traffic.) It sure would be nice to believe that.

Rider: (I was surprised, but sliding right into the opportunity, I said,) What do you mean?

Taxi: Just what I said. You know, I grew up a Christian, but when you get into the real world things aren't so cut and dried.

Rider: It sounds like you've got a story to tell.

Taxi: There's just too much wrong in the world.

Rider: There sure is!

Taxi: Right on. Me, I got a sick daughter, and two weeks ago I was held up again. Got nicked right bad too. See this cut?

Rider: It looks pretty bad. I guess things are tough on the street.

Taxi: They sure are. Sometimes I think maybe I ought to get out of this business while I can still walk. Jerks are just waiting to rip off us cabbies, and if anything happens to me, my family gets hit hard. (He paused.) But this is all I know. I've got no choice but to hang in, but after a while it gets to me. You're just catching me on a bad morning.

Rider: I get trapped too, sometimes, but your crunch is a lot tougher than mine. (We rode on in silence, and it sounded to me like we had reached the end of this conversation. Then I continued,) To pick up on your first point, would you be interested in hearing anything from me about the resurrection?

Taxi: You're the fare.

Rider: Well, I think I heard a real note of your wanting to believe it when I got in this taxi. So tell me what you think of this. Of all the fares that you could have picked up this morning, you picked me up. You were where I was, and I was going to a place that you were interested in talking about. One thing I do know: God loves every one of us, and God is always trying to help us out. So you tell me why I was where you were, and why we had this opportunity to talk a bit about things like the resurrection and what's going on in your life?

Taxi: You believe God had something to do with this conversation?

Rider: Sure. How else would you see it? (We continued this conversation for a bit, and then moved to other things, and shortly we came to the church. Our meeting was done.)

Notice how story-listening meets the cabby just where he is, and offers to him in that place a word about God's love for him. Now think with me more closely about what might have been accomplished if this hypothetical conversation had taken place?

First, the cabbie could have talked about some really important things that weighed heavily on his heart.

Second, evangelism's ministry of introductions would have identified God's ministry in the here-and-now of the cabby's life today, using as a turning point the pick-up and the cabby's longing question.

Third, had a story-listening approach been used, this evangelist would have said just enough to stir the cabby's interest and curiosity, gifts that God will work with long after she and he part.

At its best the ministry of introductions centers not on our story, but first of all values the story of the other person. It looks there for signs of God's presence and ministry, and then attempts to provide a bit of interpretation so that the other person can celebrate *their* mountaintop experience. Every evangelist has to reach a personal balance between the need to tell our story and the need to identify and celebrate signs of God's presence and ministry in the life of the other person.

Determining Your Style of Personal Evangelism

Most of us grew up with a story-telling understanding of evangelism, and even if we are scared by it, it is not easy to put this model aside. If you are now at a point of wanting to develop your capacity to offer evangelism's ministry of introductions, you'll want to pay close attention to three items.

1. You have already developed a picture of evangelism, but it may be rooted in fears of both abuse and inadequacy. Many of us have been abused by evangelists in the past, or as a result of their actions we have been made to feel inadequate. These perceptions must be put to rest, and the preceding chapters are constructed to help you do just that.

2. Your personality type will play an important part in the way you choose to exercise the ministry of introductions. All of us stand before God as equals, but before God each of us is also unique in all the world. For instance, some of us are more extroverted than others, and so have an easier time making contact than introverts do. Therefore when considering yourself and the ministry of evangelism, guard against comparing yourselves with others who might seem to be "doing it right."[3]

3. The way in which you were brought into a knowledgeable relationship with God also influences your approach to evangelism.

For example, one young woman was confronted in college by a Christian who pressed her to make a decision to accept Jesus Christ. "You have got to know the Lord," he said, with such conviction that she asked him to say more. He did, and she began to wrestle with the kinds of questions that build belief.

But because his approach had such a good effect on her, she began later to use it on others. That proved disastrous: "The more I found answers that made sense to me, the more I began to share them. I also approached other people the same way I was approached. A direct, Jesus-centered approach worked for me, and I thought it would work on everyone else.

"But soon I found there were two problems with my approach. One, I valued the task of evangelism more than the people I was working with, and because some of them felt like I was more interested in their conversation than them, they dropped me pretty fast. They resented my working "on" them, and rightly so.

"Also, I discovered that everyone was not me, and that what worked for me at a certain time in my life would not work for everyone else. I was suffering from the arrogance of thinking that my way was the only way. I learned to recognize that what happened to me was good for me and that it might be good for some others, but not for everyone.

"It took me a while to figure out that I had to meet people the same way God meets people, just as they are."

When Christians begin the task of bearing witness, the chances are good that we will do it in the same way that it was done most effectively with us. If your conversion took a sharp and rapid form, you are likely to expect the same thing to happen for others. When it does not, you might be disappointed. On the other hand, if your Christian growth and conversion were slowly accomplished over a long period of time, the chances are that you will be more relaxed, figuring that folks will "get the message" eventually.

POINT. Pay close attention to who you are and how you began to know and love God. An uncritical use of your history and the particular gifts you bring to the ministry of introductions does not take a good account of the individual needs of the person or persons with whom you may be working, and it will also blind you to the wide-ranging ways in which God meets us all, just as we are and where we are.

Checklist: Developing Your Style of Evangelism

If you're now interested in developing more fully your capacity to practice the ministry of evangelism, gather a group of similarly interested persons, and at an early meeting share your perspectives about the issues raised in the previous section.

Then use the following list of questions to help you become still clearer about the style of evangelism you value. Remember, the ministry of introductions is best learned in community. All of us are enriched when we share personal perspectives with one another, and this is particularly true when using the following questions.

1. Discuss the concepts of story-listening and story-telling. Which appeals most to you? Why? What are its assets and its liabilities?

2. How did your conversion to Christianity take shape? Was it sudden, did it result from an encounter with a person who made Jesus or God "live" for you, or has your conversion been spread out over a long period of time?

3. How does your conversion inform your approach to the ministry of introductions? Or how do you think your conversion will inform your approach to the ministry of introductions? What are the assets and the liabilities in your approach to others?

4. What do you fear most about personal evangelism, and where is this fear rooted? One of the best ways to get rid of a deep-rooted fear is to talk about it with others.

5. What is the God language you are most comfortable with? Do you talk about Jesus, God, and/or the Holy Spirit? And what are the other images that you enjoy using? Why have you chosen this language? What are its assets and its liabilities?

6. What is your style of entering into relationships with others? How will your style of relating to others serve the task of making introductions? How will it get in the way? What would you like to change?

End Notes

1. The notion of evangelism as story listening has also been recently described by Wayne Schwab, Evangelism Ministries Coordinator of the Episcopal Church, in the booklet prepared by his office, *Proclamation as Offering Story and Choice*. His office has also published a *Handbook for Evangelism, The Catechumenal Process: A Resource for Dioceses and Congregations, Faith Development and Evangelism*, and *Evangelism With the Poor*.

2. Joyce Neville, *How to Share Your Faith Without Being Offensive* (New York: Seabury Press, 1981), p. 30.

3. David Kiersey and Marilyn Bates, *Please Understand Me: Character and Temperament Types* (Del Mar, CA: Prometheus Books, 1984). These are just two of the eight categories that make up the helpful Myers-Briggs Personality Inventory.

PART III

Leadership at Work: Building Up the Church

CHAPTER 8

Worship: O God Our Hearts Are Ready

Maintenance-Minded Worship: A Short Take • Mission-Minded Worship: A Short Take • Preaching the Power of God • Always Pushing For Better Worship • For God's Sake Do Things Well • Educate, Educate, Educate • Taking Action To Make Plans

hen worship goes well so does everything else. This chapter is written to portray a picture of worship in mission-minded congregations. It is not by any means an exhaustive discussion, but it does afford an opportunity for you to compare and contrast your Sunday morning worship with both mission and maintenance perspectives.

So what can you expect from this chapter? First, it is constructed to help you catch a vision of the worship often enjoyed in mission-minded congregations, for a vision points you toward a goal. And second, it is written to show you the importance of education in relation to worship, for many congregations leave education to chance, and then wonder what's wrong. The section at the end of this chapter is to help you make specific plans.

Remember once again that I frequently exaggerate the polarities of "mission" and "maintenance" in order to make a point. Doubtless you have noted many times that I speak harshly of maintenance. It is a foil, for in fact all congregations need to value taking care of themselves, and maintain a healthy tension between the two perspectives. In mission-minded congregations, maintenance will always come second.

Maintenance-Minded Worship: A Short Take

Congregations more concerned with maintenance than mission seldom pay much attention to worship on Sunday morning. Attendance is a "duty" to some, while missing worship means guilt to others, both of whom miss the whole point of a joyful opportunity to honor One who is always richly blessing us.

Visitors and newcomers are welcomed with seldom more than a perfunctory handshake. Good-hearted ushers may never have been trained to offer any more than this. Some ushers are not so good-hearted, seeing the stranger as an "outsider," maybe even a threat. Furthermore, neither thoughtful instructions nor page numbers are offered for the inclusion of these visitors in a liturgy that's likely to be strange to them.

The service itself is planned without enthusiasm, readings are read as if they are obstacles to be tolerated—and often they are, because lay readers (and clergy) have never learned to read with spirit the greatest story ever told. If the lessons are long, people begin to worry about having to sit with "nothing to do." The sermon is often treated as something that must be endured by those listening.

Stand in the back of maintenance-minded congregations and you'll hear singing and psalm recitation that sounds like a steady drone. Little vitality shows, for the most part because these Christians have never been encouraged to value Sunday worship as any more than a weekly obligation.

Mission-Minded Worship: A Short Take

The agenda for worship in mission-loving congregations is simply this: to help God and God's people meet through words of welcome at the door, Bible readings, song, prayer, and preaching.

Take hymnody in mission-minded congregations. Now I know full well that all of us can't sing like angels. Donn Starry, an Episcopalian at St. Peter's in the Woods, admits that he can't sing a note. But he hums well, and his voice adds a tone to this congregation's singing that makes it rich. Instead of a quiet drone when hymns are sung, mission-minded clergy and their congregations sing (or hum!) as if there were no tomorrow. They sing like this because:

• they have been *taught* to do so,
• they *enjoy* making a joyful noise, and, most importantly,
• they know the more they *invest* their energy in the hymns they sing, the more likely they will become firmer in their belief.

In fact, hymns are theological education at its best, for they tell us who God is and who we are.

At a recent women's conference a middle-aged participant asked me how she could go about intensifying her spiritual life. She has children at home during the week, and a myriad of details and duties always demand attention. She seldom finds much time alone. I advised that, if possible, she draw apart to a quiet place during the week (preferably the same time every week) to read the collect and the lessons appointed for the following Sunday. I also proposed that she accompany her quiet time with a cup of her favorite tea. Next I suggested that if possible she get to church a few minutes early on Sunday morning to settle herself quietly, pick up the resonance of the congregation's fellowship as it gathers, and, in all the hymns that are sung, plunge into their singing as if there were no tomorrow.

"But people will look at me!" she said. They might. But I also tried to help her see that the more she invests the totality of her energy in the hymns we sing on Sunday morning, the more she will be lifted out of herself, the more she will feel God's presence in those moments, and the more her spiritual life will deepen.

Indeed, hymns give us glorious opportunities to join in common with the thoughts of others as God is praised. Such praise offers us the privilege of entering the mind of God. Michael Marshall writes:

> This kind of worship sets our sights and explodes the hinges right off the doors of our limited perceptions. It opens our minds to a universe of infinite light and darkness, of heaven and hell, of death and judgment. In a word, we are pointed beyond time, space and history to the Kingdom of God.[1]

It is also a good idea to teach hymns to children in the Sunday school. Just a few learned every year, later to be shared with the congregation, provide rich opportunities to help develop in your congregation a love of hymnody. If mission-minded congregations are teaching the church anything, it is this: when events of any kind are understood as playing a part in a larger whole, congregational life is likely to sound like a symphony. The more congregational life is fractured into its component parts, the more parish life sounds like noise. And no one likes noise.

Preaching the Power of God

In large measure the vitality characterizing worship in mission-minded congregations comes from clergy's enjoyment of preaching. Enthusiastic, mission-minded preaching always celebrates God's action, in both Scripture's witness and the here and now of life today.

Mission-minded clergy preach many different styles of sermons, but present to some important degree in every one of them is what I have learned to call a kingdom-of-God theme.[2] Like John the Baptist, mission-minded preachers develop their sermons from this perspective: "The kingdom of heaven is at hand." Then, like St. Paul, these preachers go on to show the presence of God's ministry in the world by identifying altars to an unknown God. For these preachers know that by proclaiming God's action today, their people are more likely to see God's action, and seeing, come to expect it.[3]

Mission-minded preachers are also guided by St. Paul's letter to the church at Philippi, which lifts this small congregation's vision to the higher things that preachers of the kingdom have learned to value.

> Finally, brothers and sisters, whatever is true, whatever is honorable, whatever is just, whatever is pure, whatever is lovely, whatever is gracious, if there is any excellence, if there is anything worthy of praise, think about these things (Phil. 4:8).

The world hungers to hear of Godly things. And these preachers meet this hunger by searching out every passage of Scripture with thoughts of God's graciousness, God's excellence and God's loveliness in mind.

Unhappily, not all sermons preached on Sunday morning center on God's action in the world. As a result, hungry Christians coming to church to be fed end up with next to nothing. For example, one English bishop wrote in the diocesan paper of a sermon he heard when he was on holiday that was, he says, a "disgrace." The congregation was there in force that day and all was going well until the vicar ascended to the pulpit:

> The preacher spoke long but said little. There was no message. As I looked around at my fellow-worshipers, I could see from the sleeping of the old and fidgeting of the young that they, like me, were finding the sermon dull, uninspiring and irrelevant. What a lost opportunity. In fact, what a disgrace.

The bishop did not reveal the content of the sermon, but observed that "the congregation does not want third-rate personal comments on public affairs, but real preaching which brings the Bible to life."[4]

POINT. For clergy not yet touched by the knowledge of God at work in the here and now of everyday life, lively issues in the daily newspaper provide far more fodder for their Sunday sermon than stories of God's action, either in Scripture or in life today.

You will not hear mission-minded preachers berating their congregations to "do better" or to "love more"—except when those admonishments are demanded. Preaching about what we "ought to do" is maintenance-minded preaching; good on occasion, but not very often. What you will hear from their pulpits is a celebration of God's power and ministry in the here and now of everyday life today. Many years ago one unknown Christian described kingdom preaching this way: "I would not give a tuppence to hear from the pulpit where my duty lies, but I would walk a long country mile to hear from whence cometh my help."

Kingdom of God perspectives appear in every Bible story, and mission-minded preachers love to use them. For example, the story of the Good Samaritan (Luke 10:29-37) provides a wonderful opportunity for mission-minded clergy to preach the power of God. When engaging a passage like this, a maintenance-minded preacher might focus on the importance of the *ministry of human beings* to one another.

But a more mission-minded approach would:

• identify *God as a good Samaritan* who visits with us all through Scripture (echoing the image of the cornerstone that the builders rejected),

• identify God as one *who in the same way visits us today* when we are in need of help (using a contemporary illustration or story), and

• conclude with a practical note. One member of clergy reports preaching from a pulpit with the words "So what?" engraved on a clearly visible brass plaque. We do well to attend to such things in our preaching. A "So what?" at the end of a sermon might be a word of practical encouragement, or the discussion of a question like "Where have you been visited by God, recently and unexpectedly?"

Mission-minded preachers use guides to determine kingdom perspectives. Because they know first of all that the Bible's witness provides a window into the universe of God's ministry, kingdom of God preachers enjoy telling the story of God's long ago, *there-and-then* ministry. And their congregations love to hear the Bible preached in this way.

Since they are never content to remain with *there-and-then* perspectives, next these clergy look for the same signs of God's ministry in the *here-and-now* of our lives today. When possible, they like to strengthen God's church by showing God's action through the ministry of their congregation to one another and the world.

Finally, if God's displeasure is evident, kingdom preaching preachers look behind it to see why. They know that God is always angry when we abuse the covenant relationship and when we abuse one another. So whenever these preachers see God's anger, they look behind it to see how love and kindness were abused.

The story of Eli and Samuel lends itself to this discussion of kingdom preaching (1 Sam. 3). The people of Israel needed a leader, and God set about the task of providing one. Using careful exegesis, the kingdom preacher would celebrate God's concrete action in the past, maybe by paying careful attention to the conversational relationship that God has with everyone of us in the world. Then this kingdom preacher will look for signs of God's conversational relationship in the world today, as leaders are raised up, whether on a national or local level. We are never alone, these preachers know, and God is more than an idea. God is a subject who acts on our behalf at all moments, every day.

Nathan's judgment of David for his adultery with Bathsheba, the murder of her husband Uriah the Hittite, and his breaking of covenant with God, also lends itself to this discussion (1 Sam. 7). The Nathan story is a clear statement that God does not tolerate abusive behavior in the world, but is always speaking out against hostile conduct and actively working to make justice reign. Kingdom preachers do not shy away from severe topics, mainly because they know it is not themselves they preach, but God's action in the world based on Scripture's witness.

Still, preaching any kind of sermon is hard work. One preacher writes in a bulletin article entitled *Sleep-Inducing Sermons*:

> What is it about a sermon that is so blamed tranquilizing? This eternal question came to mind again recently as I participated in a worship experience—not as a leader or facilitator, but as a congregant in the pew listening to the preaching. [It] drove home to me what a cosmic battle you wage week to week: the struggle to stay awake during the sermon. Being in your place, sitting in the pew, attending the proclamation of the word, resisting the temptation to snooze—I'm telling you, I haven't done anything so unbearably difficult in months.
>
> The atmosphere in worship is usually somewhat subdued. The music is soft. The tone is hushed. The room is warm. And then the preacher proceeds with the proclamation, delivered in a particular homiletical inflection, measured in a certain hypnotic cadence, and spoken in sleep-inducing waves of sonorous phrases. Before long half the sanctuary is sawing Z's.[5]

Mission-minded preachers have discovered that treating their whole sermon as a story, and preaching it in the same fashion, helps free them from sonorous tones and sleep-inducing rhythms. Manuscripts tend to lock many of us into what we must say, not what we are joyous to say. Simply look at the spontaneity present when, for example, you tell a story, and when you read that same story to someone else. Nor do kingdom preachers shy away from "harsh" sermons, and because they are not afraid of a potential "harsh" quality, they are more likely to present it carefully. This also means that their sermons are seldom boring.

In a workshop I once heard a priest despair because more and more of her parishioners were involving themselves in "Faith Alive" weekend conferences. She feared that fundamentalism was on the rise in her diocese. The discussion then turned to the task of speaking of God in today's world. But, because this participant was still feeling a pressure (that none of us could identify) from her people, one member suggested "Why not just tell these folks that God hasn't called you to this way of thinking?"

"Don't tell me to say that God would speak to me," she angrily retorted. "God just doesn't take this kind of interest in life." And then she crossed her arms and absented herself from the remainder of the conversation.

Kingdom preachers know better than this woman. They love to speak about *God in action*, not human beings doing godly actions in the name of God. And by paying attention to the good news perspectives enmeshed in every Bible story, kingdom preaching helps us meet God today.

Always Pushing For Better Worship

A sermon never stands alone in mission-minded congregations. It takes its cue from the liturgy, and it always seeks to give expression to the Bible readings chosen for the day. The sermon nestles in the liturgy, and it is to the shape of the liturgy that we now turn.

The rector of one large urban congregation describes the interest he and his congregation take in their Sunday liturgy, and the task he saw before him when he came to be rector.

> The challenge was simply this: To use all that we had been given in an attempt to make Christ's reality known in this part of New York City. With all the limitations I had to acknowledge about myself, I realize that if the claims of Christ were put cogently, intelligently, and courteously before people in a setting of worship as fine as we could achieve, people might listen and respond.

> Always we find ourselves pushing for better worship; hymns carefully chosen with tunes that people can sing whether old or new; the Holy Scriptures provided in the pews for the congregation to use as they follow the readings; readers trained to read; liturgy beginning on the stroke of the clock; service leaflets carefully scanned for mistake or omission—all these things and more which have to be done and which take an enormous amount of time. The rewards of this are that people love to come and come in great numbers, week in and week out.

> I made reference to Bibles in the pews. I am a firm believer in Biblical literacy. Lay people should be knowledgeable in the content of God's word.

On Sundays before the great liturgy at eleven there is the Rector's Forum, a forty-five minute Bible study, preparing the class for the Scriptures set aside that day for the liturgy.

It has been said that we are the fastest growing parish in the Diocese, one sadly not known for its numerical expansion. From every possible background, economic, ethnic, political and denominational, our people come, filling the church with families and single folk, old and young, the unknown and the famous, the very poor and those who have lives blessed with prosperity.

Their generosity staggers me, their humor refreshes me, their forgiveness strengthens me and all of us who make many mistakes as we try to get things right for God. And they sing! The sheer volume of song and spoken acclaim is as embracing as it is surprising. And after it all, much friendly exchange and a great deal of work for the clergy as they try to "work the crowd."

If you get worship right, the chances are you will get everything else right. Exciting, yes. Exhausting, yes. Frustrating, often. Joyful, immensely. Fulfilling, superbly. Our motto is a verse in the Psalm, "O God my heart is ready."[6]

Worship like this takes place in small and large churches, whether a few gather or whether worshipers number in the thousands. And where this quality of worship takes place, it does so because of a mission perspective and careful plans. And because of it hearts are set on fire, it "explodes the hinges right off the doors of our limited perceptions," and for a moment we are brought near to God's throne of grace.

For God's Sake Do Things Well

Mission-minded congregations cultivate an atmosphere of holiness on Sunday morning. They know that when the things of worship are left undone, or when things are done in a haphazard way, or when lessons are read from the Bible as if it's a labor the reader wishes were over, the medium conveys a message that worship really isn't much important. Nor is God.

The Rev. David White describes these counterpoints while visiting several parishes during a sabbatical leave from his Sunday morning responsibilities. The following comments are taken from his quickly penned notes to himself.

Which would you rather have? This?
The timid (or curt?) usher thrusts a bulletin in my hand. The organist makes three grand entrances, all the while chattering with parishioners. The conspicuously inconspicuous altar guild member makes several visits to the sanctuary. The acolytes appear twice to survey the scene and then return to light the candles and then return to pick up the processional cross. The parishioners never stop chattering to one another until the opening word of the hymn. This last is encouraged by the choir and clergy who speak in raised voices to be heard over the prelude.

Or this?
One is welcomed warmly by the usher and introduced to one or two parishioners nearby. Low and subdued conversation at the rear of the church, the noises of parishioners warmly welcoming one another to the family gathering. The congregation becoming quiet and prayerful, long before all have gathered. The lack of functionaries racing about. The Sense that all had been prepared well in advance...[7]

People come to church because they are responding to a God-given invitation, and they have every hope of bonding with their new-to-them community. But incorporation cannot take place if a relationship is never given a chance to develop. When strangers enter on Sunday morning, a bulletin, even when it is gracefully offered, provides only the briefest outline of morning worship. And in the Episcopal Church, if these new folks are expected to follow along with an unfamiliar order of worship by using a bare-bones bulletin, all the while juggling an unfamiliar prayer book and hymnal, and bobbing up and down between standing, sitting and kneeling, it's a wonder we keep as many of these visitors as we do. And no surprise that we lose so many.

Mission-minded congregations cultivate a spirit of generosity and welcome in their Sunday morning worship. They carefully call out page numbers and identify service books as appropriate, and they allow time for participants to find the place they are supposed to be. And if a newcomer is having trouble, mission-minded Christians are quick to offer help. There is a place for individual devotions, but when the public worship of God is joined in the church of God, there is no place for privatism. God expects from us neighborliness, and mission-minded congregations are marked by this kind of welcoming worship.

POINT. Not all, but at least part of the shrinkage in mainline churches results because worship is often poorly executed, for poorly-executed worship on Sunday morning seems to mark every shrinking congregation.

QUESTION. How does your congregation make a welcome for newcomers? What would it be like for you if you were newly in their shoes on Sunday morning? For the plain truth is if you don't make it easy for visitors to find a comfortable place in your branch of God's house, they are not likely to return. The ways and means to become more intentional about this important ministry are found in Chapter 10.

A humorous story expands this discussion of welcome. Or the lack of it. Written by former White House assistant Michael Deaver, the following vignette paints a picture of what results when strangers, in this case, Ronald and Nancy Reagan, engage the unfamiliar pattern of Episcopal worship.

> The Episcopal service is somewhat more formal with kneeling and a common chalice and considerably more ritual. This kind of Mass was very foreign to the Reagans, and within minutes after we were inside the church they kept sending nervous glances my way. They were turning pages of the prayer book as fast as they could and I was handing them loose pages to help them keep up.
>
> Nancy whispered to me in a mildly frantic voice, "Mike, what are we supposed to do?" I explained the ceremony as quickly as I could: how we would walk to the altar and kneel, the minister would pass by with the wine and the wafers. He would bless them and keep moving.
>
> The President, who as most people know has a slight hearing problem, leaned toward us but picked up little of what I was saying.
>
> We started toward the altar and halfway down the aisle I felt Nancy Reagan clutch my arm. In front of us, all I could see were people crossing themselves and genuflecting. "Mike!" she hissed, "Are those people drinking out of the same cup?"
>
> You have to remember that Nancy is the daughter of a doctor. I said, "It's all right. They'll come by with the wafers first. Then, when the chalice reaches you, dip the bread in the cup and that is perfectly all right. You won't have to put your lips to the cup.
>
> The president said, "What? What?"
>
> Nancy said, "Ron, just do exactly as I do."

> Unknown to me, the church had made its wafers out of unleavened bread, which gave them the look and hardness of Jewish Matzo. Nancy selected a square of bread, and when the chalice came by she dipped hers...and dropped it. The square sank in the wine. She looked at me with huge eyes.
>
> By then the trays had reached the President. Very calmly, and precisely, he picked up a piece of unleavened bread and dropped it in the wine. I watched the minister move on, shaking his head, staring at these blobs of gunk in the wine.
>
> Nancy was relieved to leave the church. The president was chipper as he stepped into the sunlight, satisfied that the service had gone quite well.[8]

Doubtless this small, rural congregation was overwhelmed by the Sunday morning presence of the President of the United States, with all its attendant hoopla and security constraints. But if these visitors had been strangers looking for a permanent church home, the chances are good they would never return for a second visit. Some wags would doubtless say "So what?" but they miss the point about what God expects of us.

POINT. The more complex the liturgy becomes on Sunday morning, as satisfying as it may be for those who know it through and through, the more forbidding it will be to those who hope to become a part of the church they visit.

The membership of my own denomination is shrinking, and it is partly because we seem more content to serve long-term members than the visitors and strangers God is bringing to us. Granted, a growing number of Episcopal churches are doing things differently. Indeed, some always have, and both groups do more than their share to keep this church alive. But far too many of us simply do on Sunday morning what feels good to us. We end up basking mostly in our own glory, not God's.

Educate, Educate, Educate

More than a few clergy deplore the fact that their people "don't sing," or "they don't participate very much," and bemoan that "preaching to them is like preaching to a brick wall. There's just no response." But still other clergy *do* enjoy a close relationship with their congregation on Sunday morning. And they do so because they've made all kinds of efforts to teach their people about what constitutes good worship. Nothing is left to chance.

Mission-minded clergy teach their congregation about everything, and because their congregations know they are the people of God working in concert with God for the sake of the world's salvation, they respond. A mission perspective does not develop overnight, nor does the quality of worship described in this chapter. Both must be carefully nurtured over a long period of time.

For example, mission-minded congregations enjoy being reminded that the presence of Sunday morning visitors is a response to an invitation extended from beyond themselves. As a result, these Christians offer a warm welcome not because a glad hand means the possibility of adding another "paying member" to the roles, but because in the welcome they are playing a tiny part in a cosmic drama. It is God who invites folks to church, it is God we welcome when God's people come through the door, it is God to whom we offer a service flier, and it is God whom we seat.

These leaders also know that the public school model of education generates all kinds of passivity in Sunday morning worship. For example, we often learned that it was better to be seen and not heard. And because Sunday morning worship stirs memories of school-days authority and our submission to it, mission-minded clergy make all sorts of efforts to help their congregations become joyful and spirited participants in Sunday's liturgy. Congregations who have never been helped to be anything but passive participants in their worship are generally going to be dead participants.

THE BOTTOM LINE. When plans for worship are carefully constructed, when clergy leadership takes all the pains in the world to make sure that folks know what to do and why it is done, and when a spirit of generosity characterizes the plans that take shape, God is known and hearts sing with joy.

Taking Action To Make Plans

This section is written with church leadership in mind. Please don't think that education simply means telling folks what to do. If clergy and lay leaders state that things are to be done in a certain way solely because that is the way they want them done, they are not functioning as educators. Telling folks what to do is maintenance-minded ministry. Helping folks discover the patterns of ministry to which God is calling them is mission-minded leadership.

Consider the following ideas when thinking about any renewal of your worship on Sunday morning.

1. On the Atmosphere of Worship

• Every church has an atmosphere of worship, and in part this atmosphere develops because of church architecture. The "place" of worship makes a difference. How does your building contribute to the atmosphere visitors engage in your worship on Sunday morning? Could it be improved?

• The atmosphere of your worship is affected by the attitudes and habits of your congregation. What will a newcomer think and feel as they enter into your church for worship on Sunday morning? What is likely to get in the way of their developing a warm response? Looking at your worship through their eyes will likely open your eyes.

• To help particularize worship, offer thanksgiving for birthdays and anniversaries, and offer prayer by name for the sick and those who have died. Also offer thanksgiving for the contributions of time and talent your congregation offers to God as they give themselves to service in the church and in the world. Altar guild and vestry members can be thanked, along with choir members, and the list goes on and on. And thanksgiving can be offered for the work of your congregation in the world, as electricians, engineers, teachers, nurses, and parents, to name just a few.

• Visitors with children will be most interested in how you value Christian education for their children. Occasional "show and tell" festivals, described in chapter 13, can offer the hope and promise for which they are looking.

2. On Lay Readers

• Do your layreaders read the word of God with authority? How do you assist them with their ministry? A video recorder can assist this teaching ministry, paying attention to projection, pace, enunciation and drama. Parishioners familiar with drama can assist.

• Do your layreaders offer a short summary of the reading before it is read? Do they use silence at the beginning to let the congregation settle, and do they pause for dramatic effect before announcing the end of the reading?

3. On Congregational Participation

• How well do your people sing? Do you and the choir offer opportunities for your congregation to learn to sing the doors right off their hinges? How do you practice learning new hymns with your congregation? Maybe just five minutes each Sunday devoted to singing the new hymn or becoming familiar with unfamiliar and new service music will offer just the right amount of help. Is there a healthy mix of old and familiar hymns with new and unfamiliar pieces?

POINT. Mission-minded congregations do not simply leave the introduction of new music to the organist and the choir, because in so doing worship is encouraged to become "choir-centered."

• How do you use the time before worship commences? Is there a respectful silence, and do you on occasion use this time to teach the congregation something about the liturgy or the music you are using?

• Does your congregation know how they might sound to a newcomer? When you pray the prayer book, is there an uncertain drone, or do prayers lift souls right up to the gates of heaven?

• Do you have Bibles in the pew and, if you do, do you encourage their use by helping members of the congregation find the place of the readings (perhaps in a book unfamiliar to them)? And do you give the congregation time to do so? Such a period "with nothing to do" provides a pause that helps the congregation step off confidently into the next phase of the liturgy.

4. On the Welcome of Newcomers

• How does your parish identify and welcome visitors on Sunday morning? How do you help ushers and greeters make plans to exercise their ministries? A full discussion of these ministries is found in chapter 10.

• Along with greeters and ushers, your bulletin makes a first impression that counts. Do you construct your bulletin so that visitors and newcomers can use it to make their way through complicated worship patterns?

Or is your Sunday bulletin simply a tightly constructed order of worship listing one page after another, and is the pace of your worship such that no one but the most familiar could keep up with the it?

• If the Peace is used, how is it handled? Does your use of the Peace help parishioners meet and greet one another? In these fractured times, with so many of us hungry for a community that truly cares, the time of the Peace offers a ministry that is exactly right for our age.

• How do you and your congregation handle the time of announcements? How many announcements are offered: enough to satisfy a newcomer's need to know, yet not enough to bore one unfamiliar with the congregation?

5. On Sermons

• Have you told your congregation what you need from them by way of their response to your sermon? Do you need head-nodding affirmation? Would you like to be able to say, when looking for their affirmation of a point you're working, "Let the congregation say Amen," and expect a hearty "Amen" in response?

If people don't know what you want, they are going to give you what they think you want, or nothing at all. We are talking here about an intentional ministry of education.

• Have you asked your congregation what kinds of sermons they would like to hear? A growing number of clergy now explore the lections appointed for the next Sunday with a small group of parishioners early in the week. By looking for "there and then" perspectives on the scripture, and by searching out "here and now" perspectives in life today, sermons emerge that are more satisfying to all.

End Notes

1. Michael Marshall, "The Mission High Fulfilling" in *The Anglican Digest* (Advent 1987): 62.

2. The Rev'd William Farrington, a mission-minded Episcopal priest, encouraged the inclusion of the kingdom preaching discussion. He notes that *Western Spirituality*, by Matthew Fox, distinguishes between the more traditional sin/redemption model of sermoneering, and the creation/celebration model that likes nothing better than to celebrate God's creating action in the world. Kingdom preachers lean more to the latter than to the former.

3. For a perfectly grand summary of God's here-and-now everyday action from biblical perspectives, see Walter Brueggemann, "Covenanting As Human Vocation," *Interpretation* (33):18.

4. *The Anglican Digest* (Advent-Epiphany A.D. 1989): 30.

5. Charles Foster Johnson, Senior Pastor, writing in *The Second Page*, the newsletter of Second Baptist Church, Lubbock, Texas, February 9, 1990.

6. John G. B. Andrew, "The Mission High Fulfilling" in *The Anglican Digest* (Advent 1987): 17-19.

7. David White, "Upon Entering the Church" in *The Anglican Digest* (Advent 1987): 26.

8. Michael K. Deaver with Mickey Herskowitz, *Behind the Scenes* (New York: William Morrow, 1988).

CHAPTER 9

Mission-Minded Clergy Leadership: Enthusiastic and Intentional

Maintenance-Minded Clergy: A Short Take • A Joyful Celebrant • A Skillful Liturgist • A Visionary Steward • An Able Educator • An Enthusiastic Administrator • Maintenance-Minded Clergy Burnout • Educating Clergy for Ministry • Reenvisioning Theological Education • Calling a Mission-Minded Pastor for Parish Leadership • Evaluating Clergy Prospects: Help for the Calling Committee

A mission-minded church forms only when mission-minded clergy are present. Clergy leadership makes all the difference. Not just *some* of the difference, and not just a *real* difference, as a colleague has encouraged me to say—uncomfortable with my emphasis about the absolute importance of clergy leadership.

I exaggerate the importance of clergy leadership to make a point. But from what I see in my travels around the church, a mission perspective is not likely to grow if knowledgeable and enthusiastic clergy leadership is missing. And when a mission-minded parish calls a member of clergy who leans more toward maintenance, its mission suffers.

The following pages offer brief pictures of mission-minded clergy at work. They also describe the consequences of a maintenance mindset and how it develops for clergy, and the closing parts of this chapter offer suggestions to those churches now looking for new clergy leadership. For some this may be a depressing chapter, although I wish it were otherwise. But others may engage ideas in the following discussion that not only make sense, but offer the possibility of freedom and renewal.

The plain truth is, "Where there is no vision the people perish."

121

Maintenance-Minded Clergy: A Short Take

Clergy who grew up in churches more concerned with maintenance than mission are likely to exercise a maintenance style of leadership in their adult years. Early childhood experiences are formative for all of us, and so is our experience of growing up in the church. If they grew up in congregations leaning more toward maintenance than mission—and most mainline congregations do lean in this direction—it is likely that they will exercise maintenance-minded leadership. Unless, that is, they take a careful and critical look at the past and set some *new* goals for today. For example:

• If they learned that Sunday morning Christian education was not important in their formative years, it is not likely to be valued now.

• If they learned that preaching was not much valued as a ministry by the clergy with whom they grew up, it is not likely to be valued now.

• If they learned that leadership means telling people what to do, their style of ministry is likely to be autocratic today.

• If they learned that welcoming newcomers on Sunday morning was unimportant, they are likely to perpetuate this model in their present congregation.

POINT. Without being too fatalistic but remaining sensitive to the power of personal history and education, clergy, like all human beings, are rooted in their past and, unless corrective action is taken, they are doomed to repeat it.

A Joyful Celebrant

Mission-minded clergy generally possess a mile-wide streak of optimism. God is close and they know it. Now I don't mean to say that these clergy are pie-in-the-sky optimists, but they are a hopeful bunch. Their hope is of course grounded in the steady confidence that God is always with us and, that whatever they confront, God is already richly present. Their celebrative attitude shows in several ways.

1. They have cultivated the capacity to identify God at work in the here-and-now of everyday life. They enjoy bearing witness to God's action in daily conversation, and their sermons and teachings are often illustrated with examples of God at work in the world. Parishioners often say in response, "I didn't know God was so close."

2. These clergy know that the word "celebrate" means *more* than presiding at the church altar. They enjoy presiding over the everyday, every week life of their parish. They delight in the task of keeping parishioners informed about church goings on, and their parish newsletters abound with announcements. And many of the news items in their Sunday bulletins and weekly newsletters often note God's everyday action.

3. Mission-minded clergy make it a point to praise their parish for its life and work. These members of clergy know that their congregations exist because of grace, and that the regular use of praise accelerates growth and generates even more good works.

4. Instead of seeing a problem, these leaders tend to see opportunities for celebration. No matter how much pain there is, these ministers always look for signs of a loving God doing, in the midst of everyday life, infinitely more than we can ask for or imagine (Eph. 3:20). Now I don't mean to suggest that mission-loving clergy simply say "Be hopeful" when things are tough. That's shabby care. Rather, these men and women have learned that "joy cometh in the morning," and because Another is also at work in the midst of life, they have learned to be expectant of God's ministry even when things look bleak.

THE BOTTOM LINE. A mission perspective springs from a certain hope that God is at work serving us and the world. More, this attitude is not contrived; it is shaped like the thanksgiving it is, and it springs from a gospel conversion.

A Skillful Liturgist

Not unexpectedly, worship on Sunday morning stands front and center in the ministry of mission-minded clergy. They know that adoration of God is the best kind of pastoral care, for by it they and their people are renewed to plunge into the world anew. These clergy and their congregations really do believe that Sunday is the first day of the week.

Mission-minded clergy also know that carefully planned and executed worship sets a place for the *mysterium tremendum*, an ancient term describing the tremendous mystery taking shape when God and God's people meet for conversation and communion.

"Rapture" describes just a bit of what happens when God comes near at times like these, and although these events may last for no more than a few fleeting seconds, when touched by the mystery of God's presence we are wrapped up with feelings of joy and deep peace. Tears sometimes signal these events, the gentle eye-filling kind that don't roll down our cheeks, or we may find ourselves taking a deep breath to keep control of our emotions. The story in chapter 13 of Frank and Jenny Wright captures the rapture generated by carefully planned and choreographed worship. The worship of Almighty God is the greatest show on earth, not because we make it so, but because, in our worship, we are welcomed by the Sovereign of the universe to a cosmic event.

In worship, a mission perspective's agenda is simply this: To help God and God's people meet through words of welcome, Bible readings, song, prayer, and preaching. And what results is a quality of worship that makes hearts sing with joy. To this kind of worship visitors return again and again.

A Visionary Steward

Mission-minded congregations are a spending people. Because they know that God is at work in the world, more than anything else these folks love to spend themselves in God's service. This attitude is formed by clergy leadership.

For example, mission-loving Christians spend themselves in worship by their spirited participation. They sing joyfully because they know it is their service to God, and they spend time listening to sermons and Bible readings because they enjoy hearing more about God. They also love to spend time in prayer because they have learned that God has a lot to say. In addition, mission-minded Christians spend themselves everyday in service to the world, because they know that in the world they are an important part of the greatest story ever told.

This attitude toward giving to God stands in sharp contrast to the "giving attitude" present in maintenance-minded congregations. In those congregations Christians are taught to give because it is an obligation. "We have a mission to the world," it might be said, "and we must commit ourselves to it." But note: this word *about* mission sounds far more like the law than grace.

At fundamental levels mission-minded Christians give because of love. Just as in healthy families parents make all kinds of joyful sacrifice, so mission-minded congregations respond to God in the world. That is why mission-minded clergy and their congregations every year look forward to the Every Member Canvass, a fact that blows away the maintenance mindset. The yearly canvass is not an isolated event in mission-minded congregations, but provides an opportunity for mission-minded Christians to "go on record" for God, giving them a chance to give their dreams concrete expression.

Because mission-minded congregations love to dream and because their dreams are often bigger than their financial resources, they have learned to value a deficit budget. Now deficit budgeting doesn't mean that these congregations are profligate, or in any other way irresponsible with the treasures God has given them. It simply means that they value dreams, for they know that dreams are God-inspired. Now living with a deficit budget takes courage, but the alternative is even more dangerous. Here's why.

One maintenance-minded congregation recently finished its Every Member Canvass by hassling to trim its already realistic budget by 10%. They had not met the 23% increase they had hoped for, and to do this, they cut out a contingency reserve (which probably they would have not spent anyway, and contingencies still have to be funded in emergencies) and reduced the funds available for buildings and grounds. What resulted from all this hassle? A parish of God's people ended up with feelings of failure, even though pledged income for the new year had actually increased by 13%.

There was a better alternative. Their vestry could have funded a deficit budget, thanked God for what they had been given, committed themselves to oversee pay-outs carefully during the year, and continued to pray and expect God to stir those in the parish who had the resources to contribute more. Deficit budgets do contain an element of risk. Funds are not readily at hand. But God is, and just as Jesus reached out to Peter when he stepped from the boat to walk on a raging sea, mission-minded congregations know that God reaches out to them when their budgets reflect their spirit-inspired dreams.

The church of God is not a business selling a product for profit, so business rules do not always apply. Mission-minded clergy know that dreams generate excitement, and excitement generates expectancy. As a result, the cup of parish life overflows, because the people of God actually put their treasure where their heart is. The church of God is a product of love and its resources a lot deeper than any carefully constructed budget.

An Able Educator

You will not hear mission-minded clergy delegating Christian education to others because it is a bother to them. They place a high value on Sunday school for the children committed to their charge. More, they encourage and lead classes for adults, as well as supporting the formation of Bible study and prayer groups. Along with the Sunday sermon, mission-minded clergy know that each of these activities work together to provide rich times for education.

Their teaching often includes brief sketches of God's presence and ministry. I have heard more than a few of these clergy make remarks like, "God's wind moved among us as we sang that last hymn. Did you sense it as I did?" Indeed, these leaders know that when bearing witness comprises Christian education, God has more than enough materials with which to shape Christian belief. As a result of this kind of teaching, parishioners are set free to celebrate the "fortunate" occurrences in their lives not as simple expressions of good luck, but as evidence of far more than good fortune in their lives.

An Enthusiastic Administrator

Finally, mission-minded clergy know that fundamentally administration is the work of a servant. The word administration itself means "to minister to." Hence, even mission-minded clergy who don't necessarily like administration have learned to value it.

Indeed, careful and thoughtful administration is required by mission-minded congregations. In addition to the normal requests for pastoral care that inundate these members of clergy, plans for Sunday and weekday worship must be made, the organization and maintenance of Bible study and prayer groups requires active support, and vestry and board meetings must be scheduled. To help with the important task of administration, mission-minded clergy also develop an annual program calendar for their parish, as noted in chapter 16.

POINT. Some clergy are better cut for administration than others. But the plain fact is this: without exception, mission-minded clergy make careful provision for administration, even if that means delegating administrative details to others who, by character and temperament, are better suited for the task of making daily schedules and following through on long-range plans.

Maintenance-Minded Clergy Burnout

A maintenance mindset burns out clergy. Now this doesn't mean that mission-minded clergy are immune to burnout, but the agenda of a mission-mindset tends to strengthen the spiritual life of the ordained. The following discussion develops these ideas, and goes on to show why the mainline church, itself, encourages the development of a maintenance mindset, and unintentionally sustains it.

Every year more than two hundred clergy return to my seminary for continuing education. Some stay for only one or a few days, and some for as many as six weeks in our extensive program. Not all, but many of these folk come with symptoms of burnout. If once they were mission-minded, now they worry too much worry about being a faithful caretaker; what's missing is a sense of purpose. A few may be even looking for a new line of work, or they may be thinking about changing parishes, assuming that a new situation will make everything all right.

Richard Busch, director of Virginia Theological Seminary's Center for Continuing Education, writes about the way a maintenance perspective destroys clergy.

When clergy [in my program] describe what they do...many respond with a picture of maintaining an institution.

While busy and involved in the lives of others, most clergy admit they lack depth relationships. As one put it, "My life is characterized by a wealth of acquaintances and a poverty of real relationships."

[A] weariness comes, it seems to me, not so much from the demands of ministry as from the sense of being isolated and unsupported.

[Another] observation concerns prayer. In recent years there has been a re-awakening of interest in prayer and the inner life. Across the church many signs point toward a deepening hunger in this area. Whereas one might imagine that clergy would be at the forefront of this reawakening, generally this is not the case.

Most of us with parish experience recognize that parochial life becomes weighted with a pull toward people in crisis and need and toward general busy-ness. Urgencies and activities tempt us from the work of prayer. Time spent in some regular discipline of prayer, Bible reading and journal writing gradually becomes negligible. Prayer becomes something one does with and for the sick and within a liturgical setting. Someone put it this way: "There are just so many pressing things to do that I don't have the time to pray."

Without realizing it, many in the church have accepted the idea that doing things is more important than praying.

[My last] observation concerns the faith struggle. Most clergy rarely discuss theology or faith outside of the more formal settings of worship, classes, and seminars. The language of faith rarely becomes personal and is not easily related to everyday experience. Many clergy have gradually let go the heart of their faith.[1]

By virtue of his position Busch sees many clergy after years of work without a break. He also paints a bleak picture of the natural ascendancy of a maintenance mindset.

Now these questions: Why aren't clergy better protected against this malady? Is there a secret? And if clergy grew to maturation in a maintenance-minded congregation (as most have), why aren't they offered some other alternative? To meet this inquiry we must look at theological education in the mainline church, for the theological seminaries of the church could be a natural first line of defense. Unfortunately, they are not.

Educating Clergy for Ministry

Denominational seminaries are charged with passing on the baton of church leadership to successive generations, and seminary faculty are wonderfully dedicated to this task. But mainline seminary faculties are not *well* equipped to teach the fundamentals of the kind of church leadership that growing, mission-minded communities are exercising.

POINT. Seminary faculty can teach only what they know. With little experience in the primary leadership of a parish, and growing to maturation in maintenance-minded congregations, most are simply unaware of the larger issue of preparing students to lead the church effectively.

First, because so many grew up in maintenance-minded congregations, they don't naturally make operational distinctions between mission and maintenance perspectives in course presentations. I dare say that in most mainline seminaries you can count on the fingers on one hand the total number of faculty who have had a primary responsibility for local church leadership. Still fewer are blessed with the experience of long-term parish leadership, while fewer still grew up in mission-minded congregations. As a result, the student development of leadership-for-mission suffers because faculty are not equipped to teach it.

This lack of familiarity with parish leadership shows in subtle ways. For example, with little or no full-time experience as the ordained head of a congregation, most seminary faculty have never been required to construct Sunday morning worship mindful of the tender care deserved by a congregation meeting only once each week, nor the needs and hopes of visitors. The results of this show in my own seminary's welcome when we join the liturgy in our daily chapel. In our daily morning worship we seldom announce pages in the Prayer Book, nor even the psalm to be read. Granted, seminary chapels are peopled mostly by faculty and students. But even so, generosity in response to a mission perspective demands that worship always be shaped "as if" visitors are present, for even though only a handful make it through our doors in any one week, they come as folks invited by God.

Indeed, even as God comes—all visitors arrive. But the voice of my seminary's tradition tells us that silence is "our way," for we know the shape of "our" worship. So the message conveyed to students by most seminary worship is this: the welcome of newcomers and the creation of community in the liturgy is not a substantive issue.

Secondly, since parish leadership is not taught in the classroom, students are left with the responsibility for this learning. But because many of these soon-to-be-ordained Christians grew up in maintenance-minded congregations, and because most of us don't like to give up the familiar for the unfamiliar, it is likely they will graduate with the assumption that maintenance-minded leadership is the only leadership there is.

Thirdly, faculties teach as they were taught. Most learned the content of their discipline in the academic pursuit of a PhD. In that effort they earn their degrees through a dissertation of *ideas about a discipline* later defended orally before a panel of soon-to-be peers. "A bunch of sharks they were," says one, describing the intensity of intellectual combat. Consequently, instead of the themes of parish leadership providing a context for the questions raised and answered in teaching, various academic disciplines set the context. As a result, students occasionally complain that the classroom is not very practical and they perceive it as remote from the practice of ministry.

For example, in quiet despair, one newly ordained minister noted that his parish is not much interested in Bible study: "I don't know what to do." He can't get an adult class together on Sunday morning, and there is little interest in prayer group meetings during the week. When I briefly explored what he wished to accomplish in Bible study, he said he hoped to interest his parish in some of the modern-day critical scholarship of the scriptures. Thought I, "His people don't want an exercise in critical scholarship on Sunday morning. They want to know who God is, what the Bible says about God, how God acts in their lives, and what difference a knowledge of God makes."

This pastor suffers a consequence of modern-day seminary education. In seminary he learned the academic use of the tools of modern day biblical scholarship and, because they made a difference in his life, he wants to give them to his church. The inconsistency is this: he was able to devote three years to the intensive study of Scripture in a fulltime residential environment, while his congregation on Sunday morning or during the week has only a few minutes to devote to it. And because they work hard in the world, and because they have been touched by God's love and know it, what they want in Bible study is a practical celebration of their relationship with the sovereign God of the universe.

Bishop John Howe of Florida makes just this point.

> Who cares whether J, E, D or P wrote a particular passage? People are literally dying to know what the Bible has to say to them. John Rogers of Trinity Episcopal School wryly comments, "We have discovered a way of studying the Bible in which we learn everything about it except what it says."[2]

Alan Jones, Dean of Grace Episcopal Cathedral in San Francisco, says the same thing in a different way.

> Biblical studies until recently have been in the grip of a reductionist historicism. There has been too much emphasis on the date, occasion and "original meaning" of a text with little work done on either its use *liturgically* or *devotionally* [emphasis mine] over the centuries....The results are disastrous.[3]

What the people of God *are* interested in, and what mission-minded congregations show us is this: Christians are hungry to learn about God, not *just* more about the Bible.

To the degree that normative theological discussion in the academic classroom does not identify and celebrate God's everyday presence and ministry in every course, students are not able to identify and celebrate signs of God's action in the world. As a result, the development of a mission-minded ministry suffers. Field education programs are an effort devoted to correcting this imbalance. But because many field education placements lean more toward maintenance than mission, field education continues to be little more than the practice of a practical, "What should I do now?" kind of ministry.

It is not difficult, I believe, for the reader to understand that seminary faculty tend to give to students what they learned to value in their own educational upbringing, which is an intensive exploration of the ideas most current in their several disciplines. It may or may not be relevant to mission-minded congregations. The simple *acquisition of knowledge* does not guarantee the development of a commitment to mission. In fact, if the acquisition of knowledge is not modified by a discussion of congregational leadership, and what difference any particular academic study makes in local church ministry, the acquisition of knowledge works against the development of a mission mindset.

Finally, mainline church leadership itself nurtures the hearty academic emphasis that shows in the seminary classroom. These denominations pride themselves on a well-educated clergy, and they charge their seminaries with the task of advancing an educated ordained ministry. But at issue in this discussion is the content of what it means to be "well educated" for leadership in the contemporary church. Most denominations still believe that a "well-educated" minister is one steeped in the classical disciplines. But until the classical disciplines are amended with a hearty dose of education for parochial leadership, the mainline church will continue to struggle for quality leadership.

For example, every year the Episcopal Church Foundation grants substantial study funds to carefully screened ordained clergy desiring to prepare for seminary teaching by pursuing a PhD degree. At most these candidates are likely to have only a year or two of full-time parish leadership experience under their belts. Many have none at all. Yet excellence in ministry will be promoted only by teachers with a substantial background in *both* the practice of a mission-minded ministry *and* the classical theological disciplines. Nor will this foundation support practicing parish clergy (or hospital chaplains or pastoral counselors) who would like to move toward seminary classroom responsibilities, but who prefer to complete a professional degree or board certification to finish their journey—and they are not likely to be hired by theological seminaries.

The Episcopal Church's emphasis of the academic at the expense of developing an intentional and informed parochial leadership shows in still another way. Several years ago this denomination instituted what are called General Ordination Examinations (GOE's) for graduating seniors, a week-long series of tests devised to display a student's knowledge in seven academic areas, only one of which is the practice of ministry.

Because of their focus, these examinations serve to increase the academic emphasis of seminary preparation for ordained ministry. And because some judicatories use these examinations to decide who will be ordained and who will not, harsh anxiety is generated in even the best of students. As a result, students ask faculty to provide workshops to answer possible GOE questions, and even more academic course work is elected as insurance for a passing grade.

Ordination examinations in any denomination would better support the development of a mission-mindset if, instead of the present academic focus, these tests expected students to make use of academic knowledge as appropriate while addressing *leadership* from the following perspectives:

1. What constitutes your passion for excellence in ministry, in either parochial, school, hospital or other institutional setting?

2. How will you help your people learn to identify and celebrate God's presence in the there-and-then of Scripture's witness, and the here-and-now of life today?

3. What will constitute your preaching and teaching ministry? What foci and themes will you value, and why are they important to God's people?

4. How will you equip your people for preevangelism, primary and secondary evangelism? How will you develop their confidence in the evangelism's ministry of introductions?

5. What use will you make of affirmation and praise of your people and their work in your ministry? And what theological case can you make for praise and thanksgiving as important ministries to develop?

6. How will you help your parish welcome visitors on Sunday morning, and bond them into fellowship? What do you say of God's action in the presence of newcomers?

7. What is your concept of Christian education?

• How does Sunday school fit into the rest of parish life on Sunday morning? How is the Sunday school classroom related to worship? How is the fellowship of the Lord's table tied in to Christian education? What place does the Bible have in your plans for Christian education? How do store-bought curricula materials fit into your concept of Christian education? If you were beginning a small church Sunday school program from scratch, how would you go about the task?

• What plans will you make for adult education? What is the relationship between adult education and the education of the children? How will you use both adult education and the education of children to welcome and bond newcomers to fellowship?

• What plans will you make to help your people understand their daily work as an offertory to God?

8. What provision will you make for pastoral care in your congregation? How will you provide for the sick and how will you provide for the well, and how will you provide for the stranger, the needy and the newcomer? How will you care for those whose interest has lapsed? How do each of these ministries of care relate to one another?

9. How will you help your parish organize its outreach ministry? What constitutes outreach? How do you propose to educate for outreach?

10. Why is the worship of the people of God on Sunday morning important? What will you be sensitive to, and why?

11. What is your style of leadership? Does it lean more clearly toward mission or maintenance?

Until the seminaries of the mainline church, along with denominational leadership—whether lay or clergy—give up the notion that the simple achievement of knowledge in ethics, theology, Scripture, and church history is sufficient to certify candidates for ordination, and add to that list proficiency in the practice of leadership in the local church, things will not get any better in the mainline churches.

Reenvisioning Theological Education

Happily, changes in the mainline seminary classroom may be on the horizon. The goal of the "advancement of knowledge" may soon be amended by adding to the classroom the "application of knowledge." In a recent interview, Eugene Rice, Senior Fellow at the prestigious Carnegie Foundation for the Advancement of Teaching, states:

> Since World War II, with the success of the sciences and the development of our graduate schools, the definition [of scholarship] has become narrower and narrower, so that now we understand scholarship to mean publishable research on the cutting edge of a discipline. We sense a great dissatisfaction with the way scholarship has evolved and believe the time is right to rethink what it means to be a scholar....
>
> The advancement of knowledge isn't everything there is to scholarship. We describe in the report a four-part model, with the *advancement of knowledge* [emphasis mine] as one of the quadrants.
>
> In addition to the advancement of knowledge, we see a scholarship involving the *integration of knowledge*....We fear that with the increased emphasis and value placed on specialization many faculty have lost the capacity to integrate.... We also propose that notions of scholarship should include the *application of knowledge*...we argue for a *scholarship that supports teaching*.[4]

Teaching and learning in the mainline seminary classroom are critical issues, and scholars are becoming more aware of the quadrants of *advancement, integration, application* and a scholarship that supports *teaching* as the classroom is engaged. Still another theological educator puts it this way: "Our mission as Christians begins in and is primarily moved by an explosion of joy," says John Rogers, formerly the Dean of the Trinity Episcopal School for Ministry. Observing that this is often expressed in an exuberance of life, he asked the participants in a three-day convention, "Have you been bubbling letely?"[5]

Mission-minded theological education helps students bubble with enthusiasm for God's ministry, it develops their capacity to identify and celebrate God's action in the language of the marketplace, and it makes every effort to help them think through the ways and means to *support God's ministry* by exercising leadership in both the church and in the world.

POINT. The currently shrinking numbers in the mainline church are evidence that a steady diet of highly intellectualized academics is simply not adequate to produce clergy leadership sufficient for people who hunger to know more about God, and what difference the knowledge of God makes in their everyday life.

So how can seminaries better prepare to execute their mission of preparing a next generation of clergy for work in the church and in the world?

First, they can learn from congregations growing in both spirit and numbers. These Christians have discerned an agenda for ministry that sets hearts on fire, and they know the value of being able to speak of God with spontaneity and affection. To the extent that the academic classroom nurtures the development of this leadership perspective, mainline congregations will benefit from the kind of clergy leadership mission-minded congregations already enjoy.

Second, the breadth of parochial leadership could be included as a "unit" in every academic course, whether systematic theology, Scripture, church history or Christian ethics. As a result, mission-minded perspectives would be brought more to the front and center of classroom education, and a balance struck between the rational discourse of ideas and perspectives, *and their use* by the future leaders of the church. Many students would gladly support such a change, while parish committees appointed to fill a clergy vacancy would be assured that they were being aggressively supported in their quest to provide the church with effective leadership.

Third, by cultivating the ability of students to speak gently and confidently of godly things, and because of the explicit development of a capacity for leadership, the preparation of candidates for ordained ministry could then be supervised with mission-minded perspectives close at hand. And if students cannot bubble with enthusiasm about standing with God in the welcome of the world to the church and, as appropriate, standing against the world for righteousness' sake, this attitude should count against their continuing toward ordination.

In summary, congregations operating from a mission perspective can show the mainline church what works in ministry today. Seminaries need to include these learnings in all that they teach. Indeed, the vision of ministry mission-minded congregations offer to the mainline church is a pearl of great price. And it is waiting to be used.

Calling A Mission-Minded Pastor For Leadership

Every congregation is at some time faced with the task of calling new clergy for leadership, and such a task is often anxiety-producing. "How can we agree on what we want?" wonder some, while others ask, "How can we make sure we get what we need?" This section makes no attempt to answer the breadth of your questions about calling to your parish a mission-minded pastor, but the following discussion should point you in the direction of a more thoughtful appraisal.

1. Denominational leadership will most likely have resources in place to help you through this period. But even if they are available, the following notes and suggestions are presented to help you feel more confident about this important task.

• You may be encouraged to hire an interim pastor or priest to fill the vacancy until a new leader is called. Often interim clergy have been trained as specialists to help parishes work through their grief at losing a leader whom they loved, and the anger that always surfaces when loss occurs. An interim period also gives a parish time to break away from the influence of a former pastor, and welcome afresh the leadership of a new head.

• A calling committee will be formed to help the congregation determine and evaluate the present shape of its ministry, and the kind of clergy leadership needed to modify or expand it.

Unfortunately, most search committees spend 80% of their time evaluating their present parish ministry—discerning the needs and hopes of their parish—and no more than 20% of their time meeting with their final small list of candidates. This is some imbalance, considering the importance of the selection! And still church leaders wonder why more than a few "calls" are not pleasing. Search committees also want to be democratic. "We want everyone to have a say," they declare. They count everyone's view and exhaust every resource, leaving no stone unturned. In so doing, they don't leave much time or energy for the interviews themselves.

• When a member of clergy leaves, most parishes react by looking for the pastor they *think* they need. Self-studies encourage this response, but it does not always work out. For example, upon the departure of a priest who developed them into "a fellowshipping parish," one congregation decided they wanted a more spiritual leader in the next go-round. They got what they wanted and more, for when their new priest came he proceeded to do away with all the fellowship activities they had so much enjoyed in the past. "We need to be more spiritual," he admonished them.

• Most search committees feel inadequate to the task of calling a new leader, particularly at early stages. Which means they can be at the mercy of denominational helpers.

One search committee member reported that their consultant had them role-play the interview with their prospective candidates, and then proceeded to tell the committee what responses were good and which were not, so that they could "get their man." This consultant was heavily directive throughout the entire process. And they put up with it because they were new at the task (he was the old hand), and they felt inadequate. But this committee is still angry about the way they were handled.

Still other consultants are more permissive in their leadership, offering not much information at all, but occasional comments about the health of the group's "process." There are numbers of consultants that use both process and direction appropriately. If you get one extreme or the other, watch out.

2. Prospective clergy put on their best front when being interviewed. What you see is what you get when you fill a vacant pulpit. And most calling committees and congregations see what they want to see, not what is offered. More, as the calling process draws to a close, growing affection as well as a desire to complete the job tends to dry up the spring of critical comment. When you interview candidates, be thoughtful and careful.

For example, one pastor, highly regarded by the calling committee, surprised his new parish upon arrival by expressing no interest in adult education. The calling committee had not thought to ask him about such things, and he chose not to respond to the plainly expressed interest of the parish as noted in their carefully constructed parish profile.

3. Listen to your prospective minister preach. Rarely do maintenance-minded preachers confidently declare the presence and power of God in the world and in the here-and-now of our lives today. They may tell us that God is love and God loves us, but seldom are they able to get down to the nitty gritty of pointing out the specifics of God's love in action today. Listen for how well he or she explains God's action, not in highly intellectualized language or by using abstract concepts you can't understand, but by *showing* God at work in the lives of folks like you.

Evaluate your candidates' preaching from three perspectives:

• the clarity with which they speak about God's presence and ministry in the world,

• what a newcomer or visitor would get from the sermon, and

• how accurately their sermons reflect the needs of the congregation they now serve.

4. Many clergy today are acquainted with the personality assessment tools widely used in the market-place. The Myers-Briggs Personality Inventory is a respected one. Using tools like these, discuss with your candidate the way in which she or he understands the strengths they bring to ministry, and their familiarity with their limitations. Denominational executives and staff persons can expedite discussions like these.

5. Take personal history seriously. What kind of a church did your candidate grow up in, how do they give expression to that ministry today, and if they now do things differently, what drew them to this new perspective?

6. You will also want to explore with potential candidates their vision for ministry. Inquire about the way in which they helped their present parish articulate a vision for ministry. What is it, and how did they help their people actualize this vision? Finally, having now met with you, having read your parish profile and based on their initial impression, what is their vision for ministry in your parish?

Next, how close is their vision to your vision, and by what ways and means do they see actualizing this vision? Expect them to be specific so that you can make some judgments.

• In these conversations look for signs that you would enjoy working with these candidates as colleagues. Pay attention to their style of leadership. Will they simply tell you what to do, instead of joining you in a collaborative ministry? If collegiality is left to chance, mutual ministry is also left to chance.

• How will your candidates welcome newcomers on Sunday morning, and how will they construct an hospitable liturgy?

• What is the quality of your candidates' leadership of public worship? How do you *feel* as a result of having them provide leadership for your spiritual journey on Sunday morning: confident, hopeful, quietly at peace, or otherwise?

• You will be also interested in the way your candidates make plans for worship, and the style of worship they encourage. Will they coerce (even subtly) your adoption of their style? Their track record will likely show it.

• How will your candidates make explicit plans for Christian education? Do they have an organizing principle in mind for parish Christian education, or do they just buy store-bought materials and expect you to do it all? This "I-Them" mentality, no matter where it comes from, is not a mission-minded approach to Christian education.

• The larger they are, the more that mission-minded congregations make use of small groups in the church. These groups help even the largest congregation maintain a sense of small town camaraderie. How do your candidates view the use of small groups, and how does this interest show in their present parish?

• How do your candidates show affection? Are they straightforward with their comments to parishioners, and to what extent are they able to speak the truth in love?

• How do your candidates view conflict, and how do they handle it? Do they see conflict as a collision of hopes and expectations, the edge of growth in parish life, or do they view it as frightening?

• How do your candidates view Christian stewardship? Do they enjoy celebrating the ministry of giving (whether to the church or to the world) as a joyful response to an always-giving God, or is stewardship for them an onerous, once-a-year money raising task?

• What special skills do your candidates have in the pastoral care of the church? Developing particular skills shows they are interested in their ministry. Are the skills they value the skills for which you're looking?

• How do your candidates respond to those who have dropped out of church?

• How do they help Christians value their everyday work in the world as ministry? The people of God are servants of God's daily ministry in the world, a perspective always celebrated by mission-minded clergy and their congregations.

• Finally, if your candidate doesn't draft a thank-you note for the hospitality you showed, consider afresh the importance of good manners.

To help these discussions take place, you and your candidates can also explore productively your and their concept of parish ministry using this chapter and, as appropriate, other chapters in this book.

Evaluating Clergy Prospects: Help For the Calling Committee

Every calling committee eventually reduces its short-list of candidates to one. This is always hard work, for every committee member will have an opinion. But to the extent that members don't think "their" opinion is being treated as fairly as others, to that extent the task of the committee will founder.

The following evaluative tool is not meant to take the place of general discussion, but it does provide the ways and means to poll the opinions of committee members and construct a ranking of candidates. For this is a truth: ranking opinion makes opinion easier to discuss.

To construct an evaluating tool using the criteria just listed:

1. Create 1 - 10 scales for each criteria for every member of clergy at whom you are looking.

1										10
	2	3	4	5	6	7	8	9		

2. Next, discuss *each* candidate in relation to each or any one of the criteria just noted, and on a scale of 1 - 10 rate each one at the close of your discussion as to how well, in your mind, they match each criterion. Continue this process with all of your criteria, and with all of your candidates.

3. Finally, for each clergy candidate, add the ratings from each member of your committee for every criterion. The sums will give you a picture of how you perceive the candidates in whom you are interested, providing you with both concrete data and summarized impressions as you move toward a final decision.

End Notes

1. Richard Busch, "Parish Clergy Ask, 'Who Is There For Me?'" in *The Episcopalian* (March 1987).

2. John Howe, "The Irrelevance of Theological Education" in *The Episcopalian* (February 1988): 11.

3. Alan Jones, "Are We Lovers Anymore?" in *Theological Education* (Autumn 1987): 11.

4. From a report written by Maryellen Weimer, PhD, ed., *The Teaching Professor* (April 1990): 1.

5. Barbara Benedict, "Party Atmosphere Prevails At Convention" in *The Colorado Episcopalian* (March 1990): 1.

CHAPTER 10

Helping Newcomers Find a Home:
The Ministry of Hospitality

What Brings Us to Church? • Responding to Visitors: Nothing Is Left to
Chance • Step One: Valuing God's Ministry to the First-Time Visitor •
Step Two: Talking To Newcomers • Step Three: Return the Visit While
Interest Burns Hot • Step Four: Orienting Newcomers—The Newcomers
Class • Step Five: Tracking and Sponsoring Newcomers • Step Six: Still
Later—Membership Classes • Aggressively Seeking Out New Members:
A Community Canvass Works! • Initiate A New Baby/New Mother/New
Father Ministry • Confident and Growing: Putting It All Together • Wel-
coming Visitors: A Program to Prepare Your Congregation

Mission-minded congregations never forget that it is
God who builds up the church. So when visitors
grace their doors on the first day of the week, these
congregations have a program in place to *identify*,
welcome, *orient*, *track*, and *include* these guests. If I
were ranking the importance of the chapters in this book from the
uppermost down, this chapter would be near the very top.

Briefly, mission-minded congregations construct their welcome
with the following ideas close at hand. They know that:

• unhassled clergy contact at the door of the church is crucial
either before or after worship.

• a "greeters' table" must be placed front and center at the door of
the church, for it is here that newcomers are first registered with
name, address and telephone number, and it is here that a nametag is
made.

Gene Carus, one of the official greeters at St. Peter's in the
Woods, recently saw an unfamiliar face enter the front door of her
church. "Now there's somebody I don't know," she said *with joy*,
and immediately moved their way with a smile and an outstretched
hand. Mrs. Carus also knows who brings these visitors to church.

143

• their parish must make a *total* and joyful commitment to the use of nametags on Sunday morning.

• children must be welcomed, the Sunday school explained, and the nursery pointed out to parents by *people who know*. At some point, there may be a brief tour of church facilities.

• visitors must be welcomed at the time of the announcements, either by name or in general.

• visitors must be accompanied to coffee hour. And more importantly, coffee hours with festive cookies and cakes must be held in a place that demands attention. Don't give newcomers an opportunity to flee, but happy encouragement to stay. The further that coffee hour is held from the place of worship, the more likely that visitor interest will flag.

• returning the visit of these Sunday morning visitors within thirty-six hours, or placing a telephone call within this period, effectively values their attendance and shows church interest in response. These visits and/or telephone calls are most effective when made by laypersons.

In summary, helping visitors make a second visit to the church is the most important issue there is.

What Brings Us to Church?

Developing a ministry to newcomers means getting to know who is likely to grace our doors. Many congregations think they are not growing because members don't bring their friends to worship on Sunday morning. These congregations suffer from "friendship guilt," a brand of guilt that is, perhaps, the single most important factor working against evangelism in the modern-day mainline church.

Forget bringing a friend to church. If mainline denominations simply *incorporated* 90% of everyone who visited them in any given year, church growth would be assured. We don't need to "bring a friend" to grow, as important as that may be for other reasons. We simply need to respond more effectively to the "friends" God is already and always bringing to us.

In addition to God's action, there are a number of other "reasons" that bring us to church. Many of us come because we are *newly located* in an unfamiliar town or neighborhood, and we are looking for a church to call home. Mission-minded congregations also know that our numbers are particularly high late in the summer and in the early autumn, and they make special plans to put out the welcome mat at this time of the year. Often newcomers classes are scheduled during this season.

Still others of us come because we *want to be responsible parents*. The month of September reminds us of our educational responsibilities, and as our infant children grow many of us begin to think about finding a good Sunday school. Some of us also come because we are now toying with the idea of baptism for our children.

Mission-minded Christians also know that some of us come as *non-believers*, more interested in "being social" than we are interested in God. But they know God is interested in us, and that God is perfectly delighted to meet our social needs for community. More, because God meets us where we are just as we are, so do these mission-minded Christians.

Thoughts of *marriage and a place to celebrate it* are also likely to bring us to church on Sunday morning. Mission-loving Christians enjoy welcoming "shoppers" like us. They do not disparage us either, for they know that God is playing a part in our search.

A few of us come because we have been *touched by a "coincidence" of goodness*, we have felt what the ancients called the *mysterium tremendum* of God. And we want to know more. We may be embarrassed to speak of this, fearing that others will simply "poo-faw" it. We may even call it simply "good luck," but a thankfulness to someone or something begins to form, and we are compelled to offer our presence on Sunday morning.

A few more of us make first-time visits because we are *afflicted by the stress* of troubles too heavy to bear. We come searching for a friend and some answers. And sometimes we come because we are just plain *lonely*.

Responding to Visitors: Nothing Is Left to Chance

Long before newcomers show up on Sunday morning, mission-minded congregations are hard at work putting out a welcome mat. Nothing is left to chance.

Ushers know the importance of their ministry. A few of the more extroverted members of the congregation are designated as "greeters," and plans to make follow-up home visits and/or telephone calls are not left to chance. Every newcomer visits with a full pack of expectant hope, and it demands an energetic welcome in response. For a picture of this kind of welcoming ministry in action, see the last few sections in this chapter.

But instead of being met with joy, maintenance-minded congregations tend to meet visitors with disinterest. Then, quickly thrust into their hands is a tightly-printed bulletin listing page numbers from unfamiliar service books. And finally, once the liturgy begins, there is seldom a moment of respite as worship plunges toward its completion.

If we do not care *or* if we do not show the care that we do feel, the enthusiasm of newcomers is often dealt a blow from which it can't recover. And destroyed also in that moment is the patiently constructed ministry of God in the lives of these folks.

Step One: Valuing God's Ministry to the First-Time Visitor

Mission-minded Christians know that people don't decide to come to church on the basis of solo decisions. Now don't get me wrong, personal interest and free will play their part, but the Bible says there is more in any moment of life than us. A story offered to me by a mission-minded minister makes just this point.

Stuart and Pam recently moved to Washington, DC, from Little Rock, Arkansas. It was Sunday afternoon, and I was visiting them for the first time. They had attended services just this morning.

The city of Washington is large, and a good deal more spread out than Little Rock. "Compared to this place," says Stuart, "Little Rock is a small town, and because we both grew up there we knew a lot of people. Here we know no one."

Pam and Stuart are also the parents of a two-year-old son, and hoping to add to their family, Pam says, "as soon as we get settled."

Shortly after we sat down, I asked about what brought them to St. Patrick's. Pam quickly responded. "St. Patrick's found us," she laughed, and then she told this story.

They had been on the road for three days by the time the three of them drove into town the first night. It was late in the evening, the street lights were on, and because they were on their way to a home they had seen only once before, they were fearful about getting lost.

But on a turn they passed St. Patrick's, and on our front yard they saw this sign: WE'RE MOVING SOON.

"That's exactly what we were doing," Pam says, "and the sign caught our fancy. We're not Episcopalians, but that and something else brought us to church this morning."

My curiosity piqued, I asked what that was.

"Well," Pam said with a laugh, "that's a little bit more complicated. Since we live about three blocks from St. Patrick's, one day while I was walking Todd we passed by the day school playground. I didn't see anyone around, so I figured that maybe Todd could play for a while on the swings. We don't have a swing-set yet, and he misses the swing we had just put up in Little Rock. But after we had been swinging for a few minutes, I became a little apprehensive that we might be doing something wrong, so I began to bundle him up to leave.

"And right at that moment someone stuck their head out of the kitchen door and said, 'Have fun. Make yourself at home.'

"That was the nicest thing, and that really may be the major reason we came this morning."

Parents like Pam and Stuart are always gracing church doorways on Sunday morning. And mission-minded Christians know these folks are not about to leave their small children with a stranger in a thrown-together nursery or Sunday School. They look for responsible planning and care. No matter how much money they have or don't have in their budget, you won't find a shabby nursery in mission-minded churches. And you won't find nursery care casually delegated to a couple of teenagers, no matter how faithful or well-intentioned these folks might be. Nursery and kindergarten rooms are brightly painted and spic and span clean. Parents are welcomed at the door and their children are soon known by name. As a result, there is every good reason to expect these parents to come again and again. It is also a gift that God uses with good effect to bond people to the church.

A well-working Sunday school for their children is also high on their list of priorities when parents of older children look for a church to call home. And even if, heaven forbid, greeters at the door fail to perform their task and even if clergy don't call, an attractive Sunday school conveys all sorts of welcome.

Step Two: Talking to Newcomers

It is always possible for visitors to leave church without having been engaged in a conversation by anyone. Sometimes they may leave without a personal word of welcome because church members are shy or "old timers" don't know what to say.

Welcoming visitors is not difficult, but it does require intentionality. Here's how you can go a long way toward insuring contact with your guests.[1]

1. Get their name and address. This task is best accomplished by greeters at the door who, while they prepare a nametag, are also taking down addresses and telephone numbers, and introducing these newcomers to ushers and other parishioners standing nearby.

2. Have everyone, even those who think everybody knows them, wear a nametag.

3. Post signs indicating how to go from the church to the room where coffee will be served.

4. Learn to seek out strangers. Don't be afraid of offending a long-time but seldom-attending member. A good line with which to begin a conversation with a stranger is, "My name is Jane Doe; I don't think I know you."

5. Plan things to happen during the coffee hour, such as awards to Sunday school classes, youth group presentations, displays of bazaar items, art exhibits, introduction of new members, talent shows,

music, etc. Don't miss any opportunity to "show and tell" what the Sunday school is doing.

6. On Sunday morning don't tie up your pastor's time. You will have many occasions to speak to him or her, but this may be a stranger's only opportunity. Better yet, take strangers to the rector and introduce them.

7. Prepare a concise, informative, and attractively designed document to give to newcomers *on the spot*, answering the most frequently asked questions about parish life.

Think about how you would like to be treated if you were a newcomer. I don't believe you will take issue with any one of these suggestions.

Step Three: Return the Visit While Interest Burns Hot

Immediate follow-up is important when persons make a first-time visit, and by *immediate* I mean a *same day* visit or telephone call. Or if same day contact is not possible, at least make contact within thirty-six hours. This is why.

Offering a word of welcome at the door on the day newcomers visit *begins* to confirm a call first extended by God, and a home visit or telephone call *completes* this action by helping "church" and "home" come together. Hence, the transaction begun with the decision to attend church is made complete and whole. A study attributed to the Methodist Church concludes that 90% of all visitors who are visited the same day they attend church services become active members. If new folk are visited as late as several days later, the percentage of those who become active drops to 60%. Only 30% will become active if visiting is postponed to the second week.[2]

A half-way welcome on Sunday generates the kind of quiet disappointment that shows up in the statement "Let's try someplace else next week."

To make this visiting-the-visitors ministry work, mission-minded congregations form cadres of lay persons trained to respond, preferably with a Sunday afternoon visit. And if a personal visit is not possible, a telephone call can also work wonders.

The Church of the Annunciation delivers bread on Sunday afternoon to all first time visitors. Their rector says,

"We also knew that the quicker the response by the visited congregation, the better the chance the visitor will remain and join that congregation. So we started responding with a visit on Sunday afternoon, immediately following the Sunday visit to church.

"These visits are spontaneously made, to keep things simple. And not to intimidate newcomers, these visits are made without warning. If no one is at home, the bread is left at the door with a note. It is reported that 80% of those who receive the bread telephoned the church to give thanks for the gift."[3]

Trinity Cathedral in San Francisco also sponsors a similar hospitality program called PIE (People Involved in Evangelism):

The PIE's, like their Tennessee counterparts, visit newcomers on Sunday afternoons. They don't phone in advance—the answer is almost always "Don't come" if you phone in advance.

More, these parish visitors don't stay for a visit. If invited in, they never stay longer than fifteen minutes. "Be bright, be brief, be gone" is the rule. But they always leave homemade apple pie.[4]

St. Peter's, mentioned earlier, does not make a home visit to newcomers. But their follow-up telephone call within thirty-six hours seems to work well.

The Church of the Apostles in Fairfax County, Virginia responds to visitors as follows. *Newcomers are recognized* at two points once worship begins. A first notice takes place at the time of the Prayers of the People, when groups of eight to twelve persons form. In these small groups newcomers are naturally identified and introductions made. This brief fellowship is shortly followed by personal prayers and thanksgivings. Since newcomers are usually unfamiliar and perhaps uncomfortable with this procedure, regular attendees are careful to offer explanations and guidance. Simply the sharing of a name and welcome is more than enough, but the possibility of a friendship beginning is greatly encouraged by this action.

A second introduction is made at the time of the announcements. At that time *newcomers are welcomed as a group*, some may be introduced by a member of their small prayer group, and all are asked to raise their hands to receive a blue new-member card that asks for their name, address and telephone number.

On the following Tuesday evening groups of *parish visitors* exercise their ministry. They are also trained to pay special attention to the way in which contact between new families and the parish can deepen.

Third, *the congregation itself is divided into smaller groups* of parishioners. Some of these cell groups (as they are called at the Church of the Apostles) meet weekly, some every other week, and some monthly. Similar groups go under other names at other parishes, perhaps known as Supper Groups, Shepherd's Groups or House Churches, Cousins (couples and singles), and the list goes on and on. Some include a pot-luck meal, others meet for coffee and dessert, and the program may include a brief time of study from Scripture, the prayer book or some other book commonly agreed upon, along with personal sharing, prayers and fellowship.

If interested, newcomers are quickly incorporated into these house church groups, and they are encouraged to "try out" several before they decide on one. It is much easier, the parishioners of Apostles have found, to establish relationships with a dozen persons who are seen regularly than with a thousand.[5]

Step Four: Orienting Newcomers—The Newcomers Class

You will know newcomers are serious about you once they've made their second visit, or by the time their children are enrolled in Sunday school. Now the orientation of newcomers is the ministry of choice.

So, you ask, "What are newcomers interested in knowing?" Newcoming parents will want to know how you care for their children and what activities you provide. Adults without children will be interested in why you worship as you do, along with opportunities for fellowship, adult education and service, particularly as they consider taking their fair share in the administration of the church. These guests becoming members will also want to know something about your history, how you got started and the current emphasis in your ministry. A parish brochure helpfully meets this need. And if you don't have one, write one. Keep the prose bright, breezy, and inviting, not ponderous. You want it to be read. The brochure itself can be printed on a letter-size piece of heavy paper, or made into a brief booklet.

Newcomers classes are a good place to exercise this kind of care. One large parish runs a series of four weekly orientation classes every month of the year, except July and December. Newcomers can either wait for a new class to begin, or simply join one in progress (The outline of such a class is offered in chapter 15). In smaller congregations, newcomers classes may be offered quarterly or semi-annually, recognizing that the longer the period between visit and class, the more likely burning interest will turn cold. Also remember that it's better to keep the classes small, perhaps three or four newcomer couples or singles.

If you are assigning a sponsor to your newcomer, as many congregations do, sponsors can also join the orientation class. Sunday morning is an excellent time to hold it, and so is Sunday evening. But if you offer a class in the evening, include coffee and dessert for the sake of fellowship. Such an orientation class should also include suggestions about the ways in which new folks can enter parish life. The possibility of service on committees of the vestry and on the altar guild provide just a few of the opportunities waiting to be presented in this follow-through visit. Bible study and prayer groups also provide the right place for camaraderie to develop. Such activity provides a safe and effective way for newcomers to put strange faces together with names. But mission-minded congregations have learned not to be pushy about such things; rather, they are judicious and careful in their offerings.

Don't make the mistake of welcoming these invited-by-God newcomers with tasks no one else wants to take on. That's abusive behavior. Finding teachers for Sunday school classes often falls into this category, and if this is the case in your congregation, it simply means you need to pay more attention to your Sunday school program. Don't burn out the enthusiasm of newcomers by shackling them with your unattended and ill-cared for ministries.

POINT. When we're involved in something that's *important to us,* we quickly begin to feel at home.

Step Five: Tracking and Sponsoring Newcomers

As soon as visitors give an indication that they're interested in more than the brief contact associated with their first-time visit, the task of offering companionship and encouragement comes to the forefront.

In addition to greeters and visitors, many congregations appoint carefully selected members to a *ministry of sponsorship*. Such a service is rooted in the ministry of the early Christian Church, as well as in the tradition of appointing godparents for newly baptized infants. These sponsors are parishioners who, after being introduced to first-time visitors, make it a point to welcome them to church on subsequent Sundays. They offer to sit with them during worship, particularly if the ways and means of worship are unfamiliar, they introduce their new friends to other parishioners, and otherwise help them find a home for themselves in what was formerly a strange congregation.

POINT. Many congregations, even when they undertake follow-up visits, miss the boat by simply letting newcomers fend for themselves on following Sundays.

Step Six: Still Later—Membership Classes

Eventually many newcomers will want to become strong members of your parish. Mission-minded congregations have learned to build this possibility into their welcoming ministry, and a discussion of membership classes is found in chapter 15.

POINT. In order to build a knowledgeable, articulate, lively, and intentional fellowship and ministry, membership classes offered in conjunction with classes for newcomers cannot be left to chance.

Aggressively Seeking Out New Members: A Community Canvass Works!

Some denominations pride themselves on aggressively seeking out the "lost." Although this is not a ministry often associated with most mainline congregations, I'm aware of a few churches now developing the ways and means to more actively identify and introduce themselves to unchurched members in their local community.

St. Matthew's Church in Warson Woods, Missouri, a small congregation near St. Louis, put together a telemarketing and direct mail approach for new member identification, visitation, and incorporation, and it worked even better than they first imagined. Their telemarketing campaign was set up by an outside consultant, and here's what happened.

This campaign involved defining the area to be called, identifying names and telephone numbers, and recruiting many parish members who did the calling to homes in the zip code areas adjacent to Warson Woods. Callers reported making 11,303 calls during 355 working hours. Over 750 people responded positively to an invitation to visit St. Matthew's Church, some with the hope their own church would do the same kind of calling.

> The second effort was a direct mailing to 3,800 households. A carefully worded brochure was sent to a list of people age 25-40 who have children from birth to 12 years. (These statistics and addresses are readily available from all city and county agencies.) This is the age group the parish most lacks. Recipients were invited to attend St. Matthew's church on two target Sundays and the projected estimate of 50 visitors was met almost exactly.
>
> With these contacts and names a follow-up program was developed, involving many members of the parish. Members assumed responsibility for continuing contacts. The result was a series of baptisms in June and an inquirer's class.[6]

Some churches also report good results with a "cold canvass." By that I mean a neighborhood canvass planned to invite non-church persons to attend church on Sunday morning. As a result of such a canvass, the Rev'd Richard Wagner reports that his congregation has grown by 60%. After an initial introduction and an opening question, "Do you attend a church now?," the brief conversation continues. If the answer is "Yes," the response given is something like "I'm glad you have a church home. If your friends ask about a church, think about giving them this folder." If the answer is "No," then "Here's a folder about one church. Come see us. Thanks for your time." Wagner continues, "If the person wants to talk, talk! Ask for their name, address and phone number."[7]

St. Peter's in the Woods uses a general mailing to their adjacent neighborhoods to invite newcomers to church at Christmas and

Easter. This congregation knows that when seasonal celebrations draw near, many non-church Christians think again about "going back to church." St. Peter's identifies these community newcomers by using a US Postal Service list of neighborhood addresses that have changed in the previous year. Such a list can be purchased from the Post Office and the list itself broken into mail delivery routes. With a list in hand, a brief letter of welcome is crafted, and envelopes stamped, addressed and stuffed (on Sunday morning!) with the letter and an information packet. Still other congregations use gas, electric, and water company lists of hook-ups to identify newcomers.

POINT. God is at work in the world, and mission-minded Christians pay all sorts of attention to helping God build into the consciousness of the world a knowledge of his love, presence and ministry. Membership drives do this well, and they also strengthen the church. I hope you will consider using them.

Initiate A New Baby/New Mother/New Father Ministry

Mission-minded congregations often develop an explicit outreach ministry to expanding families. Parish hall facilities are often used for Lamaze birthing classes or Parent Effectiveness Training workshops offered to the whole community. Many newcomers first became interested in the life of mission-minded congregations because these congregations were first interested in them.

As soon as mission-minded congregations hear that a member family is expecting the arrival of a new addition, they get to work preparing for a welcome. We are talking here about high quality and long-term baptismal preparation. Call this a new baby ministry, for it provides an excellent opportunity to bond families to the church of God. A note at the end of this chapter offers pointers about where to find help to develop this important ministry.[8]

So where do you begin? First, it's important to develop a cadre of interested parishioners able to track the pregnancy, birth and baptism of the new baby. These new baby ministry teams keep the parish abreast of the impending birth, and one of this cadre of parishioners is often appointed to sponsor the couple. Such an advocate offers the expectant parents an important link to the congregation.

When mother is hospitalized for the imminent birth, sponsors often are the first to notify clergy, and a hospital communion may be arranged, either before the birth or afterward. Sponsors also typically make careful provision to supply ready-prepared meals for the family still at home, and this care extends well into the first week after mother and baby return home.

Thinking toward the baptism of the child, sponsors help clergy plan pre-baptismal classes, either for a single family or, if the parish is large, multiple families. And both sponsors and other parishioners are quick to take responsibility for planning and executing a reception for this new family on the day of the baptism.

Confident and Growing: Putting It All Together

So what does a congregation "look like" that makes use of the ideas suggested in this chapter? St. Andrew's Church, a church of about 300 members, is little different from any other church on the edge of suburbia. But one of the things that does set this parish apart is the careful way they plan their Sundays so that they can welcome the world God brings to their door.

The people of St. Andrew's have been encouraged by a succession of clergy to pay close attention to the shape of God's action in the world, and they have developed an effective ministry in response. Look for yourself at how they have put things together, and catch a vision of what things could be like in your church.[9]

St. Andrew's is nestled among oak trees on a tract of land in Spring Hill, Florida. It's summertime, and we're looking in on the Sunday that the Bowen family first attends. Philip and Catherine Bowen are the parents of two children, John, who is seven years old, and Terry, who is two.

Arriving at church about a half hour earlier than the rest of the congregation, two members of St. Andrew's who have been designated as greeters stand under an archway outside the main entrance of the church. These parishioners use their time and talent to greet faithful regulars and welcome newcomers. Today Frank and Betty

Eriksen are serving as greeters for the ten o'clock service, and they are close by when the Bowen family arrives.

1. Greeters Make First Contact

Frank and Betty quietly note to themselves that the Bowens' are an unfamiliar set of faces, and so they follow their introductions with an inquiry. They also know that this family comes accompanied by God.

Small crosses are pinned on the new guests and Philip and Catherine sign the guest book. Betty informs Philip and Catherine about the nursery and the Christian education classes available, and offers to take them over and introduce them to Marie Fields. Before she leaves, she asks an usher to take her place with Frank.

2. Helping Visitors Feel At Home

Since time is an issue at this point, Marie quickly explains where John and Terry will spend the time while mom and dad are in church, the program in which they will be involved *unless* they would rather be with mom and dad, offers to accompany them on a tour of the facilities later and at that time describe the program of the church.

Terry is left at the nursery with Bonnie King, an elementary school teacher who has taken on the responsibility for the nursery. She has an able back-up when she can't be present. One or two teens often help out, but they are never unsupervised.

Catherine is impressed with the bright nursery. Later she remarks, "It looks like you really do care." John attends the second grade class in the Christian education building. This is Barbara Taylor's class. She is retired and spends a lot of time painting. Arts and crafts come naturally to her, much to the delight of the small children she teaches.

3. Words of Welcome and Inclusion

Philip and Catherine Bowen walk back to the church entrance with Betty, and she introduces them to Fred Scott. Fred is serving as an usher this Sunday, as he does on a regular rotation. Fred also serves on other occasions as a greeter, and so when he's an usher, "I sort of conceive of myself as a back-up, just in case someone isn't noticed out front. But I always look for the little crosses. I offer them a bulletin, along with a small, bright brochure that describes St. Andrew's, and I offer to show them to a seat. But if they don't want my help I don't push."

Fred adds that he will also look for them at the coffee hour, and make sure that they're introduced to the rector. "But I know he will already have their names, because Frank and Betty will have given them to him."

About midway through the service the rector makes some announcements, welcomes newcomers, and asks the Bowens, along with several others, to stand. After just the briefest background questions and some banter ("Where are you from?" and "We're glad you're here."), the guests receive a hearty round of applause. Visitors are again invited to the coffee hour, and in a short while they will be invited to begin to participate in the life of the parish in the way that fits them best.

4. Behind the Scenes

During the coffee hour the Bowens are surprised at the number of people who stop to talk with them. But what they aren't aware of yet is the behind-the-scenes preparation that goes on at St. Andrew's for visits like theirs. Fred, the usher, Pearl, Jim and Donna, and Bill and Cindy all will play a part in contacting the Bowen family.

Fred Scott, Pearl Hill, and Jim and Donna Taber are all members of the vestry at St. Andrew's. Vestry members expect one another to take the lead when welcoming newcomers to the parish. They not only engage in pleasant conversation, but they are also able to supply people like the Bowens with helpful information about parish and community life. One of the first things they do is introduce Philip and Catherine to Viola Smith. A small room adjacent to the parish hall is filled with books, mostly for children. Viola instituted the little children's library and it has been one of her ministries ever since.

Bill and Cindy Martin are members of the lay visitors group. Along with a number of other parishioners, they have worked with the rector to develop an effective follow-up visit that says "We care, we really do." They also visit the sick and shut-in. Viola prefers visiting the nursing homes to visiting newcomers on Sunday afternoon,

"But I'm happy to do it in a pinch." Bill and Cindy enjoy hospital calls, and along with several others, regularly make brief visits on Sunday, delivering the flowers from the altar when there are enough to share among so many. Today, Bill and Cindy will call on the Bowens, and they were scheduled for this task several months ago. They make arrangements during coffee hour, and set a time to pay a brief call on the Bowens today.

5. Celebrating God's Ministry: Always

We don't know all the reasons that Philip and Catherine made a decision to visit St. Andrew's today. The church may have been close by, it may have reminded them of how a church "ought to look," it may look like the church they left behind, or it may be that they heard good things about it at the drugstore. But what we do know is this: God played a part in the birth of their idea to attend, and whatever else the decision included, their decision was also rooted in a dialogue between God's Spirit and the human spirit.

The Bowens' story does not end here. Later they may choose to join a monthly supper group, and if they were one of the number of those who call themselves Single Again, they might choose to become part of that fellowship group. Or they might join the voice choir or the hand-bell choir, or they may decide to help out in the church school, or join with the ushers and greeters on Sunday morning. Or like Viola Smith, they might be stirred to an opportunity for service and develop something completely new.

The Bowens are cared for by an effective and carefully thought-through program of welcome and incorporation. It includes programs of care that show God's love to the church and to the world, and it also includes the ministry of introductions.

Welcoming Visitors: A Program to Prepare Your Congregation

If by now you're interested in organizing (or reorganizing) a welcome mat ministry in your church, use the following guidelines to construct a five-part training program for interested parishioners. It's really quite easy to equip church members for this important ministry, and it certainly takes the pressure off clergy to "do it all."

1. Preparing A Sunday Morning Welcome

It is crucial to introduce and thoroughly distinguish the ministries of both the usher and the greeter. Ushers and greeters may work similarly, but ushers focus their ministry primarily on already-enrolled members, while greeters are always alert to newcomers. Greeters also may be those designated for the follow-up home visit or telephone contact. Make sure these ministries are distinguished, and that plans are thoughtfully made to put these ministries to work.

2. Prizing God's Ministry

Help participants value God's ministry in the Sunday morning visit. Encourage them to understand that church growth does not primarily depend upon the invitation of their friends, but a response to God's already-present action. Better than inviting friends, encourage your church to welcome those newcomers that God is always providing.

To sharpen the personal awareness of workshop participants to the shape of God's ministry, I ask participants beforehand to prepare to tell about the first day they visited their present parish, or if at some point their church attendance lapsed, to describe what was going on in their lives that encouraged them to decide to come back to church.

POINT. The more we begin to see signs of God's ministry in the Sunday morning visit, the less we will feel as though we're alone in the enterprise, the more confident we will become about being God's helper, and the greater our sense of purpose when we make our follow-up visits.

3. Attending the Visitor

Discuss what visitors may be feeling, what they are fearful of and hopeful about. Explorations like these enable identification with the visitor, and they stir our imagination about the kind of ministry these folks need in response. Use the discussion found in this chapter's section "What Brings Us To Church?"

Underline *again* the importance of a careful reception at the church front door. But *next*, move the discussion of visitor welcome into a total parish context. Prepare the congregation itself to function as a welcoming community. One church charges itself with the responsibility of identifying and welcoming *all* newcomers at the time of the Peace. Once newcomers are recognized, they are introduced to others in the immediate area, and their attendance is immediately called to the attention of clergy. A general welcome is then extended.

Finally, provision must be made for effective and unhassled clergy contact as the congregation disperses after worship's close. But there is no need for clergy to do anything more than offer a greeting at this time, for the greeters themselves are prepared to obtain names, addresses and telephone numbers, and, if clergy are to visit, they can schedule the brief afternoon visit at times previously designated.

4. Valuing the Home Visit

A brief home visit is essential for follow-up, and it best takes place on the same day. Resist making a long visit. It may be counterproductive. Particularly in the autumn, Sunday afternoon football games are a pause that refreshes in the midst of harried schedules. Mid-afternoon visits can seem more like an intrusion than the gift they are intended to be. Leaving a booklet or pamphlet describing your church or denomination is often welcomed by newcomers. But if newcomers are glad to see you—and if you have the time—sit and talk for a minute or two.

I explore with workshops participants some of the topics and themes they can likely expect in these home conversations. If folks have recently moved, we can expect to meet:

• their joy upon arriving at a place of new beginnings, and the pain of leaving familiar places,

• their need to incorporate for the sake of fellowship and communion, and

• the stress attendant on being new and making their way in unfamiliar surroundings.

To explore more personally the issues with which newcomers are likely to be dealing, sometimes I make use of the story of Mike and Marty. The story itself describes a longer-than-normal visit. (This will sometimes happen!)

Mike and Marty are new in town. I visited with them the Sunday afternoon of their first visit to St. John's. We had tentatively set up the visit at the church door. St. John's ushers are trained to assist, and I confirmed our plans in an early afternoon telephone call.

Marty met me at the door and cordially invited me in. A moment later I met Mike and their two teenage children. Then the three of us sat down for coffee in a delightfully comfortable living room. It seemed to reflect their personalities.

I was surprised at how quickly some intense feelings began to surface, although because of the stress inherent in any move, I always expect them. It happened when I inquired about the reason for their move, what Cleveland had been like, and what they were finding in this area. These are the kinds of questions I think important to enable folks to tell some of the story of their lives. It allows not only moments of celebration, but also the expression of pain. All newness means pain to some degree.

Marty says that she misses her friends. It used to be that she could always call someone for company. She and Mike think it's important for her to be home for the children, and even though she wants to get back to the job market eventually—she's a commercial artist—the time is not yet quite right. But she mentions wistfully a firm in Cleveland that had their eye on her.

The children, though happy in the new school, also miss their friends. They have not yet "found their place," and it hurts. She feels their pain, but like many adolescents, they prefer to keep their own company. Unfortunately, they do not yet have a community of friends in which to confide. Marty feels their loneliness. It accentuates hers.

Mike likes his job. There's a lot more money, he's doing the things he likes best, the decision for the move was a family decision, but now he's wondering if it was the right decision. After this somewhat intense sharing, the conversation lightened a bit, and Mike remarked, "We make it sound worse than it is. We're going to be all right."

Shortly thereafter I left with a lot of things on my mind. St. John's can be a good parish home for this family, I decided. Mike and Marty are interested in some things I offered, and I'm going to get them hooked up with several folks and a monthly supper group I think they'll enjoy.

In addition to underscoring the importance of listening, I encourage discussion of this story from the following perspectives:

• Identify the issues that Mike and Marty face.

• What feelings are Mike, Marty, and the children stuggling with?

• What course of action would you recommend to them? Why?

• Look for turning points in the story, places where decisions and choices were made, and speculate about God's ministry in caring for this family and each individual.

Every Sunday morning first-time visit is an important "unknown altar to God," and by encouraging a discussion of the story behind the visit, church visitors will have more than a few opportunities to see God in action. But don't be too quick to identify the signs of God's presence and ministry in these first-time visits. First of all, value a brief visit. But if you are invited in and the invitation is genuine, and should you "see" in their story signs of God's care, I hope you will consider venturing your view. But don't be pushy. Far too often the church is viewed as an agency pressing the agenda of belief in God, and not much valuing the joy of friendship.

5. Making Newcomers Feel "At Home"

Once newcomers are identified and welcomed, a *newcomers class* is appropriate. And finally, it's important to *officially incorporate* these newcomers into the common life of both the local church and the denomination. This ministry is too often ignored, but without it the good feelings generated in a carefully constructed welcome program are more than likely to fade quickly, and enthusiasm wane.

End Notes

1. Adapted from Nancy Hammond, "The Coffee Hour: Open Arms or the Cold Shoulder?" in *The Episcopalian* (November 1988).

2. Although I have been unable to confirm the original source of these widely published figures, they are similar to figures published by Herb Miller, *How To Build A Magnetic Church* (Nashville: Abingdon Press, 1987), p. 72. "When laypersons make fifteen-minute visits to the homes of first-time worship visitors within 36 hours, 85% of them return the following week. Make this home visit within 72

hours, and 60% of them return. Make it seven days later, and 15% will return. The pastor making this call, rather than laypersons, cuts each result in half."

3. Richard Schmidt, "Has the Church Ever Delivered a Load of Bread to Your Door," in *The Episcopalian* (November 1988), p. 14.

4. *Ibid.*

5. From research contributed by The Rev'd Phillip Haug.

6. Charles Rehkoff, "Calling All Parishioners," in *The Living Church* (July 24, 1988), p. 9.

7. From "Into the World," May 1989, number 31. "Briefs, Evangelism cold calls are really warm." A bi-monthly newsletter, Education for Mission and Ministry.

8. *A New Mother's Ministry: Laying the Foundation for the Family of Faith*, prepared by Genelda K. Waggon as a project of the Episcopal Church Women of the Diocese of Western North Carolina, provides the ways and means to develop this ministry. Write Mrs. Genelda K. Waggon, 118 Macon Avenue, Asheville, NC 28801.

9. From research contributed by the Rev'd Frederick Scharf, an Episcopal priest.

CHAPTER 11

Reaching for the Drop-out, the Disappointed and the Broken-hearted

Why Do People Drop Out of Church? • Molly Leaves: A Result of Current Hurt • The Healing Conversation • Bitterness Beyond Redemption • Stress and the Dropout • Taking Action: Ministry in Response

Every year people drop out of church. Most faithful churchgoers quit coming to church because of a cluster of pain-provoking events, but this chapter doesn't simply stop at addressing the long-term member who drops out. Even newcomers may drop out of church after a couple of visits, mainly because they feel they were ignored or the church didn't seem "friendly." Many congregations simply let this event pass by. For the most part it goes unnoticed. As a result they miss grand opportunities to reach out to many visitors who are still in fact interested in them, but for whom unfriendliness now stands in the way.

Unlike others, mission-minded Christians don't simply wait passively for dropouts to return to church—which they seldom do. These congregations respond with a visit (to faithful churchgoers who have dropped out), or an inquiring telephone call (in the case of newcomers), and always there is an expression of concern.

The following pages are written to help you understand why people drop out of church, some of the issues with which these folks are struggling, how God is at work in their lives, and what you can do in response.

Why Do People Drop Out of Church?

People stop coming to church for any number of reasons. Some have to do with events rooted in personal history, and are perhaps the most difficult to counter. First, the disappointed drop-out may be

165

struggling with an unsatisfactory experience with authority during their growing-up years, perhaps with Mom or Dad, and now they project onto God and the church their feelings and perceptions. For example, if a church issue isn't resolved *their* way, they may feel as though they have been railroaded as they were when they were children. These folks may never have learned to work collegially with authority, and their win-or-lose approach to dialogue often turns conversation into an adversarial debate.

Sometimes drop-out visitors struggle with this same issue: "They don't care" might be their thought.

A second reason that people drop out has to do with the kind of stress (very current in contemporary America) that gathers steam over a long period of time. It may take the form of job burnout, marital problems, family or personal disappointments, or illness. Any of these can combine to turn people away from church just when they need support the most. Mission-minded congregations recognize that in all sorts of ways these folks are crying out for help and attention and, if their cry for help is not heeded, they will become angry and feel rejected. A genuinely-offered, listening-centered conversation is often all that is necessary.

A third reason people drop out of church has to do with a legitimate disappointment. A church action might have been taken or a comment made that makes them angry; these folks do not feel as if they were heard or their opinions much considered. Drop-out visitors might also be responding to disappointment at being unnoticed on a day that was special to them.

POINT. When thinking about reaching out to the lapsed, expect anger, but don't be misled by it. Instead, be prepared to listen to and understand the underlying hurt.

Molly Leaves: A Result of Current Hurt

Molly is sixty-five years old. Her husband Mike died in January while they were visiting relatives in North Carolina, and he was buried there in the family cemetery. That was ten months ago, and in the meantime, Molly has not heard a word from her pastor. She knows that he is aware of her husband's death, because she asked friends to ask the pastor to offer prayers for Mike on the Sunday after his death. So Molly is bitter. She calls her rector's response to her "indefensible," and she no longer attends church.

"Now maybe," you say, "Molly should have been more direct with her rector. Why didn't she telephone him in the first place?" "Maybe she was wrong to get her friends to give him the message. Maybe there's a chance that they did not." Still more, "Maybe her anger about her husband's death is being displaced on her rector, and he is getting grief that he really doesn't deserve."

Every one of those observations makes sense. But the fact of the matter is this: Molly is hurt and mad, and she has dropped out.

POINT. Most people drop out of church because of a slight or disappointment, and until the slight is corrected they will probably not return, or they may find another and more hospitable church.

The Healing Conversation

Conversation itself is the best of all therapy when responding to those who have quit coming to church. You don't need to offer advice when you visit—as if advice could be offered at times like these—and you don't need to explain to them why they shouldn't have the feelings that they have—as if feelings could be ever dealt with in this fashion.

The conversation of a friend is the best of all response, and what I have come to call a healing conversation takes this broad shape when visiting with folks like Molly. A healing conversation:

• values those who are hurt as persons with a story to tell, and helps the story be told,

• expects their story to consist of some personal pain and disappointment,

• expects the pain and disappointment to be related to the parish itself or its clergy,

• does not minimize the pain and anger by offering an explanation, although non-defensive clarification may be appropriate,

• is prepared to offer an apology if an apology is necessary, and

• knows that if the story is heard by a respected member of the parish who symbolizes the life of the parish, then the chances are good that the lapsed member will return.

So listen, listen, and listen some more. More than likely, the hurt of those who drop out of church stems from not being heard, or at worst, ignored. A healing conversation offers the possibility of restoration.

I myself met Molly because she later chose to attend a church I once served, and the following brief verbatim dialogue from our longer encounter is an example of a healing conversation. The conversation has already begun, and we are seated in Molly's living room.

Molly: He could have come by! There's just no excuse for his ignoring me. He doesn't have much of a reputation for visiting, and a lot of people are upset by it.

Pastor: It doesn't seem like there was any excuse, and the way you describe it, it sounds like it could have almost happened yesterday.

Molly: It was indefensible. Mike always loved St. John's, and we had been members for years. Our children grew up there, our daughter was married there, and a number of our friends are still members. Sometimes I think maybe I'm overreacting, but I want to tell you that what he did was not right.

Pastor: There's no missing your anger, Molly. But I'm also hearing that you miss St. John's and your friends.

Molly: That's true enough. You have no reason to know this, but Mike was the person who headed up the capital funds drive when we built the addition to the parish hall, and he was also a member of the vestry for a long time. That's what makes all this so bad for me. It's not just my feelings, but his ignoring Mike.

Pastor: And Mike deserved a whole lot better.

Molly: You bet he did. Well, enough of this talk. May I warm your coffee?

Pastor: No thanks, Molly. But I do want to offer this. A lot of your friends are still at St. John's, and although we're just delighted to have you among us, before you decide to stay I hope you'll also consider your and Mike's life there. You have a lot of memories connected with St. John's, they are rich and important, so I hope you won't make too quick a decision.

The healing conversation makes use of the continuum of *confession*, leading to *absolution*, leading to the *eucharist*. Here is how this works.

The word confession itself means "to speak with" or "to give up" our thoughts. I'm not here speaking of the liturgical "General Confession" used in the reformed church, or the private "confession" with which our Roman Catholic friends are more familiar. Confession at its roots is simply the activity of talking things out with another who cares, and in doing so giving God an opportunity for healing.

When a confession is made, this is the mystery; as painful thoughts and feelings are put into words and given up in conversation, freedom (or absolution) from their pain begins to take shape. No longer ignored nor feeling dismissed, isolation gives way to restoration, and a note of joy (from the Greek *charis,* as in eu*charis*t) begins to sound.

So it was for Molly. I felt she began the work of putting her anger behind her when, after expressing it directly, she was free to see my nearly empty coffee cup and offer more. Eventually Molly returned to her parish church, and although to this day she has been unable to make peace with her rector, I know that things are a lot better than they were. I also know that healing takes awhile, so good ministry values patience.

Bitterness Beyond Redemption

But Molly was also flirting with the danger of chronic anger, and though she did not know it, I did. Chronic anger is dangerous to human beings, and here is why. The more anger becomes our companion, the more we tend to enjoy it, and the more we enjoy it the less likely we will want to give it up. In the extreme, we can be trapped in it forever. This is precisely the reason why an immediate follow-up is important when a person stops coming to church.

Traditional theology has known about this danger for centuries, and has used the term "blasphemy" to explain it. Blasphemy is simply chronic anger turned to bitterness. Tradition has it that blasphemy is the one unforgivable sin, because it is an attitude that cuts off the possibility of any more conversation between God's Spirit and our human spirit. And without conversation, a relationship simply can't be restored.

The more we make an everyday relationship with personal bitterness and disappointment, the less we are likely to listen to what's going on around us. We turn inward and choose to see the world as we want to see it. Blasphemy is a bitterness we enjoy, and it will consume us as surely as night follows day.

There is a natural risk of blasphemy for every person who drops out of church, and if as a visitor you find bitterness too deeply ingrained, conversation will never be more than an exchange of platitudes or an expression of punitive anger. This is just the reason that childhood difficulties and trauma, long harbored in memory, are so hard to dislodge, and why their resolution may demand more help than the short-term healing conversation can provide.

THE BOTTOM LINE. The notion of blasphemy is a tool that says "take care," and a visit to the recently lapsed offers them the possibility of freedom from a bondage that can destroy.

Stress and the Dropout

Stress is an important issue in modern-day American society. Many parents work two jobs, in many locations housing costs eat up a too-significant part of current income, and children are often overwhelmed by the prospect of the future.

Stress also has a lot to do with why some people drop out of church. All of us are loaded down with stressors, things that weigh heavily on our minds and hearts. And most of the time we are able to handle them well. It is a balancing act.

When the stressors in our life multiply extravagantly—as they are wont to do from time to time—they weigh us down all the more. As a result we may feel as though we have the "world on our shoulders," or are boxed in and cut off from those around us.

Dropouts may be one person, a couple, or a family so pressed by the demands of life that involvement in the church becomes just "one more thing."

So what hope is there? When stressed folks drop out of church, a visit makes all kinds of good sense, and it offers three wonderful gifts.

First, a visit says quite simply that "I care," in much the same way a hospitalized parishioner receives the visit of a friend. As a visitor you will not likely be able to do a thing about the circumstances these stressed parishioners face, so don't fret because you can't offer explicit relief. But don't devalue your visit, for it works in just the same way a visit works to those who are hospitalized with an illness.

Second, a visit provides an opportunity for these parishioners to tell how bad things are to someone who matters, a representative of the church. A possibility for confession is offered, and absolution's gift of freedom is likely to follow, at least to a small degree.

Third, a visit offers an opportunity to reinvite a person back to church on their own terms. If they feel guilty about letting down parish responsibilities, a healing conversation offers the possibility of rethinking their commitments in light of their new and more demanding circumstances. Also, it might be that they can be encouraged to seek assistance from those in the community trained to give it at times like these.

Taking Action: Ministry in Response

All but the most insensitive congregations take notice when a regular member drops from sight. Clergy are generally the most effective respondents to the opportunity presented by those dropping out. Yet because the time of clergy is limited, ministry to the lapsed should do the following:

1. Develop a small cadre of lay persons able and trained to respond when a lapse in attendance is noticed. Some of these visitors may be those trained to provide an immediate response to first-time guests on Sunday morning, as noted in chapter ten.

2. Develop the ways and means to recognize those who are dropping out. Mission-minded congregations can spend some time in every church board meeting evaluating congregational life, the needs and opportunities present, and often such discussions will generate the names of those who are upset.

3. Remember that in our culture "squeaking wheels get the grease." So while you are responding to pain and hurt, don't become so consumed that you forget those many other parishioners who need to keep on celebrating. Many clergy tend to err in this direction.

4. Prepare lay visitors to anticipate and respond to those who have dropped out in the following ways:

• Address the reasons that members tend to drop out of church, such as disappointment, stress, or the projection of an old injury onto the church.

• Make sure your visitors are comfortable with responding to anger and helping it develop.

• Train them to be non-defensive in their listening, familiar with the shape of the healing conversation, and able to make an apology when one is suitable.

• Make sure they are alert to making referrals when appropriate, either to their minister or to a professional in the community.

5. Hold up these issues before the whole congregation on a regular basis. Notes in the bulletin, sermon illustrations, workshops for vestry and church boards, Bible study groups, prayer groups, and other church organizations can go a long way toward interesting parishioners in the ministry opportunities present at times like these.

The following books expand discussion of the issues addressed in this chapter.

Alan Harre, *Close the Back Door* (St. Louis: Concordia, 1984). Chapter 1, "Who Are The Dropouts?", Chapter 2, "Preventive Means to Limit the Number of Dropouts," and Chapter 3, "Attitudes Toward Inactives" offer helpful insight in each of these areas, and uses normative research in the field.

Wayne Oates, *Pastoral Care and Counseling in Grief and Separation* (Philadelphia: Fortress Press, 1977).

Delores Curran, *Stress and the Healthy Family* (Minneapolis: Winston Press, 1985). All chapters, but chapter 1 (family), chapter 3 (couples), chapter 5 (children) are particularly useful.

Wayne Oates, *Managing Your Stress* (Philadelphia: Fortress Press, 1985).

Donald A. Tubesing, *Kicking Your Stress Habits* (New York: NAL, 1982).

CHAPTER 12

The Church in the World: Every Day What We Do Matters to God

Helping God Take Care of God's World • Why Don't I Get What I Want? • Valuing God's Action in Our Lives: Look For Turning Points • Taking Action: Determining God's Hand at Work in Your Life • Education for Children and Teens: Looking Toward Their Future

T he matter of their daily occupations is not as important to mission-minded Christians as the quality of their Sunday worship, or clergy leadership, or the ministry of welcoming newcomers. But because they know they are God's own children, mission-minded congregations pay close attention to the way in which they work with God to take care of God's world. And when these congregations construct newcomer classes to welcome visitors, they pay attention to the way in which all of us help God provide "daily bread" in the world.

This chapter is written to help you think afresh about the work you do in God's world. It can be used as a resource in your new member or adult confirmation classes, and suggestions are offered later in this chapter to assist teenagers think about their future occupations—and God's need of them.

Recent studies show that many people, Christians and otherwise, are dissatisfied with their daily labors. If you've ever wondered if you picked the wrong line of work, you're not alone. In a recent survey by the Gallup Organization, 51% of respondents said that, if they could start their careers over again, they would choose different jobs. These figures surprise few career experts. "The cliché—and it's probably true—is that people spend more time planning their next vacation than they do planning what they're going to work at for the rest of their lives," says Jim Bowe, president of Career Management Systems Inc., a Minneapolis consulting firm.

"It's not good enough to let people stumble into careers and hope for the best," says Joleen Durken, a counseling expert at the Minnesota Department of Education. "In the first place, it's bad for productivity because people aren't doing what they're good at. Secondly, if you're not happy at work, that spills over into every area of living."[1]

Mission-minded Christian are not free of job-related disappointments. But because these folks have been helped by clergy leadership to see that what they do in their everyday occupations, whether as parent, electrician, lawyer, or homemaker, is important to God— even if, sometimes, they don't much like what they do—they know that in the economy of God's love, their contribution is valued by God.

Helping God Take Care of God's World

Not every Christian is privileged with the knowledge that in their daily occupations they work in concert with God. For example, Joan is the president of a small trucking company, a business that has been in her family for two generations. I met her several years ago at a conference I led. Joan loves God and she is active in her church, but she does not yet possess a mission perspective about her Monday through Friday work-for-pay ministry.

Joan has had a major hand in developing her church's soup kitchen for the poor of a local neighborhood, and she works in that kitchen twice a month. It's one way "we take care," as Joan puts it. She sees this as her ministry, but she does not see her presidency of the trucking firm as ministry.

"Oh," she says, "I do take a personal interest in my drivers. I help them out when things get tough. Now if that's what you mean by ministry, then I agree. But I can't see how my simply running a trucking company is ministry. It's just my job."

That's sad, I thought, so then I asked, "How do you guess this food got here?" Surprised by my question, Joan thought for a moment. Then she laughed. "My trucks may have brought it. In fact, I wouldn't be surprised if they did."

The trucking industry is an important resource in God's world. With so many of us scattered in so many places, how else will we nourish ourselves if some of us don't transport food to the rest of us? Some of us grow it, some of us drive the trucks that move it, some of us cook it, some of us pay for it, and some of us provide buildings to house the kitchens. Because of Joan's leadership God is able to provide jobs, transport food and sustain community health for those of us who would be "poor" without them. Mission-minded clergy would have helped Joan catch this vision a long, long time ago.

More than five billion human beings live in the world. So now this question: Who keeps the world functioning as well as it does?

"Now, wait a minute," you say. "With all the hunger and war there is, don't tell me God has anything to do with it." But that's precisely my point. Human freedom, sin, and natural law account for the reasons that wars are fought and why some people rejoice with plenty while others suffer without. But mission-minded Christians know full well that it would be a whole lot worse if God were not involved, and the thought that they are helping God through their salaried jobs is a source of great encouragement to these Christians.

POINT. There's a direct connection between our daily work and what the Christian church calls ministry. This notion departs from the maintenance-minded belief that ordained clergy are only those who have a ministry, and everybody else just works.

Clergy speak of a "call," a leaning toward ordination that, although it rests within themselves, is initiated from a place beyond themselves. Mission-minded Christians know that what happens to clergy is precisely what happens to all of us. When considering how we will spend our lives and put bread on our tables, we lean one way or another because our personal interests are teased by God. Mission-loving Christians believe that in the same way a shepherd balances the needs of each of the sheep against the welfare of the flock, God converses with us about the jobs that we decide to take.

When I work with Christians to discern the way their "call" to daily work took shape, I use the following considerations to get at the shape of the conversation between their human spirit and God's Spirit.

Because we are fundamentally self-interested, I suspect *our* side of the occupational conversation with God takes this shape. First, we value *our talents*, hopes and aspirations. Next, we tend to honor the *opportunities* for work before us, and finally we think about the *needs* of God's world.[2] Notice the primary focus on "me." All of us tend to think first about what we need and what's good for us, which is not bad in and of itself, but it does become bad when others suffer because of it.

God's agenda is framed differently. Because God values us as the beloved persons we are, and because there is also an equal interest in the welfare of his world, God's conversation reflects this order: *our talents*, hopes and aspirations, the *needs* of his world, and the *opportunities* for work before us.

Notice that in God's conversation the primary focus is on the community. In both cases the agenda begins at the same place, but the second and third points are reversed. The point is this: God cares for us *and* the world.

Why Don't I Get What I Want?

"But," you ask, "If God works with us and if God loves me so much, why don't I get what I want more than I do?"

Mission-minded Christians don't throw out a consideration of God's ministry simply because things don't always go their way. When a choice of occupations is considered, in addition to God's conversational ministry we must also think about:

• supply and demand,
• cultural imperatives,
• the always-present random chance, and
• personal limitations.

But still this fact remains, there is a balance in occupations in the world that transcends these four imperatives. And God's ministry supplies the difference.

First, *supply and demand* plays its part in the balance of occupations within any given culture. We have so many plumbers because of the demand for their services, and so many nurses, or lawyers, or garbage collectors for the same reason. Granted, some are unhappy and have reason to be, because of talents left unused, or racism or sexism, or because a present job was the only one available. But does this mean God is not involved? Heaven forbid. Given the infinite variables that human freedom imposes on life, God attempts to wed the talents of his people to the needs of a ministry, bringing the folk of his world, each unique, into symphonic expression. God is interested in balance and justice, and if the law of supply and demand is always at work, so too is God.

Second, *cultural imperatives* must also be taken into account. The plain fact is this: some of us take certain jobs because we were prohibited from thinking about others. Arlene's story shows what I mean.

Arlene is now a first-rate school teacher, and she has a well-deserved reputation in the community. But one day while we were talking about why and how she became a teacher, she mentioned that she had once wanted to be a doctor. I was interested in the turning point, so I asked why that changed.

"When I was growing up, it wasn't alright for a little girl to be a doctor. It was OK to be a school teacher or a nurse or a wife and mother, but in the South we didn't think any wider than this. Now don't get me wrong, I didn't consciously know this at the time, but over time I just got the message that little girls should not think about being doctors."

Together we speculated about God's stirring her interest at that early time, the way God piqued her curiosity about medicine, and God's powerlessness in the face of her culture's imperative.

She was a bit surprised by the notion of the powerlessness of God: "I thought God could do anything he wanted," she laughed. And then she continued, "You know, I never thought of this before, but the reason I'm not a doctor isn't because God didn't want me to be one, but because my culture didn't. I don't know why I didn't see this before. I just assumed it was God."

"It sounds to me like you had a call," I remarked. "I'm glad you think so," she replied, "because I've always thought that being a doctor is what I really would have enjoyed, and until now I've always wondered why God would not let me do it."

Arlene and I don't see one another very often anymore, but when we do, she still remarks about how that conversation helped her put to rest a question that had always been troublesome.

Third, *random chance* must be also given its due, for human decisions bring about consequences that may be no more reflective of what God wants than what we want.

Ted lost his job because of an economic downturn in his community. He found other employment, however, and although he stuck with it for five years he never stopped complaining. "But let me tell you, I was glad to have it because it paid our mortgage."

Ted, you see, was a small-town plumber with a family whom he loved to be with, and the five-year replacement job took him to an off-shore drilling rig. But still he had a job and, as he says, even if he didn't like his new employment, it did put bread on his family's table. And so he was thankful.

Fourth, if we find ourselves with a job we don't want, it might be because God doesn't see things our way, or it might be that we are reaching for something beyond *our capabilities*. In other words, God may be less excited about what we want to do than we are.

But even when we make decisions and they don't work out, maybe because God doesn't support them (and God would be trying to tell us that) or they are not supported by the world, God does not point a critical finger. Even as we suffer the legitimate consequences of our dilemma, God is already at work with us looking for a new way to handle things.

POINT. God is interested in balance and justice, and if we are reaching beyond our capabilities, God is not going to deceive us to keep our hopes alive. For this reason, prayer is better understood as listening than talking.

Valuing God's Action in Our Lives: Look for Turning Points

From birth to death every life is a journey, and all along the way decisions are made that turn us one way or another. Look for turning points in your life as you think about your present occupation. Mission-minded Christians value them as signs of God's caretaking action. These turning points appeared at times when you sought out consultation and conversation with others, when you depended upon intuition within yourself, and when your faith in what was right for you was little more than the substance of things hoped for (Heb. 11:1).

Jack's life story shows several important turning points, and they may be somewhat like yours. He grew up in New England and was the first of his family to attend college. Now Jack's father wanted him to study engineering, an occupation the world would always need, and faithful son that he was, Jack agreed. Later, however, he changed his major to business administration, for it seemed to be a better fit. Graduation passed and Jack settled into a business career.

Several years later Jack's next door neighbor began to hound him to apply for a new position in a large multinational corporation, and Jack listened. His friend was convinced that a match between Jack and this corporation would be perfect, although Jack was not. Although the position required more technical proficiency than Jack liked, he decided to interview, and he was hired on the spot.

Some say Jack has the gift of gab. He can persuade and inspire, and under Jack's leadership the department began to orient itself more toward marketing than research. Sales accelerated, the department grew, and everything fell into place. Jack settled down for the long haul to retirement.

But then his father suffered a heart attack, and after lengthy conversations he and his wife decided to move, if possible, to a city near his father's home. A job was found and the move made, but still another neighborhood friendship began a conversation taking Jack to yet another interview. Jack says this job is the "best yet," and the light in his eyes confirms it.

Now try to picture God's action in this story. Look at this narrative from the perspective of Jesus' visit with two of his disciples on the road to Emmaus, and you'll get some hint of God's action in Jack's life, the same kind of action that also appears in our own. Jesus had been crucified, and two of his disappointed disciples were traveling the seven-mile road from Jerusalem to Emmaus. Their lives were in shambles. Everything was fractured. Like a wind-blown banner, what had been so promising was now in tatters.

Disappointment is always eased by talking it out, and so these two reminisced about the crucifixion, probably trying to make sense of it, and maybe even figure out where they all went wrong. Perhaps they might have thought, "If only we had not done that."

The road was probably filled with travelers, and as they trudged along they were joined by another. Now he seemed no different from anyone else, and he soon pitched into the conversation. In a while the stranger began offering some clarifying comments, and without realizing it, they found themselves consoled. His perspectives made good sense. The day's end was close, however, and as they drew near to Emmaus they invited him to join them at the dinner meal. He had made the journey so much easier, and they were grateful. Not that any of their "problems" were solved. They were still disappointed and dejected, but his presence had been a moment of respite from the lonely trials of the last several days.

So they sat down at table, and because he was their guest he took the bread, gave thanks and broke it, and in a twinkling their eyes were opened and he disappeared. Without waiting for even a minute they rushed back to Jerusalem with the news (Lk. 24:13-35).

The road to Emmaus is as long as the history of the world, and when any of us look back at our history, with only a little bit of faith and Scripture's witness, signs of God's presence and ministry begin to show, particularly in the turning points.

So what do we learn from Jack's story about God's action? This young man was the first in his family to go to college. Because he grew up just after the Great Depression, it is not difficult to understand his father's concern about a practical preparation for the future. His father's concern also reflected God's interest. So one can also imagine Jack questioning his course in life. He knew that "most of us simply took jobs after high school, and an eighth grade education was good enough for my dad!"

But God is always about the task of networking the world's needs to ministry, and as Jack was toying with the notion of higher education, comparing one path with another, God was offering helpful clarification, in just the same way Jesus did for the disciples.

Now Jack has the best job yet, but is this the last stop? The future is always rich with possibility, and every year Jack's circumstances will subtly change. But God will be present. Like the parents of children, God is interested in how we choose to spend our lives, for our sakes and for the sake of the world.

Taking Action: Determining God's Hand at Work in Your Life

A rich tapestry of turning points is created by God's action and our interests, and both bring us to the jobs we hold. Newcomers classes provide excellent opportunities for brief discussions like these, and so does occasional Sunday morning adult education. And what results is this: increasing confidence that in our daily work we do indeed make a difference in the world.

The following questions are designed to help you deepen your awareness of the ways in which God works with us to take care of the world. You may choose to consider these questions all by yourself. Better yet, ask a few others to join you, and explore your everyday God-called ministries using the following questions as guides.

• Look back over your life for turning points, times when new vistas opened or new possibilities suddenly presented themselves. How did they happen? What persons contributed to them?

• Are you now doing what you expect to do for the rest of your life, and if you are not, do you see at this point other possibilities beginning to show themselves? What action on your part will it take to help God actualize these possibilities?

• Was there once, a long time ago, the dream of a job that was never realized? What stood in the way? What opportunities did God need that were not available? Remember also that God works with what God has, and if you're not doing what you want to do, it may be more a result of human freedom preventing doors from opening than a sign of God's desires. But it may also be that you are simply reaching beyond your capabilities.

• How does your daily toil help God take care of the world?

The Book of Common Prayer provides an excellent opportunity to celebrate what you learn about your daily ministry, so take a look at "A Form of Commitment to Christian Service" as a grand opportunity to celebrate before God's throne of grace the wonderful ways every one of us plays a part in God's caretaking ministry. But if you include this liturgy in your Sunday morning worship, don't hide it away in a corner of your order of worship. Build the entire event of Sunday morning worship around this affair, include your Sunday school (both children and adults), and do this every year. In only a short while your people will know the shape of God's presence and ministry in ways which they never before dreamed.

Education for Children and Teens: Looking Toward Their Future

Children begin at an early age to ask themselves questions about their future life's work. For adolescents, the topic of occupations provides an opportunity to explore how they are likely to spend their lives in their adult future. And for adults, explorations can happily center on God's providential care of his world—through us, and the ways in which he has called us to our occupations.[3]

We are, of course, everyone of us, saints of God, and Sunday school provides a particularly good time to celebrate our daily occupations. For smaller children, think about scheduling the Police Canine Corps, the Fire Department, or Rescue Squad Members for Sunday visits. Members of other professions can also be invited. An electrician can hook up a simple circuit and describe how she helps God take care of the world. Or an artist might sketch some classroom impressions and talk about the ministry of creating beauty in God's world.

One year John Stewart, veterinarian extraordinaire, visited classes with his dog Sam. He showed his skill, talked about the care of animals, and explained in his own words how believed he was serving God in his daily job. Dr. John was also able to describe some of the decisions he made along the way that got him to vet school, and speculated about the way he believed God nudged his interest here and there—which included the support of his wife. He later thanked the teacher for asking for his help. "It was one of the nicest things I ever did. Nobody's ever used me as a saint before."[4]

At the time, I myself wondered about the number of children who, in those Sunday morning moments, were stirred by God to begin to consider taking care of animals in the work-for-pay future. We may never know, but God does. And God rejoiced at the opportunity for ministry in that Sunday school event.

Or a member of the medical helping professions can give a simple physical with a stethoscope. St. Luke's feast day falls October 18, and tradition has it that Luke was a physician. The Sunday closest to his day is a good one to explore the way God is with us through the lives of those he has called to healing ministries: nurses, medical physicians, social workers, counselors, and the list goes on and on. I hope you'll also use a mom or dad as a teaching vehicle. They're saints too, and the most important persons in our children's lives.

THE BOTTOM LINE. God uses these educational events to spark our interest in our future and to introduce us afresh to his everyday care for us. Renewed congregations know this, and as a result the world is beating a path to their door.

End Notes

1. Washington Times. Page C-10. Tuesday, April 11, 1989
2. Hanchey, *Creative Christian Education*, p. 103.
3. A discussion of these topics is encouraged during the All Saints term in my nine-month program of Christian education, briefly discussed in chapter 13, and developed more fully in *Creative Christian Education*.
4. *Ibid.*, p. 99.

PART IV

Education in the Mission-Minded Church: Equipping the Saints for Ministry

CHAPTER 13

Organizing a Parish for Christian Education

Escaping Failure • Prayer Book Perspectives on Christian Education •
One of Many Success Stories • Wedding Worship and Sunday Morning
Christian Education

ll across the country mission-minded congregations make careful plans for Sunday morning Christian education. Indeed, Sunday school for both children and adults plays a major part in sustaining their common life.

Sunday school in these congregations sounds like a nine-month-long celebration. Bible stories are explored through plays and drama that include both children and adults; banners line the walls of hallways and classrooms; there is a weekly "mini-celebration"—in the bulletin or at the time of announcements—about what the Sunday school is doing and, on regularly-scheduled occasions, a full-blown parish celebration shows and tells the fruit of classroom explorations.

No matter what their size, whether large or small, mission-minded congregations never leave Christian education for adults or children to chance. More, mission-minded Christians have learned this: to the degree that they welcome children on Sunday morning, the parents of these children are likely to return again and again.

This chapter is mostly devoted to helping any size parish evaluate the Christian education of its *children*, and in the following discussion you will find specific suggestions and all kinds of encouragement.

Escaping Failure

Mark this point: Mission-minded congregations are not wedded to "classroom-intensive" Christian education, an educational procedure

189

hampering many Sunday school programs. Maintenance-minded congregations often conduct "classroom-intensive" Sunday school because "That's what we're supposed to do." They've had no one to help them catch another vision.

What is "classroom-intensive" Christian education? Almost every store-bought curriculum is "classroom-intensive." These programs present finely tuned *teacher-centered* lesson plans, but as a result they end up sounding a lot like the school lesson plans that most young students thought they left behind on Friday afternoon.

Moreover, ready-made materials are *created to be implemented*: they are not generally written to be amended or personalized. They do not encourage the development of a goal for the year, nor do they provide for determining objectives. This work has already been done. As a result, teachers generally implement these programs working in isolation, a fact soon apparent to students and their parents, and when this news gets around the parish, year after year it becomes more difficult to enlist a teaching staff. Still later these parishes go hunting for another curriculum "savior."

POINT. Mission-minded congregations have learned that what is good for the public and private school during a six-hours-a-day, five-day-a-week program is not good for the thirty or more minutes we have on Sunday morning. Classroom-intensive Sunday school will likely fail, even if it begins strongly in September, because children on Sunday morning hunger for a *note of celebration*, not "learning more,"—whatever "more" is.

But even when mission-minded congregations use store-bought materials (and they do), these congregations change them by including occasional intergenerational learning events (involving parents, children and singles), they set a few modest learning objectives for each year, they often celebrate what was learned in the classroom, teachers work in an atmosphere of teamwork, and there is always close clergy contact and support.

Prayer Book Perspectives on Christian Education

Mission-minded Christian education in the Episcopal Church generally honors the Prayer Book. Although the remainder of this chapter is written with the Episcopal Church in mind, the ideas discussed are pertinent to any denomination using the common lectionary of Bible readings on Sunday morning.

This kind of education:

• takes into account themes drawn from the *liturgical year*, which provides a sensible and familiar context for education in the whole parish,

• embraces the theme of *eucharist*, with specific plans for celebrating the work of classroom Christian education,

• generates a feeling of *communion* among teachers, students and parishioners, and

• loves to explore *Bible stories*.

If your Sunday school program is floundering more than you like (recognizing that nothing in the world is perfect), and if you want to make some changes that satisfy, don't simply spend more money on a new set of study materials. Even if they are purchased by the truck load, they will likely disappoint you after a year or so of use.

Instead, brainstorm about what you need, and use the following questions and discussion as guidelines.

1. *Does your Sunday school program break the nine-month school year into manageable segments?* Nine months is a long haul. But when the school year is broken into several time periods, everything begins to work together smoothly.

This kind of organization is much helped by the sequence of the church year. For example, many Episcopalians sang as children:

> *Advent* tells us Christ is near;
> *Christ-mas* tells us Christ is here.
> In *E-pi-pha-ny* we trace
> All the glo-ry of his grace.
> Then three Sun-days will pre-pare
> For the time of fast and prayer,
> That, with hearts made pen-i-tent,
> We may keep a faith-ful *Lent*.
> *Holy Week* and *Easter* then
> Tell who died and rose again:
> So we give him special praise
> After those great forty days.[1]

This hymn was listed first in the children's section of The Hymnal 1940, and it helped more than a few generations fix the Bible's witness and the church's great remembering firmly in mind. I hum the tune still, and so do others who grew up in the Episcopal Church. Mission-minded congregations still honor the flow and movement of the church year. They trust the rhythm and cadence it provides to their program, and in large measure it is the reason they are more successful than not.

I myself am wedded to a five-term modification of the church year, each term about six weeks in length. All together they provide a helpful framework upon which to hang the whole year's teaching, learning and celebration. The idea for such terms isn't really new. For example, Advent/Christmas and Ash Wednesday/Lent/Easter are universally recognized as the two most important seasons of the church year. Learning from mission-minded congregations, my *Christian Education Made Easy* and its companion, *Creative Christian Education*, make six-week terms of both these seasons. They build on these two terms by adding three others, beginning in September with:

• *All Saints* term (6-8 weeks), and concluding with an All Saints show-and-tell festival on the Sunday closest to All Saints day, followed by

• *Christmas* term (7 weeks),

• *Epiphany* season (5 - 8 weeks),

• *Lenten* term (6 weeks),

• *Easter/Pentecost* term (6+ weeks).

2. *Does your present program offer opportunities to celebrate what is taking shape in the Sunday-morning classroom?*

The more everyone in the parish knows what is happening next, the more likely Sunday-morning Christian education will sound like a happy parade. This is the plain truth: If you don't celebrate the fruits of Sunday-morning Christian education, you are flirting with despair. Children will lose a sense of purpose, teachers will feel alone, and parents will increasingly think that nothing much is happening.

What I've come to call "show-and-tell" festival worship generates the celebrative atmosphere characterizing Christian education in mission-minded congregations. These occasional festivals insure success by providing an opportunity to display what's been going on in the classroom.

"So," you ask, "what do these festivals show and tell?" If a class makes a banner about a Bible story (and making a banner is a good way to learn any Bible story), it can be shown to the parish with appropriate hoopla on a designated Sunday. Or if a classroom play of a Bible story is written, what better place to offer it later to Almighty God than before the altar of God's church on Sunday morning? Parishioners will love it; so will parents, visitors and children.

POINT. "Show-and-tell" festivals are not just for the Sunday school community. They are meant to be a celebration of the previous term of study by the *whole parish at the main Sunday service.* Furthermore, parents visiting for a first time are attracted to congregations who show pride in what their children are doing in the Sunday-morning classroom. Store-bought curricula materials don't offer this kind of programming, mainly because ready-made curricula materials aren't written with evangelism and church growth in mind.

Adult and teenage classes can also present their labor and love in these festivals. For mission-minded adults, show-and-tell is not "kiddie work." Indeed, these Christians know full well that in their play and presentation they bear witness to God's love and their belief in it. As a result, their children not only hear their parents speak of God's love, but see their parent's belief "in action." Do you see how simple it is?

Mission-minded congregations have discovered that when Sunday school is relegated to a back hall classroom, it is out of sight and out of mind. And when teachers and students discover this, students will quit coming and teachers will quit volunteering. If you want the Sunday school program to bless you with spirited enthusiasm, you must first bless it with regular acknowledgement and affirmation. Occasional "show-and-tell" festivals provide this gift.

3. *Does your present program celebrate Bible stories of God's action?*

If your current curricula materials don't pay close attention to the Bible, I would close them up. Parents bring their children to church hoping that in church their children will come to know more about God. And they themselves want to hear more about godly things. Bible stories provide just the right resource to accomplish this goal, and if you choose to break the nine-month school year into five terms, one Bible story can easily last for a six-week term. Simply celebrate the story with arts, crafts and drama. Then, when you "show-and-tell" to the parish what you and your children have been doing in the classroom, enthusiasm and joy will shine.

Studying Bible stories (with attendant crafts activities and their later "showing and telling" to the congregation) tends to encourage the attendance of children. It offers a short-term goal toward which to work, and arts and crafts provide the note of fun that makes Bible stories come to life.

4. *Does your present program encourage your teaching staff to make plans and work together?*

Most store-bought curriculum materials don't offer an opportunity for teachers to make plans or work together, mainly because all the plans necessary are already provided. As a result, teachers often end up feeling lonely and isolated.

5. *Does your present program include occasional intergenerational parish events for everyone?*

If parents, children, teens and singles are not occasionally joined in a common activity, then you are missing out on a procedure that can fire parish life with joy.

Materials meeting every one of these important criteria are not generally available, for most store-bought curricula are designed with the public school model close at hand. They are "classroom-intensive." But of those ready-made materials available (and all are full of good ideas), every one of them will work better and generate more satisfaction by using the following guidelines:

• Schedule in terms or blocks of time to focus student and parish attention on common themes.

• Plan regular parish events to celebrate what is happening in the classroom.

• Focus on joint planning by the teaching staff to make these store-bought materials "your own."

• Occasionally schedule events for all ages.

One of Many Success Stories

I hear much about disappointment in Sunday morning Christian education. But I also hear much about success. One small North Carolina town boasts this story.

> Ours is a small but vibrant, growing parish. We typically see 75-80 people on Sunday. Our physical plant is small, and limits us to a "one room schoolhouse" approach. But we find a "one room school" works wonders for us. The children enjoy the working like one big family. And to keep the children's interest high, we choose open-ended activities that tease the imagination.
>
> We use a Bible story every week. We emphasize a simple story-line and the characters, we reinforce and repeat the learnings through the use of a children's chapel program (informally telling the story), and we always present a creative project for the day.
>
> The energy and the enthusiasm just keep building. We work in teams for month-long blocks of time. That helps our teachers stay fresh. We've noticed, too, that new children seem to be incorporated quickly because we are working and learning as one big family, and this in turn seems to help with the rapid incorporation of their parents.[2]

There are all kinds of ways to adapt the suggestions made in this chapter to meet the needs of your congregation. They do work, and every year more and more congregations are finding this out.

Wedding Worship and Sunday Morning Christian Education

Mission-minded congregations make every effort to include children in mainline worship on Sunday morning, and they do so in two ways. First, on regularly scheduled occasions they celebrate in Sunday's worship what's being learned in the classroom. Second, their children are also welcomed for at least a part of every Sunday morning's worship.

Look first at the occasional inclusion of classroom materials in "show-and-tell" festivals. I once helped a couple, Frank and Jenny Wright, celebrate their sixtieth anniversary in Sunday morning's worship. Careful preparations for the festival ranged over several months, and every Sunday school class was involved in this task. A zoo, you say? It did take careful administration, but that too is an important part of Sunday morning Christian education.

Classes explored modern-day marriage and family life. In some cases children interviewed their moms and dads. Photographs of parents' weddings were brought to class. For children of single parents, it was an opportunity to find out what it had been like "once upon a time," an important by-product we had not anticipated.

One class made a great big bright banner highlighting important milestones in the Wrights' life, like their births and marriage, the purchase of their home, and the births of their children. Since Frank had once worked for the United States Postal Service, the town's Post Office was also pictured. To this day that banner still hangs in the parish hall, bringing back many happy memories.

The big Sunday finally came, and our worship not only celebrated Frank and Jenny's sixtieth anniversary, but every marriage in the parish. The church was packed with friends, many of whom came for a first-time visit. It was a day of remembering and celebration, and it was glorious.

> Later, a 37-year-old member of St. Andrew's who'd known the Wrights all her life said she'd cried a bit during the service, but "I never felt closer to them or to myself than today. I wish church were like this more often."[3]

Though she makes no mention of God, it was God's presence she felt. Furthermore, the smiles of Frank and Jenny radiated God's glory, and hinted at the joy of the congregation. God was at work in the midst of this celebration.

Children in mission-minded congregations often worship with their moms, dads or sponsors, and enjoy the fellowship of bread and wine. But because many maintenance-minded congregations seldom make provision for all-family worship, this notion is likely to generate some (or even much) apprehension. Many older people simply can't tolerate the threat of disruption that small children easily pose. Nor should they. More, sermons for adults are too important to be lost on children, whose attention spans and personal interests are not yet at adult levels. But mission-minded congregations also know that children can be taught to respect the needs of others (commonly called socialization), and that, as necessary, provision can also be made for a children's chapel to be held during the time of the sermon.

An interesting study of growth patterns in mainline Australian churches from 1963 to 1975 corroborates what I have learned. This research found that membership in Roman Catholic, Lutheran and

Mormon churches increased, while that of Episcopal, Presbyterian and Methodist churches declined. There was only one common denominator: when children were separated from the worship of the community and sent to another place, membership in those churches declined. Growing churches, this research discovered, expected children to take part in worship, and provision was made for their participation. Declining churches "hid children away."

> I am not preaching a "gospel of children," but I question whether the Gospel can be heard in congregations that refuse to allow children's presence. One trend which is particularly destructive and demoralizing to children is the practice of having Sunday school groups meeting at the same time as the main worship service. Constantly dividing up the church on the basis of age and sex copies a worldly, high-school model of education.[4]

POINT. In churches where Christian education flourishes, careful provision is made to welcome children in Sunday morning's worship, and Sunday morning worship is closely allied with the classroom.

End Notes
1. Hymnal 1940. Hymn 235. This hymn is, of course, left out of The Hymnal 1982 by the same folks who also tried to delete "I sing a song of the saints of God."
2. Written by Mrs. Jocelyn King of New Hope, North Carolina.
3. Hanchey, *Creative Christian Education*, p. 61.
4. *Ibid.*, p. 65.

CHAPTER 14

Education for Adults and Teens: Skill Building for Evangelism

Why Do Episcopalians Fear Evangelism? • Three Kinds of Evangelism •
Episcopal Church Evangelism: What It Looks Like • Organizing an
Evangelism Study Group: For Adults and Teens • Always Use Stories •
Taking Action: What Next for Episcopalians?

any mainline adult Christians want help with the
ministry of evangelism. This chapter is written to
provide help, and it is written with adult education
in mind.

Adult education is a high priority in mission-minded congregations; to some degree every occasion for the education of adults encourages the capacity to speak of God in plain, everyday language.
Bible study and prayer groups, evangelism study groups, Sunday
morning adult education classes and sermons—each one plays its
part.

This is a hands-on chapter, written to help you develop your
capacity to speak confidently of God. The following pages discuss
the three kinds of evangelism generally valued and distinguished in
the mainline churches. This chapter also notes the importance of
prizing stories, and includes a discussion about the particular approach of Episcopalians to evangelism's ministry of introductions.

Help is available in this chapter to assist even the smallest congregation in forming a small group to explore evangelism. It can be
used by any congregation looking for ideas about developing its
capacity to exercise evangelism's ministry of introductions.

Why Do Episcopalians Fear Evangelism?

Like members of other mainline denominations, many Episcopalians fear the ministry of evangelism. Maybe you were once harshly handled by a fervent Christian "pushing Jesus," or maybe you've seen too much of the TV evangelists.

> Evangelism is associated—at least in the minds of many Episcopalians—with emotional fervor, intellectual bankruptcy, partisan politics, and naiveté. Others, more favorably inclined toward the term, are tempted to confuse it with renewal movements, the need to increase church membership, or even the visitation of new members.[1]

Many Episcopal clergy also fear the thought of evangelism. Because most of them grew up in a denomination whose leadership was opposed to it, or at the least unfamiliar with it, thoughts about evangelism generate defensiveness. Many clergy attended seminaries whose faculty (for the most part) were also children of the Episcopal Church, and no one can teach what they do not know.

POINT. Because many Episcopal churches have not paid much attention to the task of evangelism's ministry of introductions in recent years, they are at a loss when thinking about evangelism's rich possibilities today. As a result, they tend to expect too much of what is often called *preevangelism*, and often they have been turned off by the use of *secondary* evangelism.

Three Kinds of Evangelism

Evangelism in the mainline Protestant Church is generally fashioned in three ways.

Preevangelism, primary evangelism, and secondary evangelism each help us value the rich opportunities we are given to reach out to one another and to God's world. Each of these concepts is different from the others, and few of us will be skilled or even much interested in all three. For the sake of the world and God, however, we do value all three as parts of a whole.

"So what is preevangelism?" you ask. *Preevangelism* is evangelism directed toward ministry in the world. Starting a day care center, sponsoring concerts, community drama groups, and public lectures, establishing a food pantry, and other kinds of outreach qualify as preevangelism. This kind of evangelism introduces the world to the care and interest of God by providing care to the world in God's name. The Episcopal Church generally does well with this form of evangelism, and often uses it to justify its neglect of primary evangelism.

Primary evangelism identifies and celebrates God's action in the world to those not in the church. Acting from the perspective of Scripture and the tradition of the church, and with a healthy dose of reason, primary evangelism looks at life experiences to discern God's here-and-now everyday action, celebrating this action with a word of explanation or witness. Primary evangelism is essentially positive, telling the good news of God in the "small change" events of life, but also able to explain, as appropriate, why bad things happen even though God is good.

POINT. The core of Christianity is not a program of good works, as important as good works are. It is not a philosophical world view, and it is not a human yearning to simply know more. The core of Christianity is an announcement that God has intervened in the history of the world, and intervenes even now to take responsibility for us because we are not able to help ourselves. Primary evangelism is also enjoyed by many Christians in daily conversation, in conversations on Sunday morning, in sermon illustrations, and it always celebrates the goodness of God.

Primary evangelism is also the style of evangelism with which many Episcopalians seem to have the most trouble. Because many Episcopalians have never been encouraged to use the Prayer Book, Bible and hymnal to identify and celebrate God's everyday presence and ministry in the world, the ministry of primary evangelism is often not even an option.

Secondary evangelism is the ministry of evangelism the church directs toward itself. It might be called "graduate school" evangelism. Here the celebration of God's ministry takes a more complex shape. The life, death and resurrection of Christ is celebrated, Bible study—even if it is often devotional—uses the critical tools of academia, and such ideas as creation, sin, redemption and salvation are explored.

Too often, however, fervent Episcopal Church evangelists excessively visit on the world and one another the ministry of secondary evangelism. And while they satisfy themselves that they are acting as evangelists, their ministry is often characterized as too aggressive and argumentative by people not equipped to respond to or understand what they are talking about.

Episcopal Church Evangelism: What It Looks Like

Far more than an argument or the explanation of a complex theological doctrine (Is it any wonder that many Episcopalians fear thoughts about evangelism?), primary evangelism in the Episcopal Church values story. And it does so because of the witness of Scripture, the Prayer Book and the hymnal. The Prayer Book and hymnal are not esoteric discussions about who God is and who we are. Indeed, each one is quite simple in its approach to life and theology.

For example, in the Prayer Book God is One whose "unfailing providence sustains the world we live in and the life we live..." and God's care watches "over those [who], both night and day, work while others sleep...." This is not a picture of a God sitting high and lifted up on a throne somewhere, uninterested in our daily lives. The Hymnal 1982 also celebrates the story of God at work in the world: "Come, risen Lord, and deign to be our guest...." God is an ever-present help in times of trouble, and in all the times of our lives.

One recent Episcopalian convert, her highly developed intellectualizations challenged by such imagery, retorted, "I simply don't believe God takes that much interest in what we do every day." The Prayer Book and hymnal say otherwise. But if they value the story of God's action so much, why aren't Episcopalians more comfortable with the ministry of primary evangelism and its value of story and identification? In fact, they are becoming so, and mission-minded congregations around the country are showing them how.

Whenever Episcopalians practice primary evangelism, they give expression to four perspectives important to Anglicans everywhere: *Scripture, tradition, reason* and *experience*. Remember these four items, for they not only stand at the center of this book, they stand at the center of Anglicanism itself.

Scripture tells who God is by showing God at work in the history of a particular people. Without Scripture we would be unable to perceive God at work in the world. We would simply be touched by good fortune or good luck without ever knowing its author. The Bible is a window into the universe of God's action. God's love does not change, and so today believers expect the deaf to hear, the blind to see, the lame to walk, and the poor to hear a word of good news, precisely the ministry Jesus describes for God (Luke 4:16f).

The *tradition* of the church provides the second perspective when describing evangelism for Episcopalians. Just as one family has one way of celebrating Christmas and another family has another way, through the Prayer Book and hymnal the Episcopal Church has a particular way of celebrating God's love for the world. They are the "official" theological texts for our church. Both books make explicit and practical the discussion of God's ministry in our lives today in prayers like this: "Open our eyes to behold your gracious hand in all your works; that, rejoicing in your whole creation, we may learn to serve you with gladness...," while the Prayer Book catechism develops this idea of God's grace: "Grace is God's favor toward us, unearned and undeserved; by grace God forgives our sins, enlightens our minds, stirs our hearts, and strengthens our wills."[2] Episcopalians have learned to expect God's action in the world because we have been taught by our tradition to expect God to show care in the world. God enlightens our minds (with better ideas), stirs our hearts (to generate action), and strengthens our wills (to follow through).

A similar description of God's action is found in the collect for Advent 3: "Stir up your power, O Lord, and with great might come among us; and, because we are sorely hindered by our sins, let your bountiful grace speedily *help* and *deliver* us...." And if this collect doesn't paint a picture of grace, the notion of God's grace is developed still further in Proper 23: "Lord, we pray that your grace may always *precede* and *follow us*, that we may continually be given to good works...."

Every story in *Church Growth* shows God's stirring grace at work in life today, helping and delivering us. Mission-minded Episcopalians know that we are surrounded on every side by the love of God, and every time we pray the prayer book or sing the hymnal our tradition teaches us to look for the love of God.

Experience offers a place for Scripture and tradition to meet for discussion. Indeed, the interpretation of personal experience makes the ministry of evangelism both friendly and immediate. The use of personal experience troubles many Episcopalians, however. Many suffer from an overbearing sense of the remoteness of God. God is often presented by clergy leaders and preachers as so much "out there" that most folks in the pew can't appreciate God at work in the "here and now" of life today. Maybe they have been running scared from charges of "fundamentalism," or are frightened of the accusation of being too "literal." Some say that the church's inability to celebrate God at work in the world today results from an undue seminary emphasis on philosophical and systematic theology, with its valuation of reason and God's transcendence at the expense of experience and God's immanence.

Mission-minded congregations don't fret with concerns about the use of experience. They love to tell stories about God, and they know God is close because they have been taught by their clergy to see the "small change" miracles always present in the midst of life. Indeed, modern-day Episcopal Church evangelists, teachers and preachers don't "deny the place of reason, tradition or scripture. Rather, [they] know that those 'authorities' are always mediated through specific contexts and particular people's experience."[3]

POINT. The use of personal experience makes evangelism sound less like an argument and more like a song. So use stories. And enjoy.

Finally, by the use of *reason* the Anglican tradition brings Scripture, tradition and experience into close conversation with one another. Anglican evangelism knows that human beings have been created in the image of God, that we are free "to love, to create, to reason," and that God has blessed us "...with memory, reason and skill."[4]

If biblical perspectives tell us about God—who God is, what God intends, and how God is present in the world—and if the tradition of the prayer book and hymnal celebrates these same realities in a more devotional fashion, reason helps us make the connection between what our sovereign God did once upon a time and still does in our lives today.

Reason gives Anglican evangelism its full shape. Taking its cue from both the prayer book and the hymnal, reason devotes itself to a simplicity of witness. Modern-day Episcopal Church evangelists do not present complex theorems about God. They leave such things for advanced Christian education and academics. What Episcopal evangelists do best is sing the song of God's love that shows on every page of Scripture, those same signs of God's love showing today.

Organizing an Evangelism Study Group: For Adults and Teens

Mission-minded congregations know that teaching and learning the ministry of evangelism is an important part of their ministry. As noted earlier, items such as sermons, Bible study groups and prayer groups provide a broad context and encourage the ministry of evangelism in mission-minded congregations. But if you want to be more specific than this, use the following guidelines to set up an evangelism study group.

First, gather a group of interested people, perhaps as a Sunday morning adult or teen class. Consider also the possibility of working with a teenage youth group over a six week (or longer) period, exploring stories from their lives from faith perspectives. The exercises at the end of chapters 5 and 6 in this book are designed to be helpful. Then, because enthusiasm builds when everyone knows where they are headed, carefully present to your class the outline of your journey together, or present a course schedule you've already prepared. Suggestions in this chapter are offered to help you with the task of constructing such an outline.

Early in your first meeting, note the importance of story-listening as opposed to story-telling. Then introduce the concept of evangelism as a ministry of introductions. Briefly discuss this ministry and come up with an operational definition of evangelism that your class can agree upon. Brainstorm for impressions. There is a lot of misinformation about evangelism, and if it is not noted right off, the development of new perspectives will not easily take place. In this initial meeting (or meetings) you will also want to distinguish between the ways in which small children, teens and adults picture God. The discussion in chapter 6 is designed to help you get off on the right foot.

Always Use Stories

When you're ready to begin the task of practicing the ministry of introductions, commence with a story, perhaps one chosen from your own life or experiences or one presented in this book. "Canned" stories are a good place to begin.

When I'm presenting the ministry of introductions to folks who are not familiar with it, before I introduce the story I like to bring up just a few of my favorite metaphors and images. Story interpretation is much aided by the introduction of just one or two metaphors offered before the story is shared.

POINT. Never neglect to use a story when you teach about evangelism. If you simply try to explain the ministry of introductions by talking about "how it can be done," your work will likely be too abstract to make much of a long-term difference. Christians want practical ideas and methods that make a difference.

Later, once your class has explored a story introduced by you, most everyone will be interested in presenting a personal vignette of their own. But if your group is too self-conscious about using their own stories, encourage them to consider presenting one they recently read in a newspaper or magazine.

To help workshop participants feel as confident as possible about presenting their stories, I've found the following story subjects helpful.

1. Tell the story of your return to church if you have ever lapsed. What was going on in your life at the time, and what interested you in a return?

2. Tell the story of joining the church you presently attend. When was your interest stirred, and what encouraged its growth when you came?

3. Tell the story of a time in your life when you felt God's presence in a special way.

Then ask participants to type their stories, limiting their length to one or two paragraphs. Encourage class members to be alert to turning points (no matter how insignificant they may seem to be), and have copies of the typewritten stories available for everyone.

As the story is read:

1. Invite your class to identify turning points.

2. Ask questions such as "What else was happening?" or "What were you wearing?" or "Did you think of doing this instead of that?" Questions like these flesh out the story, they encourage more elaboration than the written word permits, and more deeply involve the whole group.

3. Offer comments and invite comments from the class.

4. Visualize the story on a blackboard or newsprint, drawing simple stick person pictures or noting key words on the board, or circle the group and ask for observations or insights.

The following "canned" story was presented in a workshop I led several years ago, and it illustrates the kind of narrative I like to encourage.

"We got away from going to church after we were married. Because we both worked, Sunday mornings were just a good time for us to be together. But we did go to church at Christmas and Easter. Then when our children came along we occasionally visited on Sunday, and we usually went to large churches because we could be sure of a good nursery.

"But the reason we're now deeply involved in church is as a result of one Christmas Eve. It was special. Maybe it was because the children were now old enough for Sunday school and we needed to "get active," or maybe it was because we were simply needy. No matter what it was, on this Christmas Eve we were touched by the music and pageantry, and we decided to return later for more regular worship. Within a year we had become active members, and the adult fellowship group, which shares a once-a-month potluck dinner in parish homes, became a major part of our lives."

Although more than a few Christians scorn the so-called secularization of Christmas, and some even make fun of Christmas and Easter Christians, calling them "Santas and Bunnies," this story plainly suggests that God uses every bit of holiday hoop-la and nostalgia to touch our lives.

Now look for turning points. All stories include points where, because of decisions made or events that happened, things went one way and not another.

One turning point in this story has to do with pageantry and music. "How did God use pageantry and music to touch this family's interest, and how did it fuel their enthusiasm?" Now make this question about their life personal to your class: "How does God touch you with music and pageantry at times like these, and why are such things so important to human beings?" And still another turning point is revealed when one begins to speculate about God's conversation as the magnificent music of Christmas given voice by a congregation of the faithful. "What did God say," might be the question, "when the brass joined the congregation's voice during the closing hymn?" Because whatever God said changed the lives of this couple.

POINT. Any story from human life, even the most harsh, contains signs of God's peace-producing ministry. Most Christians don't realize this. Granted, when tragedy strikes it may be difficult to see signs of God's ministry, but with just a bit of careful searching, they will appear.

Taking Action: What Next for Episcopalians?

Wayne Schwab, Evangelism Ministries Coordinator for the Episcopal Church, says that two questions unlock the ministry of evangelism for Episcopalians. The first is: "What is an evangelizing moment?," and the second is: "What does an evangelizing person look like?" Says Schwab, "An evangelizing moment occurs whenever we encounter unchurched people." He is, of course, speaking about the ministry of primary evangelism. Because we believe that God is already at work in their lives, we come alongside them to listen to their stories, offer interpretation about God's here-and-now action, and share our own stories. An "evangelizing person" is one conscious of God's everyday action in the midst of life, one who can identify, explain and celebrate signs of God at work in both Scripture's witness and the here and now of life today.

Then Schwab continues, "Our purpose in evangelism is not to meet our power needs for more people and money. Our purpose in evangelism is to share in God's restoration of all humanity and the whole creation to right relationship with God."[5]

Episcopal Church evangelism should be marked by the following characteristics:

1. God is always about the task of inviting and accompanying visitors to church. Hence, visitors come "hungry" to know more about God, and when these newcomers find a church that loves God and knows how to talk about God, they are likely to return again and again. If the ministry of primary evangelism is not enjoyed in the church on Sunday morning, it will not be exercised in the marketplace among the unchurched. This is the reason many Episcopalians are not confident with the ministry of primary evangelism.

2. Episcopal Church evangelism also knows that Jesus shows us the nature of God at work in the world today. Because of Jesus, speaking about God in the midst of life is always concrete and easily grasped; it is never vague or nebulous. Almost every collect in the Prayer Book ends with something like "through Jesus Christ our Lord," and most begin with an address to a sovereign God, One whose nature Jesus shows us.

3. Episcopalians enjoying the ministry of evangelism have learned that this ministry begins by listening to the stories of others. Evangelism in the Episcopal tradition is never coercive, nor does it restrict the freedom of the other person to believe. Rather, Episcopal Church evangelism teases the mind with images, pictures and coincidences, each of which serves God's own evangelizing ministry.

4. Episcopalians believe that a newborn and growing Christian faith cannot be left to fend for itself, and hence evangelists act to nurture it. Classes for newcomers are carried out with joy, parents and sponsors of infants to be baptized are welcomed with information, the Lord's Holy communion is explained to the parents (or sponsors) of children taking their rightful place at the communion rail, and classes are held for those wanting to make an adult affirmation of their faith through the Rite of Confirmation.

5. Episcopalians believe that evangelization is "completed" when the seeker knows the shape of God's action in the world and can speak about God's love in plain, everyday language with confidence. For such a person the Bible, prayer book and hymnal are made flesh. In other words, good evangelism makes natural evangelists of others. To celebrate the arrival of this time of maturation, the Rite of Confirmation or adult baptism is an appropriate expression of evangelism's ministry "come of age."

Put these five perspectives to work in your parish. The next chapter will show you how. Then watch evangelism's ministry of introductions take an easy and comfortable shape, and watch your parish grow in faith and confidence.

END NOTES

1. The Evangelical Education Society, *Outlook* (Winter 1988), p. 5.

2. The Book of Common Prayer, p. 134; The Hymnal 1982, 306.

3. For and insightful discussion of the Anglican use of experience, see Lyn Rhodes, *Co-Creating* (Philadelphia: Westminster Press, 1987), p. 38.

4. The Book of Common Prayer, pp. 845, 370.

5. Wayne Schwab to Stephen Muncie, 3 October 1989. The notion of evangelism as story listening has also been recently described by Wayne Schwab in the booklet prepared by his office, *Proclamation As Offering Story and Choice*. His office has also published *Handbook for Evangelism, The Catechumenal Process: A Resource for Dioceses and Congregations, Faith Development and Evangelism*, and *Evangelism With the Poor*.

CHAPTER 15

Making Believers of Christians: Newcomer and Membership Classes

Classes to Welcome Newcomers • Classes to Make Members of Newcomers • The Portrait of a Mature Christian • Constructing a Membership Class: Working Toward Maturation • Believer's Confirmation • "Kiddie" Confirmation: Robbing the Church of Strength

trengthening the faith of Christians, and particularly adult Christians, stands at the center of a mission-minded congregation's common life. This chapter follows on the educational focus of the preceding two in developing both the *newcomer* and *membership classes* mentioned in chapter 10. Each class is different, and *both* are important.

Now listen to this point: It is of enormous importance to this chapter's discussion.

A huge, landmark study, involving completion of a 374-item questionnaire by 10,000 church people,…notes that what matters most in building mature faith are not the commonly emphasized classes for the young—important as they are—but adult Christian education. Further, this most important stage of learning is found to be widely neglected in (mainline) churches.[1]

The consequences of little or no adult education are two fold: *First*, the interest of many mainline adult Christians wanes, and more than a few drop out of church. *Second*, with no vision of the Christian life and witness, a maintenance mindset assumes a stronger shape in those who remain.

Classes to Welcome Newcomers

Every mainline denomination will approach the development of a newcomers class with different hopes in mind, but when you do, consider the following items.

First, there is a subtle distinction between a visitor and a newcomer. A visitor is still uncommitted. They are still wondering whether they want to stay or not. A newcomer is one who has made a commitment. It may not be a large commitment, but they are beginning to think of you as their church home, and it is likely that they want to know more about you. A visitor is not yet commited to your church. Hence, mission-minded congregations make every effort to meet newcomer interest with a lively discussion that offers satisfying answers.

Second, personally invite newcomers to this class. A general invitation will likely get no response at all.

Third, a class no longer than four weekly meetings can be both brief and illuminative. If you conduct these classes on Sunday morning (perhaps the most convenient time for most Christians), you may have only 30-40 minutes of quality time available. Although the time is short, it is certainly better than nothing. An evening meeting offers more time, but it may be less convenient.

Fourth, remember that you are not offering full-scale theological education in these classes for newcomers. You are offering an opportunity for bonding to take place and questions to be answered. If this happens, and if your program is lighthearted and upbeat, members of your class will begin a process of learning that will last for years. Also include in this class the sponsors of your newcomers. If you do not use sponsors, perhaps you should consider it.

Then, as appropriate, use the following ideas to construct your program.

First Week

Goal: To introduce newcomers to one another and to your parish.

1. Make introductions all around.

2. Ask about first impressions:

• What do newcomers like about your church?

• What do you do that differs from their last parish?

- What don't they like?
- What don't they understand?

3. Include brief remarks about the history of your congregation: when you got started, the historic foci of your ministry to your town or community, and the special marks of your ministry today.

4. Discuss your style of worship, including the participation of children at the Lord's Table.

5. Discuss the ways class members can take their share in the responsibility of caring for their new church, serving as ushers, host or hostess at the coffee hour, Sunday school teachers, etc.

Remember to pay first-of-all attention to newcomer questions and opinions. Few congregations are going to be absolutely pleasing across the board to every newcomer. Many are likely to wish for a few changes to remind them of "home," wherever home was. If newcomers are given an opportunity to express their views and if they find an understanding hearing, they are more likely to be happy in their new home than if their grief is not given an opportunity for expression and conversation.

Finally, remind everyone that next week your class will share their stories about coming for a first time to worship with you, and learning to use the Bible and, for Episcopalians, the Book of Common Prayer to identify and celebrate God's action in these stories.

Second Week

Goal: To offer newcomers an opportunity to tell the story of why they are present and how they heard about you, and to introduce them to the Bible and the Prayer Book as tools to celebrate God's action in their lives.

1. Ask sponsors and/or newcomers to share their own stories.

2. Because newcomers may be a bit bashful, if necessary use your story, a sponsor's story, or one of the stories provided in this book to introduce a discussion of God's action.

3. Employ the following Prayer Book perspectives:

- What does the story show us about God's grace?
- What does the story show us about human freedom?
- Luke 4:16f: What does Jesus suggest about God's action in the story?

• Use other perspectives of your choice.

3. Be alert to questions like "Why do bad things happen if God is so good?" Hear the story out and, as appropriate, show how Episcopalians use the Prayer Book to understand these stories, using the notion of freedom (BCP 845), sin (BCP 848), and the forces of evil that seek to destroy life (BCP 302).

Discerning signs of God's presence and ministry is especially important in mission-minded congregations, and a class for newcomers provides a grand opportunity to both introduce the Prayer Book *and* to discuss God's action.[2]

If your class wishes to expand this discussion into another week, ask class members to share a story about God's power in their lives.

Third Week

Goal: To learn something about your denomination's history. Many congregations suffer from low self-esteem simply because members don't know who they are.

• Present a short history of your denomination, using lecture materials, if necessary, a video if possible—with bright written materials to supplement it. See page 219.

• Introduce selected lay members of your congregation, and ask them to discuss their ministries, in the church and in the world. Have them tell about why they enjoy doing their church ministry, and why it is necessary.

• Explore for a second time possibilities for the participation of newcomers as they take up parish responsibilities.

Fourth Week

Goal: Formal welcome.

• Once this program is completed, these now no-longer newcomers and their sponsors should be presented formally to the congregation. To the extent that visitors are effectively welcomed, they are likely to become active members. And to the extent that these folks are left to their own devices and desires, they are likely to drop out.

THE BOTTOM LINE. With this kind of commitment to theological education, these visitors now becoming members are more likely to stay around for the long haul, fed with living bread.

Classes to Make Members of Newcomers

As a continuation of your welcoming program, give every consideration to the development of more lengthy and comprehensive membership classes. Some church executives suggest that a lack of newcomer and membership classes may be one of the reasons that the size of many mainline denominations has declined in recent years.

Thomas Carson, Executive for Stewardship in the Episcopal Church, suggests that a lack of newcomer and membership classes may be one of the reasons the size of his denomination has declined in recent years. I think he is right.

> We in the Episcopal Church have never been strong on new membership instruction. Most clergy minimize baptismal as well as confirmation instruction.
>
> The hundreds of congregational bulletins that cross my desk affirm this. We read time and time again that the bishop will be coming for his annual visitation in the next three or four weeks, and all persons desiring to become members of the congregation should contact the clergy as soon as possible for instruction.[3]

A half-way encouragement develops half-way interest or no interest at all. Mission-minded congregations know otherwise. They make plans every year to conduct membership classes, and they constantly remind parishioners about the wonderful opportunity to become an "official" member of their denomination.

The Portrait of a Mature Christian

Rather than leaving the development of a mature Christian faith to chance, and to meet the interest of newcomers with even more discussion, mission-minded congregations construct membership classes to help a sturdy Christian faith develop. But what is a mature Christian faith? The following description outlines its basic shape of a mature Christian faith, a baseline picture. For just as a twenty-one-year-old man or woman doesn't yet look as they will at sixty years of age, so a baseline mature Christian faith for adults marks a beginning of the mature adult pilgrimage.

One, a sturdy, mature Christian faith has at hand an overview of God's saving action in the world from the first to the last chapter of the Bible. Now this doesn't mean that these mature Christians are Bible scholars, but they do know the biblical shape of God's love for the world, the way it shows in the event of creation itself, how the Bible pictures sin entering the world, God's attempts through the ages to raise up a loving and righteous people, and finally the coming of God into the world to accomplish this task. This overview also includes knowledge of the early church's witness to incarnational, God-with-us faith.

Two, a sturdy, mature Christian faith can identify and discuss without embarrassment God's action in the world today. These sturdy Christians know who God is and what difference God makes in life. As a result, they are familiar with exercising what the church calls the ministry of evangelism. They believe that God is with us, that God cares aggressively for our welfare, working on behalf of communion and community, and that Jesus shows us all we need to know about God.

Three, a sturdy and mature Christian faith is not afraid to tackle such questions as "Why do bad things happen in the world if God is so good?" Mature Christians know that freedom in the universe, and God's value of it, is likely to play an important part whenever bad things happen, along with those "evil powers of this world which corrupt and destroy the creatures of God," and what the church has traditionally called sin.[4] These notes are elaborated in Susan's story in this book, chapters 4 and 5.

Four, a mature Christian faith knows the history of its local parish church, how it got started, the history of its ministry, and the special shape of its contemporary ministry. It also knows something of the history, polity, and liturgical tradition of its own denomination, as well as the shape of local church governance.

Five, sturdy and mature Christians know that everyday they help God take care of the world in their daily occupations, whether in their jobs, their hobbies, or their roles as parents and partners. They know that serving on the altar guild or the vestry is important, but it is not the primary way they help God take care of the world.

Six, these Christians know that the notion of spiritual gifts embraces far more than simply speaking in tongues, for example. They have been moved by their teachers to see that their unique personality is an important gift from God, and each of us brings particular gifts to relationship and to community.

Constructing a Membership Class: Working Toward Maturation

When the task of developing a strong Christian faith is at hand, mission-minded congregations know that frequent membership classes are a crucial tool. A membership class devoted to the criteria just noted cannot be accomplished in a week or a month. But if you regularly *welcome newcomers* with the kind of brief program suggested in this chapter, the interest of newcomers will likely be whetted to take advantage of this more lengthy membership program.

"So," you ask, "how long should a membership class be?" Rather than set a length of time, consider the criteria above and construct your class with these ideas in mind.

The following course takes almost six months. It can be shortened, but I don't see how a membership class designed to make sturdy believers out of already-baptized Christians, or to prepare adults for a believer's baptism, can take much less time. The program itself can be conducted on Sunday morning, if time permits, during a 45-minute period, or it can be expanded to 1 1/2 hours a week on a week-night, perhaps with coffee and desert.

Six Weeks

Goal: Learning to use the Bible and the Prayer Book to identify and celebrate God's presence in the world.

First, extend introductions during the first two class sessions. Help participants get to know one another, because the more they know one another, the more likely they will commit to the full responsibilities of taking care of their new congregation.

Second, using the Bible and, for Episcopalians, Prayer Book perspectives, present a brief overview of God's saving action through history. Begin with creation, briefly move through the the history of Israel, explore the ministry of Jesus, and conclude with the work and witness of the early church. For a wonderful summary of God's action in community of faith, use Hebrews 11-12:2, perhaps in conjunction with the canon of Eucharistic Prayer "C" in the Book of Common Prayer.

Third, help these interested Christians begin to discern God's everyday action in their lives today, using stories like those found in this book. This may be a new activity to some, but hunger for a knowledge of God is a major part of the reason we come to church in the first place. So while interest burns bright, meet it.

Every story included in this book can serve as a guide to this activity. Episcopalians can also use the catechism of the Book of Common Prayer to explore issues of grace, freedom, evil, and the Incarnation. Help participants begin to answer the question "Why do bad things happen in the world if God is so good?" Invariably I find that even the briefest discussion of God's love generates this question, and there is no better time to explore a question than when it burns hot.

Two Weeks

Goal: Learning the history of our local parish.

Participants will want to know a little something of the history of their new (to some) parish, how it got started, the history of its local ministry, and the special shape of its contemporary ministry. To help with this task, draw on the experiences of older parishioners, or ask members of the congregation to come in and explain what has happened in the past. And if you don't have a cogent and brief parish history, now is the time to devote to the task of creating one, perhaps including photographs.

Three Weeks

Goal: Appreciating God's action in calling us to our present jobs, and how we help God take care of God's world.

Prepare to help participant discuss their ministry in the world through their daily occupations. The ministry of the laity is more than just a synonym for serving on the altar guild or the vestry, and when mission-minded Christians know that they serve God in their work, they don't feel nearly so isolated in their jobs as they might sense otherwise. Use as a resource the discussion in chapter 12 of this book.

Three Weeks

Goal: Identifying the personal gifts these Christians bring to ministry, community and relationships.

Some clergy and congregations like to use a tool like the Myers-Briggs Type Indicator (or a much used, abbreviated Myers-Briggs Type Indicator called the *Kiersey Temperament Sorter*) to explore the differing gifts each of us brings to everyday life and ministry.[5]

Three Weeks

Goal: Learning the history of your denomination.

Use books, pamphlets, study guides, and films provided through your denominational offices. For Episcopalians, Cathedral Films has developed an excellent 40-minute video showing the history of the Episcopal Church in America. By using their accompanying study guide, congregations report that learning history is both easy and fun. More, this same organization has created a three-part video entitled *The Story of Anglicanism*, narrated by Michael York and including a study guide.

Three Weeks

Goal: Examining and learning about liturgical worship and the pastoral resources in the Book of Common Prayer, and particularly the way liturgical worship is shaped in their local setting.

For the liturgical traditions such as Anglicanism, the shape of worship is probably of much interest to participants, particularly the way it is shaped in your local setting. Newcomers are probably quite taken with the way in which your congregation worships on Sunday morning, and they want to learn more about it. And if they aren't pleased with some of the things that take place, discussion is likely to ease their aversion to a point of happy toleration. Membership classes like this one help that happen.

Three Weeks

Goal: Learning the polity of your church at national and local church levels, the shape of local church governance, the ministry of vestries and parish councils, and the relationship of national leadership to your parish.

Such a subject as this provides a magnificent opportunity to meet parish leaders, have them tell about why they enjoy doing their church ministry, and why it is necessary.[6]

Once this program is completed, participants can be presented to the congregation for a formal welcome. For Episcopalians, if this membership class doubles as a confirmation class, participants can be presented to the bishop. And if an episcopal visit is not scheduled near the completion of the course, the presentation to the congregation can provide just the note of affirmation that is momentarily deserved, perhaps using an adaptation of A Form Of Commitment To Christian Service in the Prayer Book.

Believers' Confirmation

Use the criteria suggested in this chapter to build your own *believers' confirmation class.* Such a class could run from the first Sunday in Epiphany until the Sunday of Pentecost, when confirmation itself is scheduled. Mission-minded congregations know that adults like Connie (whose story was told in chapter 3) want far more than milk toast when thinking about who God is and who we are as children of God. They want to know what the church is, why we worship the way we do, what the Bible says about God and what difference a knowledge of God makes in the here and now of our lives today.

As a result of treating confirmation as an opportunity to make articulate believers of newcomers and infant-baptized Christians, mission-minded congregations are attracting more than a few Christians who are tired of limping though life unaware of what they sense everyday in their lives. Christians should be given every opportunity to deepen their faith through a program similar to this, and should have committed themselves to such a program (or its equivalent) if they aspire to vote in parish matters, or if they wish to assume a leadership role.

"Kiddie" Confirmation: Robbing the Church of Strength

Unfortunately, *believer's confirmation* is not the norm in the Episcopal Church; "kiddie" confirmation is. So listen to this point:

routinely presenting adolescent children for confirmation has done more to harm the Episcopal Church than any other Prayer Book practice. What it has done is raise up a people who don't know who they are.

For example, clergy leadership in one shrinking congregation (located in a growing neighborhood) every year invites twelve and thirteen year-old children to their confirmation class by promising coke and cookies. Now you tell me why the Episcopal Church is shrinking!

Why do we make use of "kiddie" confirmation? Until the thirteenth century baptism was the only requirement necessary to take communion. That was before the enthronement in 1279 of John Peckham as Archbishop of Canterbury. Angered that many adult Christians baptized as infants were not presenting themselves to the bishop for confirmation, he decided to change the church and decreed that no Christian would be admitted to the holy communion without confirmation; as a result, confirmation was inserted between baptism and admission to the Lord's Table and this became Anglican practice. Until recently the Episcopal Church has been shackled by this system, perhaps the single most important reason that we have not in recent years much attended the nurture of an adult Christian faith.[7]

Instead of using age as a criterion, and instead of using confirmation as a rite of passage into the church (whether for adolescents or adults), mission-minded congregations use the criteria of *readiness to* and *interest in* handling the things of God as the goal toward which to work. These congregations and their priests are more than willing to present anyone to the bishop for confirmation if these criteria are met.

But still this fact remains: A host of store-sold, ready-made "kiddie" confirmation programs pack the shelves of Episcopal Church bookstores. These materials are bought with the hope that Christian maturation will occur if they are used. Or worse, adolescent folk are tracked through confirmation because "that's what we are supposed to do," or the rite of confirmation provides the substance of a junior or senior high Sunday school class because "we've got to do something with these young people." The routine and un-critical confirmation of adolescent children does not nourish God's church.

This said, some adolescent children are ready for a believer's con-firmation. Though in a minority, they have, by their investment in the life of the community of faith, been met by God in such a way that they are alive to God's presence, and they want to know more.

So now you ask, "If we don't confirm our children at an early age, what are we to do with them?"

First, give your children a year-round Sunday school program that works. Don't expect a kiddie confirmation class to do in a few months what you're unable or unwilling to do every Sunday of the year. The discussion in chapter 13 is designed to help with this task.

Second, consider this point: Mission-minded congregations are re-covering an ancient tradition by saying that no baptized person ought be denied feeding once they are born into the Christian family.

Infants in mission-minded congregations are admitted to the Lord's table from the earliest age. Gently over the course of Sundays and through their early years, natural curiosity, the mystery of the Eucharist and God's action at the table combines to form children as Christians. Powerfully engaged by God at such moments as these, childhood imagination combines with God's action to generate the nativity of Christian faith. And why can this conclusion be drawn? I've heard more than one small child say "Jesus" as the host is offered.

Mission-minded Christians also know that with a parish-wide vi-sion about what makes a full-blown believing Christian, children will have a goal to aim for as they grow older, instead of a hoop through which to jump. When a solid program of Christian educa-tion for children takes place on Sunday morning, confirmation can be unapologetically used to celebrate a mature Christian faith.

Third, one hastens to add that all adolescent children deserve some rite to celebrate their passage into young adulthood. Their parents also both need and deserve this support from the community of faith. Happily, the Book of Common Prayer provides a useful ve-hicle. *A Form of Commitment to Christian Service*, with careful preparation, readily lends itself to the important work of affirming the growth of our children, as youngsters commit themselves to being good students, or baby-sitters, or the task of earning money with work-for-pay tasks, or taking responsibility for the family automobile, and the list goes on and on.

End Notes

1. From *Effective Christian Education: A National Study of Protestant Congregations*, published by the Search Institute of Minneapolis and sponsored by six mainline Protestant denominations through a grant from the Lilly Endowment Inc. Also cited in The Washington Times, Friday, February 9, 1990, page B5.

2. Gospel drama provides a method to make this discussion satisfying and lively. See Howard Hanchey, *Christian Education Made Easy*, chapter 9.

3. *Stewardship Report*, Episcopal Church Center, Spring 1988.

4. The Book of Common Prayer, pp. 845, 302, 848.

5. David Keirsey and Marilyn Bates, *Please Understand Me: Character and Temperament Types*, (Del Mar, CA: Prometheus Nemesis Books, 1984). The Keirsey Temperament Sorter is easy to use, and each of sixteen personality configurations is discussed with a page of insights, celebratory in tone.

6. For Episcopalians, Forward Movement Publications publishes booklets and pamphlets devoted to this discussion. One 6-page pamphlet is simply entitled *The Episcopal Church* and still another *Vestries in the Episcopal Church* by Robert R. Hansel (27 pp.). Available from The Forward Movement, 412 Sycamore Street, Cincinnati, Ohio 45202.

7. See Ronald S. Fisher, *When Chirldren Receive Communion: A Return to the Original and Historic Practice* (Forward Movement, 1987).

PART V

Making Plans
for the Future

CHAPTER 16

From Maintenance to Mission: Making Local Plans

Generating a Mission-Minded Parish Conversation • Learning From the Trends in Your Congregation's History • Becoming Intentional: Celebrating Your Patterns of Ministry • Announcing the Kingdom of God: The Ministry of Publicity • A Clergy/Parish Annual Evaluation • Creating a Program Calendar • Worksheets

mission-minded congregation won't be formed simply by demand. Change comes by grace and through graceful parish leadership.

Note the importance of leadership. One pastor, for example, decided he would no longer preside at the marriage of "church shoppers," nor would he offer baptism to shopping parents. He forgot, if he ever knew it, that it is God who first invites us to church, and that he is choosing to stand against the ministry of God in the world. In his own words: "I want my people to become more sturdy in their faith. We have got to have more commitment. I simply won't water down the faith of the church by admitting to our ranks folks who are not serious about who we are and who they are."

This pastor does have a vision of a mission-minded congregation's common life, but he will not help his parish become a mission-minded congregation by simply telling them so, or by withholding the ministry of the church from those whom God brings to us.

His parish will become more mission-minded the more he celebrates God's presence and ministry in his sermons, in his teaching, and in his pastoral care. As a result, over a long period of time his people will come to know the presence of God in powerfully per-

227

sonal ways, and soon, their common life will shine with all sorts of enthusiasm and old-fashioned commitment.

POINT. Instead of demanding that their congregations become what they are called by God to be, mission-minded clergy inspire visions and dream dreams of what already is. And all along the way they watch God move their people from bondage to freedom.

This is a chapter for making plans. It is written to help both clergy and lay leadership put to work some of the ideas found in this book. Here clergy will find the encouragement to:

1. Ask the lay leadership of your congregation to *commit* itself to a discussion of the topics in this book. For example, what ideas in the preceding pages provide encouragement to:

• identify and invite newcomers in your community to come to church?

• develop and implement plans to welcome newcomers, and follow up on their visit with a return visit or telephone call?

• welcome children with an effective Sunday school and nursery program so that parents will continue to come?

• provide newcomer and membership classes to strengthen the life of your congregation?

2. If a commitment is forthcoming, you will next want to work together to develop in your congregation a *discussion of ministry*—the ministry of both your congregation and God to the world.

3. Next, you may wish to make plans for the future of your parish by learning about what worked in your past.

4. Then, to fine-tune your already present programs, you may wish to evaluate your current *patterns of ministry*.

5. Finally, you will want to develop a year-long *program calendar*.

Make use of the worksheet found at the end of this chapter. If you are a member of a committee, photocopy it for others. It is designed to help you organize your ideas and begin to make plans.

But if this positive and affirming approach does not work, perhaps because a part of your parish (or even a majority) is simply content with their maintenance mindset, it may be necessary for you as a member of clergy to put the already present maintenance perspective to critical scrutiny, show where it is found, and explore why it does not work. This legalistic approach, however, sounds mainly like the nagging it fundamentally is.

THE BOTTOM LINE. Some congregations may be intractable in their commitment to a maintenance mindset. Having grown accustomed to maintenance thinking, they are not at all interested in changing. As a member of clergy, if you are not content to work with this situation patiently, you should consider leaving before you burn out.

Generating a Mission-Minded Parish Conversation

If you find that your congregation *is* interested in developing a new vision of mission, or simply wants to become more precise with the vision that they already have, here's how to proceed.

Put a copy of this book into everyone's hands. Next, devote ten weeks in the fall or ten weeks in the spring to a parish-wide study of it. Preach to mission, use the book in your adult class(s), devote time to ministry conversations whenever your board or vestry meets; in short, use this book to help your congregation plunge into a discussion of mission that takes its breath away. Then proceed as follows.

First, determine where you would place your congregation's present ministry on a scale between maintenance and mission. Next, where would you like it to be, and what will help you get to that place? Remember: Every church contains some of each perspective.

Mission _____ Maintenance

Second, ask yourself these questions: What signs of "static triumphalism" so we see in our congregation? When did it begin? How can it be diffused? If you are a member of clergy, how is your current ministry formed by the maintenance (or mission) perspectives you engaged as a child growing up in (or outside) the church?

Third, using Chapters 1 and 2, at every board or administrative committee meeting pay some attention to the mission marks in your congregation that you would like to strengthen, and which are not at hand that you would like to have present. For example:

• Attend your congregation's ability to speak of God's everyday presence and ministry, and the mission mindset's love of the ministry of introductions.

• Revalue the welcome and incorporation of newcomers, and your response to the lapsed.

• Critique education in your parish, both your Sunday school program for children, and the relationship of the worship of the parish to the education of children and adults, opportunities for adult education, and your support of the ministry of the laity.

• Examine pastoral care in your parish, and the way you use, or do not yet use, small groups for Bible study and prayer.

• Look at your outreach program, and the assistance you offer to the community that surrounds your church building.

• Is your Sunday worship a welcoming celebration of God's love, offered to the world? What are your strong points, and what would you like to see improved?

• Clergy, examine your leadership style, and the style of ministry developed in this book. What is happening in your ministry that you'd want to see continued and strengthened, and what still seems out of reach?

Informed discussion makes knowledge explicit. So let these discussions simmer on the front burner of parish life. If you do not, your parish will likely revert to the least common denominator—a maintenance perspective.

Learning From the Trends in Your Congregation's History

Renewing a parish's ministry can also be helped by examining your congregation's history. For example, most every parish has fat and lean years. By picturing the history of your parish as a decades-long journey, both fat and lean years will clearly show. Next, search for the shape of your parish's ministry during the rich years and, as appropriate, seek to recreate that shape today. But don't forget the lean years; to the extent that you're able to discover what made them lean, you may be able to avoid repeating past mistakes today.

Of course what we are talking about is the ongoing oscillation of history as mission and maintenance perspectives play themselves out against one another, one generation giving way to another. There is a naturally occurring pattern of dying-and-rising in the life of all churches.[1]

Becoming Intentional: Celebrating Your Patterns of Ministry

Every parish is a combination of many *patterns of ministry*. No parish has just one pattern, and these patterns combine to give every congregation a unique personality. "So what are the components of a pattern of ministry?" you ask. The presiding minister has his or her part to play, lay leadership plays its part, and so does congregational history.

By determining your patterns of ministry you will be well on the road to finding out how you minister to others and how you do not. Make use of the worksheet at the end of this chapter, and by discerning and evaluating the patterns of ministry in your congregation, you will be more ably equipped to make changes if changes are necessary.

POINT. *Patterns of ministry* celebrate the shape of current ministry in your parish, and they answer the operational question "Who are we?"

St. Peter's in the Woods, first mentioned in chapter 1, provides a case in point. Like many congregations, St. Peter's published a series of objectives for itself and its ministry. Those had to do with such things as obtaining the services of a full-time minister and breaking ground for a building. Such objectives are often used to give focus to parish life. But as helpful as they are, objectives also subvert the celebration. Objectives are future-centered, and although they give focus to hopes and aspirations, they also assert the judgment that we are not yet where we want to be. *Patterns of ministry*, on the other hand, celebrate by articulating present practice and implicit hope.

At my behest, St. Peter's began to consider some of their patterns of ministry. The following four were identified as the most important. Also noted are the revisions of these patterns that St. Peter's considered in early 1990, and some of the issues that asserted themselves when those patterns were revealed.

1. THE MINISTRY TO NEWCOMERS (Present pattern). Newcomers are welcomed at the door, name-tags are made, there is a follow-up telephone call, and newcomers are given every opportunity to participate as fully as possible in all aspects of parish life.

Possible revision of the pattern:

• Newcomers' names could be printed in the next week's bulletin.

• Newcomers could be introduced in the liturgy—perhaps at the time of the Peace by others who have met them, etc.... But this means we need to be more intentional about welcoming newcomers, and introducing them to one another.

QUESTION. Because late summer, Christmas and Easter are three periods of accelerated first time visits by newcomers, should we mail an announcement of our worship to every zip code adjacent to our meeting place? Perhaps we could join with several other denominations to design and execute such advertising, since advertising to individual zip code addresses proves to be an excellent method of generating interest in a local congregation.

2. THE MINISTRY OF CHRISTIAN EDUCATION FOR CHILDREN—AND THROUGH CHILDREN TO THEIR PARENTS (Present pattern). Children are given Sunday school instruction, they are welcomed into the liturgy at the time of the Peace to dine at the Lord's Table with their parents, and in their procession into the liturgy they are given opportunity to offer to the parish the results of their classroom labors. Because of this recognition they are affirmed, even blessed. And so are their parents and so are their teachers. Newcomers with children are especially looking for this kind of feeling.

Possible revision of the pattern:

• The presentation of arts and crafts in already in place. But the number of children present on one Sunday could be printed in the next week's Sunday bulletin, and called to attention in the announcements on regular occasions. Success breeds growing interest.

• Occasional and brief intergenerational activities during the coffee hour could involve the parish in a common activity. We could make a banner, or chrismons, or butterflies. The children would prepare for this event in the Sunday school classroom, we would act together as a community, and then show and tell the following sunday what we had done the week before.

3. THE MINISTRY OF STEWARDSHIP (Present pattern). Money, time and talents are important at St. Peter's. We currently celebrate this aspect of our parish life at the time of the offertory.

Possible revision of the pattern:

• At the offertory, or at the time of announcements, selected members of St. Peter's could be thanked individually each Sunday for their contributions of time and talent (the vestry, the choir, the altar guild, those who prepare the refreshment table in the foyer, etc.), and prayers and thanksgivings offered to God for their life and labors.

• Compile a list of committees and individuals (a cycle of prayer) to be identified on consecutive Sundays, their gift of time and talents praised, and prayers and thanksgivings offered to God.

RESULT: a spirit of celebration in the parish, an important ministry identified, the gift of time and talents valued, and the need and opportunity presented to others for participation.

4. THE MINISTRY OF FELLOWSHIP (Present pattern). St. Peter's enjoys fellowshipping on Sunday morning, not only in the liturgy where a spirit of enthusiasm reigns, but before worship when we greet one another often for the first time since the previous Sunday, and in the coffee hour after worship, when goodies are provided without a schedule.

Possible revision of the pattern:

• Those who explicitly provide for fellowship could be recognized in Sunday's worship; for example, those who bring the food, set up the food, and welcome the newcomers.

• We need to guard against talking about church business at coffee hour, which invariably excludes visitors from conversation.

How do your own patterns of ministry match up to both need and opportunity? Consider your present patterns and their possible revision, paying attention to such items as your:

1. Capacity to identify and celebrate God's presence and ministry in the world.

2. Equipping of parishioners for preevangelism, primary and secondary evangelism.

3. General use of praise and celebration; the ways in which you say thank you to one another and to God.

4. Identification, welcome and inclusion of visitors.

5. Recognition of the difference between a visitor and a newcomer.

6. Pattern of worship on Sunday morning, and the companionship your worship offers to newcomers.

7. Affirmation and celebration of Sunday morning Christian education for children.

8. Membership classes.

9. Stewardship of time, talent and money. Are you wedded to an annual Every Member Canvass, or is Christian stewardship an all-year affair?

10. Programs for adult education.

11. Outreach ministry.

THE BOTTOM LINE. Identifying, evaluating and revising *patterns of ministry* goes a long way in helping a parish become more articulate and intentional about its ministry, about what is working and what is not, about what is important and what is less so. Inevitably God creates through such discussion all kinds of new perspectives.

Announcing the Kingdom of God: The Ministry of Publicity

Mission-minded congregations have an announcement to make to the world: God is close, they know it, and they are honored to offer the rich patterns of their ministry to the world.

How do you publicize your ministry to your community? A weekly announcement in your *local newspaper* or *community newsletter* can keep your presence before the public. Such a consistent announcement provides a constant background for community consciousness, so that when someone thinks about going to church for a first time, they are likely to remember "that ad." In this same vein, the yellow pages in your local *telephone book* are also worth valuing.

But there are still other ways, and in large measure they are eveι more effective than the newspaper of the telephone book. A *community canvass* at Christmas, Easter, and late summer provides just the right information for newcomers in the community, or for those who have lapsed and are now thinking about a return to church. Seasonal mailings work. This *mailbox ministry* is discussed in Chapter 10.

Roadside signs also produce results, sometimes on a grand scale. Most every congregation will have a sign immediately adjacent to their building. But merchants have long known that a narrow field of advertising generates narrow interest. Growing congregations announce their presence by placing their signs at local shopping centers and service stations.

And if these congregations can't find a place for a permanent sign, they are not chagrined. Late every Friday afternoon, members of St. Peter's in the Woods place eighteen signs in the communities adjacent to their meeting place. These same signs are put away on Sunday after church by the parishioners who have "adopted" them. St. Peter's learned that state road crews cannot permit signs on the roadside during the week, but on the weekend their signs can show for forty-eight hours. And forty-eight hours is just enough time to offer an "idea" to the weekend traveler. St. Peter's reports that of all the advertising they do, and they use every one of the ideas mentioned in this section, *movable signs* get the best response. And note: this brand-new congregation grew by 400% in its first year, and they are new in an area of established neighborhoods. Movable signs are not expensive to make, they will last a long while, and they seem to be an idea exactly right for the 1990s.

Evaluate the way you publicize your ministry to the world, and use the ideas in this section and chapter 10 to take action.

A Clergy/Parish Annual Evaluation

An annual parish evaluation of present patterns of ministry and clergy leadership provides an excellent method for continued growth, and the ways and means sharpen current ministry. When evaluation is made from mission-minded perspectives, parish ministry is honed to a fine edge.

If you are a member of a mission-minded congregation and you want to make your ministry even more intentional than it is, this section is written to help. And if you are a member of a congregation leaning more toward maintenance than mission, and if you want to become more intentional about the development of a mission-minded ministry, this section will also serve you well.

Intentionality marks ministry in mission-minded congregations. Every year these communities pause to take a look at what they are doing and how well they are doing it. Congregations marked more by a concern for maintenance, on the other hand, don't much value evaluation. And often when evaluation is made, there is a punitive note to it, on the order of "You should have..." and "We ought to...."

There is a better way. To make your parish's ministry more intentional, make explicit plans on an annual basis to explore your ministry form the following perspectives.

1. Consider what you are doing presently in the following ministry areas:

• learning to speak of God,
• evangelism and its ministry of introductions,
• the ways in which praise and thanks are offered to one another,
• stewardship of time, talents and treasure,
• welcome of visitors,
• welcome of babies to your nursery,
• use of newcomers classes and membership/confirmation classes,
• ministry to the lapsed,
• Christian education for children,
• adult education, including the use of small groups for study and pastoral care (Bible study, prayer groups, fellowship groups, supper groups),
• encouragement of members to value their daily occupations as callings by God to ministry, and
• outreach ministry.

2. If there is a gap in your overall ministry, explore it. Does this ministry deserve your attention (and not every ministry may), and if not, what need does God have of it, if any?

3. If there is a gap in your ministry and it does need to be addressed, develop an action plan. What kind of leadership (both clergy and lay) will it take to get this ministry off the ground and flying?

4. What signs will show that this ministry is functioning and effective?

An annual and explicit discussion of these items will much enhance the spirit of your common life, particularly as they come to reflect the on-going shape of your ministry through the year.

Creating a Program Calendar

Mission-minded congregations make plans for ministry. They set objectives for themselves, and they take every opportunity to make their plans known.

For example:

• when a community canvass for newcomers is set for September (using mailing lists from the post office), Christmas and Easter,

• when there is to be a community Blessing of the Animals scheduled for the fall or spring,

• when plans for a Lenten study program are developed,

these items end up on the parish's year long program calendar. This schedule of events helps mission-minded congregations see the totality of their year's ministry, and it helps them critique it. Making a calendar of events highlights priorities.

A program calendar moves parish ministry from general perspectives and ideas into specific, intentional foci. Long range planning and scheduling are not left to chance in mission-minded congregations, no matter what their size.

For clergy, a program calendar means taking better care of their time and the time of their parish by organizing more effectively. As a result, the general ministry of the parish becomes more specific, and parish life becomes coherent. For parishioners, a program calendar gives explicit shape to the full range of their ministry, particularly when it is published or displayed for all to see.

As a result of discussion in all parts of the parish, a program calendar is likely to include such things as:

- seasonal preaching and teaching themes,
- the parish homecoming,
- the year's schedule of Sunday school activities.

If the nine-month school year is broken into terms, each term will:

- announce themes in Sunday morning Christian education,
- highlight Sunday school registration,
- schedule the installation of Sunday school teachers,
- note parish educational festivals,
- cite the year-end Sunday school celebration,
- note the ministry of welcome and inclusion, with the dates set aside for the parish visitors training programs, the dates of new member classes designated,

as well as the Sundays designated for:

- the recognition and reception of new members,
- the installation for the vestry, board of deacons or stewards,
- the recognition of acolytes,
- recognition of the church basketball team,
- the recognition of other parish organizations.

Also noted will be:

- church staff meetings,
- deadline for information in the Sunday bulletin and/or parish newsletter,
- Bible study and prayer group meetings,
- dates of choir rehearsals, and
- meetings of parish governing boards, along with a note citing their goals and objectives for the year.

A program calendar makes a vision of parish ministry concrete for everyone. It should list every parish event during the year (like evening supper groups, weekly prayer groups, etc). Newcomers particularly will be interested in the overall ministry your parish values. Every staff meeting ought to center some of its attention on the program schedule to date, events should be anticipated in the newsletter Sunday morning announcements, and they should be regularly included in the Sunday bulletin.

THE BOTTOM LINE. Because of a program calendar, every member of your parish will know what the year offers, and at any point in the year just where the journey will next lead.

Details like Program calendars and explicit parish conversations about such things as God's presence and ministry, distinguishing between mission and maintenance perspectives, and the host of other issues noted in this book mark congregations proud of who they are and confident of God'd ministry. And attention to details like these generally separates mission-minded congregations from those just limping along. So make plans, invite everyone in on their development, lift them up before God and God's people like the grand offertory they are, and the results will be wonderful.

End Notes

1. If you're interested in developing this study, help is close at hand. Making use of data first set before the Church by Bob Waymire and C. Peter Wagner in their *Church Growth Survey Handbook*, the Episcopal Diocese of Southern Ohio has published a manual to help congregations and clusters of congregations evaluate their history so that they can see what worked in the past: Timothy West, *Workbook for the Decade of Evangelism* (Cincinnati, OH: Episcopal Diocese of Southern Ohio, 1989).

WORK SHEET #1
BECOMING INTENTIONAL IN MINISTRY

**Solving Problems You Didn't Think You Could
or Didn't Know You Had.**

This work sheet will help you organize the ideas in this book that you found interesting.

1. What ideas in the preceding chapters did you find interesting? Choose from the following list, and add the others that stirred your thoughts.

• Learning to enjoy the ministry of identifying and celebrating God's everyday presence and ministry.

• Valuing evangelism as a ministry of introductions.

• Publicizing the ministry of your parish.

• More firmly grounding your ministry of praise and thanksgiving for God's blessings throughout the parish.

• The welcome of visitors, identifying them when they become newcomers, and providing classes to orient newcomers and later to make them members.

• Developing a more intentional ministry to the lapsed.

• Your program of Christian stewardship.

• Enhancing your educational ministry:

in the Sunday school for children.

enabling adults to identify and celebrate God's presence and ministry.

Valuing daily occupations as calls by God to ministry.

• Valuing pastoral care as care for the shut-in and the sick.

• Valuing pastoral care in small group settings.

• Valuing your outreach ministry, and the use of your parish hall by community groups.

• The quality of your Sunday worship.

• Constructing a year long PROGRAM CALENDAR.

• Your own ideas...

2. Rank the top five ministries from most to least important. Why are they ranked in this order?

3. What would you like to change? Why?

4. What problems can you anticipate if you seek to make changes in any of these ministries?

5. What help can you find in the parish to implement these changes?

WORK SHEET #2

Identifying Your Patterns of Ministry

This work sheet will help you identify the patterns of ministry already present in your congregation, and the emendation they may need.

1. What patterns of ministry do you want to examine? Choose from the following list:

• Equipping parishioners to speak of God's everyday presence and ministry.

• Your ministry of introducing God to God's world.

• Your ministries of preevangelism.

• Publicizing the ministry of your parish.

• Giving praise and thanksgiving for God's blessings.

• The identification and welcome of visitors.

• Your support of newcomers.

• Classes for newcomers and members.

• Your ministry to the lapsed.

• Enhancing your educational ministry:

    in the Sunday school for children.

    for adults.

Valuing daily occupations as calls by God to ministry.

• Your ministry of care for the shut-in and the sick.

• Your ministry of pastoral care in small group settings.

• Your outreach ministry.

• Other ideas.

2. Briefly describe your most important patterns of ministry.

3. What purpose do these present patterns of ministry serve?

4. How could these present patterns be improved?

    Why do they need improvement?

5. What problems can you anticipate if you make revisions?

6. What help can you find in the parish to implement these revisions?

Index

A

Adam and Eve 85

advertising, the ministry of 153-54, 207, 232-35

altar guild 11

Andrew, The Rev. John G. B. 119

Angels 8, 10, 40, 43

Anglican Digest 2, 14, 15, 31, 91, 118, 119

Arn, Win and Charles W. 15

Association of Theological Schools 142

Athens, St. Paul at 41f

B

Bakker, Jim and Tammy 2

baptism, believer's 217

Bates, Marilyn 99, 223

Bell, Martin 30

Benedict, Barbara 142

Bethge, Eberhard 92

Biblical citations, Old Testament
    Gen. 2:15-17, 3:4-6 85
    Ex. 13:21, 16:13-16, 17:3-7 70
    Deut. 32:10-12a 67
    Ruth 1:16-17 70
    1 Sam. 3 108
    1 Sam. 7 109
    Prov. 29:18 121

Biblical citations, New Testament
    Mt. 5:48 10
    Mt. 10:29-31, 18:12 55
    Mt. 11:28 90
    Mt. 23:37 86
    Lk. 2:8f 41
    Lk. 4:16f 45, 203, 214
    Lk. 10:29-37 107
    Lk. 12:16-21 22
    Lk. 13:34 86
    Lk. 24:13 83
    Lk. 24:13-35 182
    Jn. 3:1-20, 7:45-52 47
    Jn. 19:31-42 48
    Jn. 20:27 66
    Acts 8:26-39, 21:8 44
    Acts 17:34 41
    Acts 24:2 70
    Acts 25:13-26:32 49
    Rom. 8:28 89
    1 Cor. 9:19-22 42
    1 Cor. 13:11-12a 79
    1 Cor. 14:11 49
    Eph. 3:20 18, 23
    Phil. 2:9-11 46
    Phil. 4:8 106
    Heb. 11:1-12:2 218
    Heb. 11:1 181
    1 Pet. 5:8 88
    Rev. 3:20 68

Bitsberger, The Rev. Donald 200

Boaz 69

Bonhoeffer, Dietrich 92

Book of Common Prayer
    Eucharist Prayer "C" 218
    Form of Commitment to Christian
        Service 184
    on beauty and God's gracious hand
        203, 210
    on destroying the works of the devil 92
    on freedom 91, 213, 216, 223
    on God the Son 50
    on God's Grace preceding and follow-
        ing 203
    on God's Grace 203, 210, 213, 216,
        223
    on God's power to stir up 203
    on God's providence 68, 202, 210
    on sin 83, 91, 214

243

on the "forces of evil" 88, 92, 214, 216, 223

Bowe, Jim 176

bring a friend, the danger of depending on this approach 145

Brueggemann, Walter 72, 119

Busch, Richard 127, 142

C

Career Management Systems 176

Carnegie Foundation for the Advancement of Teaching 135

Carson, Thomas 215

Carus, Mrs. Gene 143

Cathedral Films and Videos 219, 223

cathedrals 42

checklists, worksheets, and other helps
    becoming intentional in ministry 240
    Christian education, Episcopal Prayer Book perspectives 190
    church growth survey 14
    Clergy/Parish annual evaluation 235
    determining God's hand at work in your life 183
    developing your style of evangelism 98
    lapsed members, developing a ministry in response 171f
    membership classes, an outline of 217
    newcomers classes, an outline of 212
    organizing and evangelism study group for adults/teens 205
    patterns in ministry, identifying your congregation's 242
    planning worship, becoming intentional for visitors 115
    solving problems you didn't think you could 240
    taking action to diagnose your congregation's mindset 29
    welcoming visitors, a program to prepare you congregation 159

Church Growth, Inc. 12

churches used as illustration 4, 8, 12, 14, 20, 24-30, 104, 119, 143, 150, 154, 156, 161, 231, 235

clergy burnout 29, 122, 127-28

clergy leadership 6, 12-13, 109, 121-27, 166, 227, 230, 233, 235

clergy vacancy 137-41

Colorado Episcopalian 14

Conaway, James 49

confirmation
    See Episcopal Church

Curren, Delores 173

D

daily occupations, value of 175-80, 183-84, 216, 218, 220, 223

Deaver, Michael K. with Mickey Herskowitz 119

Diocese of Colorado 3

Diocese of Connecticut 20

Diocese of Southern Ohio 239

Durken, Joleen 176

Dykstra, Craig 23, 30

E

education 79-81, 211
    teens 98, 175, 205, 217

Edwards, Jonathan 31

Emmaus 83, 181f

Episcopal Church
    baptism 217, 220
    Christian education Anglican style 190
    confirmation 217-22
    Holy Communion 221-22
    marks of evangelism in 202f
    new member instruction 215
    preparing for the decade of evangelism 208

seminary education for leadership 129f
size 19-22, 114
Episcopal Church Annual 30
Episcopal Church Foundation 132
Episcopalian/Professional pages 30
Evangelical Education Society 210
evangelism
definition 40, 201
Episcopal Church 203-5
learning ministry of 44, 49, 52-59, 63, 66
ministry of introductions 10, 43-44, 51, 62, 66-67, 78, 86, 202
personal 62, 74, 96-98, 183-84, 205-9
preevangelism 12, 200
primary evangelism 201, 204
secondary evangelism 201-2

F

Farrington, The Rev. William 119
Ferguson, Doug 38
Fisher, Ronald S. 223
Forward Movement Publications 223
Fox, Matthew 119
fundamentalism 204

G

Gallup, George 2-3, 175
General Ordination Examinations 133
Golding, William 65
Gospel drama 223
Great Awakening 31

H

Hammond, Nancy 163
Hanchey, Howard 91, 185, 197, 223

Harre, Alan 172
Haug, The Rev. Phillip 164
Hirst, The Rev. Dale 59
Howe, John 131, 142
Hymnal 1940 191, 197
Hymnal 1982 197, 202, 210

I

images and metaphors 74, 80-81

J

James, David L. 30
Jesus 10, 22, 353, 41, 45-46, 55, 66, 69, 83, 86, 90, 203, 216
Johnson, Charles Foster 119
Jones, The Very Rev. Alan 131, 142
Joseph of Arimathea 48

K

Kiersey, David and Bates, Marilyn 99, 223
King Agrippa 49
King, Mrs. Jocelyn 197
Kolb, Erwin J. 15
Kung, Hans 9, 15

L

lapsed members 11, 165-70
Lilly Endowment, Inc. 223
Living Church 2, 14, 31

M

maintenance mindset 4, 6, 8, 9, 17, 19-20, 103-5, 113, 122, 125, 140, 227, 229

making members of Christians
believer's confirmation 175, 215-23
kiddie confirmation 221
teen confirmation 220-23

making plans for mission-minded ministry 228-31, 237, 242, 249

Marshall, Bishop Michael 91, 105, 108

Miller, Herb 163

ministry of introduction 53, 62-66, 72, 146, 161, 207

mission-minded Christian education 14, 116, 147, 157, 189-96, 232, 240

mission mindset 4, 7, 9-10, 12, 17, 23, 29, 103-6, 113, 122, 125, 140, 196, 227-28, 232-33

Morse, David 223

motivating "Sunday-only" people 3

Muncie, The Rev. Stephen 210

Myers-Briggs Personality Inventory 99, 219

N

Naomi 69

Neville, Joyce 99

Nicodemus 46

nursery for infants and toddlers 147, 157

O

Oates, Wayne 172-3

Oden, Thomas C. 92

Orpah 69

P

pastoral care, importance in mission-minded congregation 12

Peckham, John, Archbishop of Canterbury 221

preaching 106-9, 118, 122, 139

program calendar 127

R

Reagan, Ronald and Nancy 113

Rehkoff, The Rev. Charles 164

Rhodes, Lyn 210

Rice, Eugene 137, 142

Rogers, The Very Rev. John 131, 135

Ruth 69

S

St. Luke 185

St. Paul 35, 41-42, 44, 49, 79, 89

St. Philip 35, 44

St. Thomas 66

Scharf, The Rev. Frederick 164

Schmidt, Richard 164

Schwab, Wayne 15, 99, 208, 210

Starry, Donn 104

Stepp, Laura Sessions 14

stewardship 7, 22, 124, 233

Stewardship Report 223

Stewart, Dr. John 184

study groups 10, 74, 90, 98

supper groups 29

Swaggart, Jimmy 2

T

theological education for mission 2, 127, 129, 131-36, 200, 204

Trinity School for Ministry 131, 135

Tubesing, Donald A. 173

V

Virginia Theological Seminary 127, 129

W

Waggon, Mrs. Genelda K. 164

Wagner, C. Peter 15, 239

Wagner, The Rev. Richard 154

Washington Post 14

Watkins, Bill 92

Weimer, Maryellen 142

welcoming visitors and newcomers, the ministry of 4-8, 11-12, 15, 22-23, 26, 117, 122, 129, 143-61, 211, 232-33

West, Timothy 239

Westminster catechism 18

White, David 119

White, The Rev. David 111

worship
    education 105, 112-18
    pastoral care 4, 104-5, 116, 123, 208, 233
    planning 6, 110-113, 124

Wright, Frank and Jenny 124, 196

Y

York, Michael 219, 223